the Lazy Goddess

the Lazy Goddess

The quick and easy way to look amazing and be fabulous at everything

HANNAH SANDLING

Published by Metro Publishing
an imprint of John Blake Publishing Ltd
3 Bramber Court, 2 Bramber Road,
London W14 9PB, England

www.blake.co.uk

First published in paperback in 2008

ISBN: 978-1-84454-649-7

British Library Cataloguing-in-Publication Data:

A catalogue record for this book is available from the British Library.

Design by www.envydesign.co.uk

Printed and bound by 🐾 Grafica Veneta S.p.A., Trebaseleghe (PD) - Italy

1 3 5 7 9 10 8 6 4 2

Papers used by John Blake Publishing are natural, recyclable products made from
wood grown in sustainable forests. The manufacturing processes conform to the
environmental regulations of the country of origin.

Acknowledgements

I WOULD LIKE to thank all my goddesses out there who have helped me with this book, especially the queen of all the lazy goddesses, my amazing muma! Without you and all of your lazy tips, this book would never have happened. Plus my amazing dad, whose inspiration for the DIY side is what really got me going on this book! I'd also like to thank my two 'ugly sisters' Katrina and Perfect One Emily – they really are the ultimate and coolest butt-heads in this universe! Rojy, you've been amazing too, you give me strength and direction in life. I would also like to thank Diane Banks and all the team at John Blake Publishing who have been off the scale fantastic! And last but certainly not least, Sue Rider, the BEST agent that has EVER existed – thank you for everything and for constantly taking me to the next level. Here's to conquering the world!

Contents

A Note From The Lazy Goddess

DO YOU SOMETIMES feel like a raging dog with rabies: slightly scabby, slightly possessed and full of aggro? Well, that used to be me. I worked 24/7, styling celebrities worldwide and making them look breathtakingly beautiful; I designed and transformed tired, out-of-date homes into heavenly palaces; I ate ready-made, crap food due to lack of time, thus making my poor old oven truly redundant and my energy levels as fast as a slug; plus, I was sorting out everybody's love life except my own. Yep, I spent the best part of five years living and looking like a trog. My life was so busy that I was sacrificing all those lovely little essential things that make you feel so good and special – girly lunches, exercise, pedicures, facials and even some good old retail therapy.

If this sounds remotely like you, then you'd better read on as I've got all the speedy solutions to combat those beauty and fashion disasters. I've got excellent short cuts to spring-cleaning your home and I'll show you how to drop a dress size without having to go anywhere near the gym. Yep, this book is now your bible and will show you how to multitask your way through a hectic day, leaving you more time to live life to the max and look drop-dead gorgeous at all times.

This hot babe bible is full of sneaky, one-off unique tips that me and all my celebrity friendies want to share with you. And believe you me, they work!

Love
Hans
xx

Introduction

WE'VE ALL BEEN there: Monday morning, staring into the mirror at crusted-up eyes, complete with carrier bags underneath so they hang halfway down a pale and patchy, pimply face. Or perhaps your breath is so stinky that one puff would leave pretty little flowers fighting for their lives, while your hair's so straw-like that it would be an incredibly desirable environment for first-time homemaker birds. And the view down below might not be much better: glancing up and over a bloated stomach to a wig-like muff (which could be mistaken for a small rat stuck in your crotch) and toes so grubby you could grow some rather exotic mushrooms in between them.

As for trying to get a man, forget it! You have to ask yourself, what man in his right mind really wants to date a hairy cavewoman who can't cook (her best dish resembles steaming cat sick), whose house looks and smells like a skip, and whose fashion sense... well, does she always get dressed during a power cut? And has no one told her about VPL?

But, you know what? The week really doesn't have to start like this. You could quite easily wake up next to Mr Perfect in your oasis of a home, looking like you've just stepped out of the glossy pages of *Vogue*, all glam and gorgeous with glowing skin, silky lustrous hair and dainty little piggy trotters that really only deserve to be slipped into luxurious fluffy satin mules.

The best thing about this book is that it demonstrates how you can get all this without having to shake the last dregs of life out of your piggy bank and without having to spend hours in the bathroom, or on your hands and knees scrubbing. Most of the answers to your beauty and household problems are already lurking somewhere at the back of your fridge or kitchen cupboards, which means they're quick and easy to solve. Even better, they're dirt cheap, too!

So, you grim goddesses: get up, glam up and be prepared to say goodbye to all those prehistoric beauty, dating, household and cooking regimes because trapped within that gorilla-like body of yours is a gorgeous girly gagging to be set free!

1

Beauty

HAIR

'YOUR HAIR LOOKS worse than the dog's!' ranted my father, year after year, sounding like a stuck record as he waved his favourite bossing-around tool, his pen, first at my hair (a semi-dreaded do, which I thought quite cool at the time and very much suited my hippy lifestyle) and then at Mia, our rather porky family dog, who had hair so wiry you could have used her as a scouring pad. In fact, the only reason she had such unkempt hair was down to the fact that she kept herself busy out in the barn all day long, catching rats.

It was only when a good friend turned round to me one day and very politely said, 'Hans, I hope you don't mind me saying, but your hair really does look like a Worzel Gummidge, flea-infested haystack,' that I realised I had to ditch my constantly dried-out, bad-hair-day barnet and start donning sleek and glossy Jennifer Aniston-style tresses instead.

But I knew this would not be an easy journey, more an uphill slog, if anything. It not only meant a trip to hairdresser-to-the-stars Richard Ward's super-deluxe salon for a cut and colour, but if I really wanted a red-carpet glossy mane, then I also had to start stuffing my face with delicious foods like salmon and lobster (apparently very nourishing for your hair) and keep my fridge bulging at the seams 24/7 with the finest beer since a good old rinse with it would bring me one step closer to getting my Jen locks! So I wrote up my shopping list and hit the supermarket to get my hair sorted...

How to Get Lustrous Locks

- Due to its calorific content, you may not keep mayonnaise in your fridge, but you might just have to start buying it as it's amazing for re-hydrating dry and damaged locks. Simply massage it into your hair, wrap your head in a plastic carrier bag, leave for twenty minutes and then wash as normal. Apply a light amount of conditioner afterwards, then rinse out. (For all you calorie-watchers out there, low-fat mayo works just as well!)
- To keep your mane glossy, rub castor oil into the roots once every two weeks, leave it in for fifteen minutes, then wash as normal. Apply a light amount of conditioner afterwards, then rinse out.
- Dilute fresh lemon juice into a large bowl of lukewarm water and dunk your head into it. Rub the mixture into your head, as this stimulates hair growth. Lemon juice really enhances the colour of your hair if you are blonde – and also helps to remove dandruff.
- If you've run out of regular hair conditioner, use a soft fabric conditioner as a substitute. This trick is also fine for those with sensitive skin.
- After you've washed your hair, always do the last rinse with cold water to encourage it to shine. The hot water you use when washing your hair

opens the hair shafts, making it easier to wash and clean your barnet. Cold water closes the hair shafts and stops them from producing oil for a bit, plus it flattens the cuticles and prevents them from splitting – meaning no more frizzy locks!

- When you or your man buy your six-pack from the offy, make sure that at least one of them doesn't end up down your throat! Beer is brilliant for conditioning dry and damaged hair. Simply rinse wet hair in beer and leave to soak in for fifteen minutes. Shampoo and condition, then rinse in cold water.

- Give your hair a real pampering session: rub a mixture of warm water, a touch of salt and two teaspoons vinegar into it and leave for a couple of hours. Rinse with cold water to keep oiliness at bay.

- Because you're a hot babe-in-the-making, only silk will do when it comes to your bedding. Not only will it make you feel like a rather spoilt princess (because we're worth it, right?) but it's also incredibly good for keeping your hair looking glossy and smooth while you get your beauty sleep; it keeps your hair flat and doesn't make it static or knotty.

- Mix 1½ teaspoons coconut oil and 1½ teaspoons honey together, massage into the scalp and all over the hair. Leave for twenty minutes, then rinse. This will re-hydrate and soften dry hair.

- Eat salmon on a regular basis (swizzled down with a glass of vino, of course!). The fish oils it contains will nourish the cuticles of your hair, making it thicker and stronger.

- If your barnet's looking a little on the thin side, maybe you need to look at your lifestyle. Are you stressing, over-styling or on the wrong diet? All of these can affect your hair quite dramatically. Eating the right foods will make your locks glow. Because hair is made up of protein, it's really important that you eat lots of protein-rich foods, such as fish, eggs and meat. If you don't eat red meat, then make sure you include foods that contain lots of iron in your diet so that you don't become deficient in it. Add watercress, pumpkin seeds and kelp to your meals as a substitute.

- Rather than buying a dandruff shampoo, make your own: just add a little castor or olive oil to your shampoo.
- When washing your hair, focus on the roots while massaging the shampoo in – that's where the dirt tends to build up. Only lightly wash the lengths to avoid drying them out.
- For immediate glam, glossy hair, spray hair gloss onto it.
- To bring dull hair back to life, mix 200g (7oz) plain yoghurt with an egg. Rub it into your scalp, leave for five minutes, then wash as normal. When I'm at home working, I leave this mixture on my hair all day. Just tie your hair up in a bun or hide it under a shower cap.
- Make sure you wash your brush and comb with hair shampoo every two weeks so you don't pass on old grease to fresh, yummy-smelling locks.
- Massage your head every time you wash your hair to stimulate hair growth.

When You Can't Be Bothered to Wash It... Grubby Hair Tricks

- For the ultimate lazy-girl option, spray dry shampoo into your hair (from most chemists and supermarkets). Leave for five seconds to allow it to do its job and absorb all the grease, then brush out. Hey presto! You'll look like you have just stepped out of the salon. What a god-sent gift, hey?
- Spray last night's smoky party hair with your favourite perfume.

CELEBRITY TIP!

Caprice - Model and Businesswoman

Invest in a pair of hair straighteners. They are brilliant for giving your hair some Hollywood glam, but they are also great for getting unwanted creases out of clothes that have been stuffed in a suitcase while travelling.

- Sweep your hair back off your face and up into a ponytail. Don't brush it up as you'll only highlight the fact that you've got lard-like hair! Instead, rake your fingers through your locks to give a textured, non-greasy look. Also, having your hair up off your face helps prevent spots.
- Wear a hat or scarf on your head to disguise the grease.
- When you're in a hurry but your hair's horribly greasy, put it up into a loose bun, pull forward as much or as little of the front section as you like and wash that bit under your sink tap. Dry as usual. The clean hair at the front gives the impression that the rest of your hair is lovely and clean, not dripping in grime.
- Another good way to camouflage manky hair is to put sections in rollers, apply a little hairspray to them and leave for five seconds to dry. Gently remove the rollers so as not to break the hair. Your hair will now be boasting a rather voluminous Hollywood style.
- The more highlights and colour you have, the longer your hair will look cleaner.

- You can also give your barnet a little blast with the hairdryer to lift the roots and encourage more volume. You don't need to dampen it at all – just blast it on the hot level, which will give it a helping hand to bring it back to life. (Only for a few hours, mind you!)

Coping With Hair Disasters

- This tip is one I learned from experience, out in the middle of nowhere in Bali when my bleached blonde hair decided to go green after I jumped into a heavily chlorinated swimming pool. Luckily, I had brought with me a stash of my must-have groceries that I can't live without: Earl Grey tea bags being one of them and tomato ketchup the other. It was my trusty ketchup that saved the day! I just squeezed a quarter of the bottle onto my damp hair, massaged it in, left it for ten minutes to neutralise the colour and then washed it out with shampoo and conditioned afterwards.

- To prevent hair from going green in the first place, simply cover your damp hair in conditioner before you throw yourself into the pool to stop your hair from absorbing the chlorine.

- If your hair has gone AWOL and you don't have any serum in your bag, tame it down by smoothing a mini-blob of hand cream over the surface instead.

- Lightly dampen flat, limp hair with your garden plant spray bottle, then stick your head upside down. Blow-dry it while scrunching away for instant volume.

- Always carry a handbag-sized hairbrush and styling spray on you in case you get caught in the rain without a brolly. All you have to do then is dash to the ladies' room and dry your hair under the hand-dryer.

- If your hair turns into a static Afro after you've blow-dried it, smooth it over with a silk scarf to remove flyaway hairs and to give a glossy finish.
- Alternatively, you can calm down uncontrollably static hair by spraying hairspray onto a brush and groom it from top to bottom.
- We tend to have more bad hair days during our time of the month when our hormones wreak havoc. Don't pull it out in desperation, just do the best you can and be patient!

CELEBRITY TIP!

Richard Ward - Celebrity Hairdresser

Short of time? If you don't have time to wash your hair and totally blow-dry it, just shampoo and re-blow-dry the fringe/front and sides. Even if you just take a 2"-wide section and give it a quick wash over the basin and style it. Any length hair can look revitalised with this quick trick and, best of all, you can feel fresh and more groomed, too. It is always the fringe and sides that look the most bedraggled or greasy if not freshly washed and, especially with curly frizzy hair, the sides and new hair growing around the hairline is a tell-tale giveaway if caught in the rain. Long hair is great for this, as you can sleek the remainder back in a ponytail and look amazingly groomed in an instant.

- A good hairdresser is like an LBD – if you trust it, love it and know it makes you look good, what's the point in trading it in for a new one? If, however, you get a bad haircut, you must complain and get the salon director to re-style your hair for free. If, however, it was the boss who gave you bad hair, you should pay nothing and go to another salon to get it fixed (preferably one that a friend has recommended).
- A cool hat will always hide a bad haircut and will allow you some time to grow out the offending style.

Coloured Hair

- If you have red hair and it's looking a little dull, purée eight carrots in your kitchen blender. Now bend your head over the sink, massage it into your hair, leave for eight minutes then shampoo. The carrot pigment will boost the red in your hair.
- To perk up blonde locks, rinse them in chilled camomile tea after you shampoo.
- When you're sunbathing on holiday and want a few natural highlights, squeeze lemon juice onto your hair. It's quick, cheap and great for blonde or light-brown hair.
- If you're going on holiday and don't want your lovely colour to fade, wear a little silk scarf or a hat to prevent the sun from zapping it.
- I always get my highlights and lowlights done after I've been on holiday to a sunny destination as opposed to before. Why? If I'm out swimming and diving, etc. the sun really dries my hair out and any lowlights will fade big time, meaning a trip to the salon before I go on holiday would be a complete waste of time and money. If you go afterwards, you can have

your hair colour re-balanced and have a luxurious moisturising treatment. But if you're worried that your hair's going to look like a manky old mop while you're away, I suggest you use a colour-enhancing shampoo to liven up those locks and tide you over.

- When you go to the salon to get your hair coloured you're better off going with greasy hair. Why? Because the natural oils will prevent your head from becoming sore (from bleach, especially) and your hairdresser will be able to see where the roots start and end more easily.

- If you don't have time to go to the hairdressers, do your own DIY highlights. It's so easy: just put a dab of facial hair bleach onto a toothbrush and stroke it through your lovely locks. Wash out when developed.

- Go easy on styling mousses, especially if you shampoo every day as they will dry your hair out and encourage the colour to fade more quickly.

- If you have coloured hair, you are better off spending more on your conditioner than your shampoo – cheap conditioner can leave a plastic residue on your hair. My advice is to buy the best you can afford.

- Did you know that if you wash your hair every day then the colour fades much more quickly? If you can bear it, try to skip a few washes a week and use dry shampoo to tide you over.

A Little TLC For Your Barnet

- After washing your hair, stick your locks in a homemade turban (this helps to soak up excess water), leave to dry 75% (you can easily fill in the waiting time gossiping to a friend on the phone or putting on your make-up) and then blow-dry it on a medium heat. Never blow-dry your hair when it's soaking wet or you cause long-term damage by over-drying it. Plus, wet hair is very fragile and prone to breaking.

- You can do a bit of DIY hair-cutting anywhere, whether you're at work or at home. All you have to do is wrap a small piece of hair around your finger until the split end is visible, then snip it off with a pair of sharp scissors.

- Eat plenty of fruit, vegetables and protein to encourage healthy hair growth.

- If you've used hair products in your hair after you have blow-dried it, don't put it up in a ponytail for at least six hours. You'll ruin that fab straight style you've just spent ages doing and instead have nasty old kinks.

- To re-condition damaged hair, separate an egg, add a tablespoon of water to the yolk and mix. Then whisk up the egg white till it stands in peaks and add it to the yolk mixture. Get in the shower, wet your hair and massage the mixture into your scalp and hair. Leave for ten minutes, then rinse with cold water.

- To sort out Worzel Gummidge tangles, always use a comb and work from the bottom upwards.

- Always brush your hair before you wash it as brushing wet hair can lead to split ends. If you want to de-tangle wet hair, however, use a comb instead. A comb won't damage your hair as much as a brush will.

- When I want an instant Pamela Anderson to-die-for hair do, I get my real hair extensions out. Although they look fab and are worth the money, they really do need looking after. You can brush them like normal hair, but when it comes to washing them, take them out, wash as normal and then lay them out to dry flat on a towel.

- If you get chewing gum in your hair, soak it in full-fat cola until it comes loose.

- Avoid buying hairbrushes made from synthetic bristles and opt for a natural-fibre brush instead. They are a lot kinder to your hair and scalp.

- Stress can cause dandruff, so, if you suffer from it, you may need to re-assess your lifestyle. Just so you know, dandruff occurs when the oil-producing glands go into overdrive, making the dead skin cells on your scalp fall off in large sections rather than one cell at a time. And if you haven't sorted the problem out yet, do everyone else (and your clothes) a favour and don't scratch your scalp, otherwise you'll shower everyone and everything.

Getting to Grips With Your Hairdryer

- Keep your hairdryer moving at all times. Don't stop in one patch to make it dry more quickly – the heat will do huge damage to your hair.

- Don't turn your hairdryer onto full heat. You may as well dry your hair in a clay oven – it'll just become very dry, brittle and will easily snap.

- So you don't look like you've electrocuted yourself after blow-drying, point the hairdryer (with the nozzle on) down along your lengths of hair. This will encourage the cuticles to flatten, resulting in hair that reflects lots of light.

- If you've absolutely no idea where to start when using your hairdryer, ask your hairdresser to give you a quick lesson on how to do an easy blow-dry (PS: that's my mother's tip!).

- Before you style your hair, dry it roughly until it's almost dry to avoid cindering your hair. It'll be quicker and easier to style, too.

C E L E B R I T Y   T I P !

Richard Ward - Celebrity Hairdresser

Invest in a professional dryer – our salon dryers are 3200 watt (most consumer ones are 1800 watt). You will literally be able to blow-dry your hair in half the time.

Simple Hairdos

- Add some diamond hair clips to your hair for instant night-time glamour.
- Wrap small sections of hair round non-heated curlers and while you're waiting for them to set, soak away in a hot bath. The steam will help set and style your hair. After your bath, give your hair a gentle blast with your hairdryer to ensure that it's completely dry. When dry, gently remove the curlers and, hey presto, a complete halo of curls!
- For lustrous curls, plait your hair into two French plaits down the side of your head and leave to dry.
- To create tumbling tresses, take 2.5cm (1in) wide sections of damp hair and add mousse. Coil round your finger, pin to your head and blast with the hairdryer.
- For the ultimate Hollywood hairdo, try hair extensions (especially if you're down to the woodwork!). Shop around for a good salon so you don't end up with a synthetic hair stack – if you went anywhere near a ciggie, you'd end up in smoke!

FACE

To a lot of people the word 'fridge' means snacks, nibbles and pork-out sessions. I know it did to me back in my industrial vacuum-cleaner days (eating everything in sight!). But what you need to drum into your head is that fridge also means 'beauty'. Yes, all those yummy treats that start off in your mitts and end up down your throat can now be blitzed, blended and basted onto your skin resulting in babelicious, beautiful skin.

Ugly Mug Busters

- For tighter-looking skin, give your face a two-minute massage every day using facial oil or facial cream. Gently massage upwards and outwards. Do not drag your skin.
- Sleep with your head on two pillows at night so that your face is up high. Never sleep face down, always sleep on your back, if you can. This prevents your face from looking puffy when you wake up – everything keeps circulating and fluid won't have settled.
- To reduce puffy eyes after late-night partying, soak tea bags in iced water and place on your eyelids. Or try chilled cucumber slices instead. It's a cheap and easy way to soothe them instantly.
- Little hard spots around the top of your eyes or around your cheeks are likely to be a build-up of trapped fatty deposits. If you want to get rid of these spots, otherwise known as Millia, then hold a hot, wet facecloth over your skin for 3–4 minutes – the temperature should feel comfortable, not painful. This creates a kind of sauna which will help to remove the dead skin cells around the spot. Another way of removing these little blighters is to gently exfoliate them; this will help to entice

the small cysts out. Ask your pharmacist for the relevant facial scrub.

- Don't forget to drink water regularly. It not only cleanses your complexion but helps you to lose weight too, as it flushes all the toxins out. Often hunger is due to dehydration (which can cause premature wrinkles), so drink before you eat. Aim to drink about 1½–2 litres of water each day. But fear not, you don't have to force water down your throat on the hour, every hour – you can drink healthy herbal teas too.

- Condition your eyelashes once a week with a cotton bud dipped in vitamin E cream or olive oil. Like your hair, they also need a bit of TLC.

- If you have dry and cracked lips, put some eye gel under your lipstick to fill in the cracks, leaving them smooch-able.

- Treat your skin to a deep-cleansing mask. It will draw all the dirt out of your pores, dislodging the blockages that cause spots.

- For a brilliant DIY facial scrub at home, mix two tablespoons each of sugar and lemon juice together and massage gently over your skin. Exfoliate away till you look like a gleaming goddess! If you're strapped for cash, there's no need to bother about expensive facial treatments.

- Face, hands or body, keeping your creams clean is really important. That's why it's better to buy pump-dispenser creams rather than a big pot that you can shove your mitt into. After a while your pot of cream will become quite contaminated, especially if you may dip your paw in it without having washed it!

- If you get facial hair and are worried about waxing it, try bleaching it instead. Always do a patch test on a small area of skin first when trying out a new product.

- We lose a lot of our bodily fluid during the night while we are

sleeping and this results in dehydrated, wrinkly skin. To prevent this from happening, put a large glass of water by your bed to re-hydrate the atmosphere.

- Help stimulate the production of collagen (which brightens the tone of your skin) by eating lots of citrus fruits such as oranges, grapefruit and limes.
- If you wake up with puffy eyes in the morning, blend up a roasted apple. Apply around the eyes, leave for fifteen minutes and then rinse off.
- Gently tapping your fingers around your eye sockets helps to reduce puffiness.
- To treat spots on your face and neck, chuck a raw carrot into your kitchen blender and apply to your skin. Leave for twenty minutes and rinse.
- For a quick face lift and tightening of the skin, splash cold water onto it. This stimulates circulation and brings a healthy glow to your complexion.
- Take one cod liver oil tablet every day for glowing skin.
- Thread veins on your face can be caused from eating spicy foods, booze and over-squeezing. To prevent them, massage your skin regularly – disguise with a good foundation. Or you could go and see a non-invasive surgeon to have them removed.
- Smoking really speeds up the ageing process and gives you purse-like lips, so either look for a cream that fills in feathery lines – or preferably give up altogether.
- My mum swears by it: she always drinks a mug of camomile tea in bed at night. She says it reduces puffy eyes and dark circles, and you know what? She's right – she looks fab!
- Mashing up a banana with a little milk makes a great natural moisturiser.
- Do you get dry and irritated eyes? This may be due to a lack of vitamin A.

CELEBRITY TIP!

Lisa B, - Model

My tips for looking your best start with the basics – keep to these and you will always look your best:

- *Eat a balanced diet – this doesn't mean dieting and foregoing certain foods, it means try to eat all the nutrients your body requires and definitely treat yourself now and again!*
- *As often as possible, get 7-8 hours of sleep a night.*
- *Cleanse & moisturise your skin everyday – face and body.*
- *Avoid taking the sun; use a form of sun protection with an SPF of 15 or above if you will be exposed to the sun for any extended length of time.*
- *Don't smoke!*
- *Drink alcohol in moderation!*
- *Drink lots of water each day, especially if you drink lots of tea or coffee. Water is vital for maintaining normal bodily functions, good health and well-being, growth and development. By drinking enough, you also reduce your risk of all kinds of conditions including dehydration, kidney and liver problems, skin complaints, constipation and breast cancer.*

Drink water to lubricate them and use eye drops to make you feel more comfortable. Eat lots of dairy products and oranges, too.

- To zap the first signs of a cold sore, press an ice cube on it for fifteen minutes. To kill it off in the final stages, apply a mixture of ½ teaspoon lemon juice and ½ teaspoon salt. It hurts, but it works – no pain, no gain!

- Eating a little liquorice every day will not only help your bowels run more efficiently (it eases constipation) but will also delay the ageing process.

- To cleanse and tighten a grubby city face, cut a couple of grapes in half and rub them all over your face. Rinse with cold water.

- Be really careful when cleaning your lugs! Don't go shoving cotton buds down them otherwise you may end up piercing your ear drums, plus you could be ramming even more wax down your ear.

- If you get dry and cracked lips, rub a little of your moisturiser onto them and gently brush with a soft, dry toothbrush to remove a layer of dead skin cells.

Goodbye, Pizza Faces... Fabulous Facials

- For a quick little DIY steam at home, fill a large heatproof salad bowl with boiling water and the juice of a lemon. Cover your head with a towel and lean over it for ten minutes. Wipe your face dry. Now, although I think squeezing your spots can do more harm than good, there are occasions when you have to, and deeply buried blackheads are a good example of this. So, once you've steamed your face, you can zap them out with your fingertips (making sure your hands are super clean so as not to spread germs). After a good old juicy picking session, splash your face with cold water to close up the pores.

- Another good way to get rid of blackheads and to give new life to dull-looking skin is to mix two tablespoons water and two tablespoons baking soda together. Massage into your skin and leave for three minutes, then rinse as normal.

- Always wash and exfoliate your face before you do a facial or a mask. The face masks will work a lot better and you'll get better results.

- I eat a mackerel fillet once a week in a lovely salad for a clear complexion and a healthy glow.

- For oily (not sensitive) skin, blend two ripe tomatoes with two tablespoons natural live yoghurt. Massage into a cleansed face and leave for fifteen minutes. Rinse off and moisturise. (You're probably better off doing this at home, alone, when your boyfriend's out – this treatment makes you pretty rough-looking and may scare him!)

- Here's another quick DIY exfoliator when you're in the shower: rub lots of soap into your hands, dip in sugar and scrub away all over your body.

- Blend a massive slice of watermelon in your kitchen blender and apply it directly onto a cleansed face. It's an excellent natural cleanser.

- Blast a small cup of porridge oats in your kitchen blender along with enough warm water to form a thick consistency. Massage into your face to exfoliate the skin.

- To tighten up skin and help reduce wrinkles, whisk up an egg white and apply it to your face. Leave for ten minutes and then rinse off with cold water.

- Lemon is brilliant for getting rid of blackheads. Rub lemon juice onto them before you go to bed, leave on overnight, and then rinse your face in the morning. Continue doing this each night until all of the blackheads have disappeared.

Spots – How to Deal with 1,000 Whiteheads

Spots can be the bane of a woman's life. While some girlies are going out with glorious, glowing complexions, others are stuck at home, too scared to leave the house and display their Mount Vesuvius-like spots! Poking, prodding, squeezing and picking aren't always the best options. Here are some very effective DIY home remedies to banish those blemishes.

- Put a little fresh lemon juice on a spot to speed up the drying process.
- Squeezing spots may look better in the short term but in the long term it will damage and scar your skin. You're better off applying a good foundation to hide them.
- A facial massage will help stimulate the blood circulation in your face and flush those nasty old toxins out which cause spots. You can do this yourself at home with your face cream: gently massage in upward strokes.
- To speedily dry up a whopper of a spot, first cleanse your face and then stick a blob of toothpaste on it before you go to bed. The mint extract will help to dry it up.
- Grind eight almonds with a little warm water to make a paste. Apply to the affected area and leave for twenty minutes. It's a great, natural way to dry spots out.
- If your spot is about to erupt, clean your hands thoroughly and put a hot wet flannel over it to open up the pores. Now gently pull the skin away on either side of it. Try to avoid squeezing as you will break and damage the skin. Rinse with cold water to close the pores back up.
- To remove blackheads, blitz up a bunch of fresh parsley in your kitchen

blender for a few seconds and massage it onto the affected area. Leave it to do its work for 15 minutes, then rinse. Parsley is a great natural cleanser.

- For a new arrival, place an ice cube on your zit for five minutes to reduce the redness and then lightly cover it with concealer.

- When covering up a spot, always pat on your concealer rather than wipe it on. It will only end up looking really unnatural and also you may open up the spot again and re-infect it.

CELEBRITY TIP!

Dr Christian Jessen - Presenter of Channel 4's
Supersize vs Superskinny and Embarrassing Illnesses
Troubled by cold sores? One of my special secrets is that you can use live yoghurt to help get rid of them quickly. Smear some on as often as you can and the bugs in the yoghurt will quickly attack your cold sore virus and help it heal faster.

BODY

How to Get a Babe Body in an Instant

- Drink three cups of green tea each day. It's really good for helping you to lose weight as it speeds up your metabolism.

- If you get little spot-like bumps on the backs of your arms, they could well be fatty deposits. They are very easy to get rid of – just exfoliate them daily with your body brush.

- To get rid of warts, go for a walk outside and look for dandelions. Pick

one, extract the white gooey part of it (in the stem) and apply to your wart. Do this daily until it has disappeared.

- If you get headaches regularly, avoid reaching for pills every time. Instead try massaging lavender oil onto your temples or you can use a cold, wet flannel (straight from the fridge). Put it on your forehead to soothe the pain. Also, try drinking a large glass of water as you may just be dehydrated. If your headache persists, go and see your doctor.

- 4head is a great headache treatment. It comes in the form of a little stick that you rub over your forehead and into your temples. Magic!

- Body creams are like your naughty knickers: a little bit of enjoyment that only you know about – and, as with your knicks, nice girlies never go without them!

- Do you wake up with a pregnant-looking stomach every morning and you haven't done a poo in ages? Well, you've got constipation. So, to help entice the little blighters out, drink a cup of boiling water with one third of the juice from a lemon and a dollop of honey in it half an hour before you have your breakfast.

- Another way to get rid of the bloat is to eat watermelon as it helps prevent water retention.

- Missing out on beauty sleep (under five hours a night) can make you put on weight because it slows down your metabolism (the rate at which your body burns calories). So get an early night!

- To make your skin cuddly and soft, put three tablespoons of powered milk into your hot bath, then lie back and relax. This helps to get rid of dead skin cells.

- If you have trouble trying to reach those difficult parts on your back to give it a good old scrub, then get a pair of old tights, chop one leg off and pop a soap halfway down inside it. Tie a knot either side of the soap. Then simply throw it over your shoulder and scrub away! You'll notice how all the dead skin comes loose and sticks to the tights.

- Those who exercise at least three times a week are more likely to enjoy a good night's sleep than lazy couch potatoes.

- Before you go down the plastic surgery route to get your boobies enlarged, try shading in a pair. All you have to do is put some bronzer onto your bronzing brush and swish it down your chest where you would normally see a cleavage shadow. If you can't think how to do this, then get your weekly celebrity magazine and check out the girls' boobs to copy the shadowy lines.

- Use a full-length mirror to see if you have a spotty bum. If so, then you need to exfoliate it. Simply wet your hands, cover and lather them in soap, then dip your hands in sugar and scrub. This is also really good for getting rid of cellulite. Great for pert little bum cheeks!

- Turn your bathroom into the Tropics. Run a bath, light some candles, put your favourite CD on and exfoliate. Afterwards, slap on a layer of fake tan and climb into bed. When you wake up, you'll not only feel totally relaxed but also like you've just stepped off a beach in Thailand with a golden glow. (Chuck some old sheets on your bed first, ones you don't mind getting stained, rather than pristine white ones.)

C E L E B R I T Y   T I P !

Jerry Hall - Model

*Lying in bed stretching is
the best exercise!*

The Perfect Set of Pins

There are those lucky cows in life who are born with the most blessed pins – long, up to their armpits, the ones that cause men to crash their cars into lamp-posts. Then there are the girls who aren't so lucky, the ones born with gravity-defying tree-trunk stumps, legs so short that when they step off the pavement their bum cheeks hit the kerb! Whatever category you fall into, here are a few helpful hints to make your pins look more stretched and streamlined.

- It might look as if you've got two loaves of bread tied to your trotters, but MBT (Masai Barefoot Technology) is what it's all about these days. The embarrassment of wearing these chunky, orthopaedic-looking shoes is so worth it: it's like having two mini-gyms welded to your legs. Not only do they improve your posture, but they also give your legs a toning workout with very little effort.
- Ever wondered why Giselle Bundchen, Kylie and Pamela Anderson have the hottest bums in Tinseltown? Well, I can promise you that they will all have

a pair of 'Fit Flops' tucked away in their bags. Like MBTs, they sort out poor posture, reduce the appearance of cellulite on your trunks, plus they tone your bum cheeks into ones that can strut down the beach with no discomfort at all. The best thing about them is, they do all the work for you – all you have to do is walk and hey presto! Cute cheeks in no time!

- Hair-free legs always look thinner, sexier and more shapely than hairy beasts.

- Try not to sit cross-legged. This only creates thicker-looking ankles due to your lymphatic drainage not being able to work efficiently. Having said that, you shouldn't sit there with your legs akimbo, either!

- Tights with vertical stripes make chunky legs look a lot thinner. Avoid horizontal stripes at all times!

- To make your legs look thinner and longer, rub a little shimmer cream down the centre of your calves and shins to highlight them.

- Help eliminate most of your varicose veins the natural way, goddesses – eat lots of grapes and citrus fruits. The white membranes of citrus fruits are a rich source of bioflavonoids. These natural compounds help to strengthen your blood vessels and therefore reduce the appearance of the dreaded varicose veins.

- For instantly thinner-looking legs, brush them in bronzing powder.

- Wear vertically striped trousers – they will streamline your legs.

- Always take the stairs rather than the lift to tone your legs up.

Hairy Beast Removal – From Muff to Moustache

Looking as if you could house an entire zoo of animals in your jungle of hair (whether it's under your arms, in your crotch, all over your legs or around

C E L E B R I T Y   T I P !

Alesha Dixon - Singer

If you want to make your legs look longer, wear a shoe that matches your skin tone with a higher-waisted skirt or trouser. Black shoes draw the eye to the floor and cut your legs off at the ankle whereas skin-coloured shoes make them look much longer.

your mouth) isn't a particularly attractive sight for your fellow humans to have to witness. I understand – it can be a real fag, very time-consuming and also extremely painful in certain areas to remove a rug of hair, especially if you're using wax. But as the old saying goes, no pain, no gain. And it's true! You'll look thinner, feel minxier and if you aren't a Bridget Jones and have a boyfriend then you'll make him a happier man because once you've had a good old deforestation, he won't have to use his mining tools or head lamp any longer to find his way around your body!

- First, if you cannot stand pain and you're planning a big waxing session then I strongly advise you to take a couple of mild painkillers to help ease it. I have to note here that waxing hurts even more just before and during your period so those little painkillers will go down a real treat if you really must have a wax during this time.
- If you have a massively overgrown muff that's totally out of control then you're better off getting your scissors (or the garden shears!) out and

trimming most of it down first. Trying to wax a mass of hair can be extremely difficult and might leave you squirming in a lot of pain.

- If you are a virgin to waxing and feel embarrassed, try to look at your beautician as you would your gynaecologist.

- I always exfoliate before I wax, because then the wax has a much better chance of sticking directly to the hairs rather than your dead skin cells. This also prevents painful in-growing hairs. Don't exfoliate just before you wax, or the skin will be warm and the wax will be more painful – anything up to two hours prior to waxing is fine.

- If you really are body-shy and envy those girls who can walk around the bedroom totally naked in front of their man without feeling a bit of embarrassment, then here's a way to practise losing your inhibitions. Go and get yourself a bikini wax at your local salon. There just isn't the time to be shy because they're used to seeing hundreds of muffs every day, plus they will do you front ways, back ways and see everything from your bum cheeks to your front cheeks.

- Also, when you're next at the gym, walk around the changing room naked and don't try to cover up. Nobody cares, everyone goes around naked. Over time, you will build up loads of confidence and, before you know it, you'll be the one walking round the bedroom in your birthday suit with not a worry in the world. Plus, he'll LOVE it!

- To remove in-grown pubic hairs, simply soak a small towel in hot water, press against the area for ten minutes to warm up the follicles and eventually they'll ease out. You may have to repeat this a couple of days on the trot.

- Keep your armpits clean and shaved. Hair traps bacteria, which will stink to high heaven. Shaving is quick, easy and cheap but the downside is that hair grows back very quickly. The results of waxing last for longer, but you run the risk of unsightly ingrowing hairs. I'm a shaver lady myself!

- Always throw your razor blade out after ten shaves. A blunt blade will give you razor burn and may cause infection.
- To help the wax to adhere to the hairs better, lightly dust the area with talcum powder.
- If you have a moustache, go for hair electrolysis to remove it long term or try facial bleach.
- If you haven't got time to go and get your moustache sorted out, but you can't bear the thought of being seen out and about looking half-man, do your own little DIY number. Simply mix 1 teaspoon honey with 1 teaspoon lemon juice; gently apply to the hairy slug in the direction of the hair growth. Leave for 10–12 minutes then rinse off with warm water.
- Always shave in the morning at the beginning of your shower or bath. You'll get a far closer shave at the base of the hair.

Cellulite – How to Keep Orange Peel in the Kitchen, Not Stuck to Your Behind

You're in the changing room, trying on some sizzling hot underwear and everything is looking pretty good until you catch the reflection of what you hoped would be a set of pert little bum cheeks. As you stand there in your bra and dental-floss thong (which incidentally has been gobbled up between your cheeks), the ghastly 360° mirrors lit by the most unflattering lights above highlight just how much cellulite you have. It's every woman's nightmare, but you'll be glad to hear that you are not alone as 75% of us ladies suffer from orange-peel skin.

So here are some clever mini-miracle tips that will help reduce the lumps and bumps on your body and save a fortune on expensive anti-cellulite creams.

- Coffee is a massive culprit in causing cellulite so, rather than brewing a cup in the morning and drinking it, transfer it to a bowl. Now jump into your empty bath and start to massage it into the affected areas to exfoliate, then rinse thoroughly.
- One of the most effective ways to get rid of cellulite is to dry-brush skin using a natural bristle body brush. Using firm strokes, work up towards the heart all over your body in circular movements to stimulate the blood flow and the lymphatic system.
- You can also exfoliate while taking a shower. Having said that, don't exfoliate and dry-brush on the same day or you'll zap your skin of its natural oils.
- Instead of getting the bus to work, walk! Put your trainers on and stash your smart work shoes in your bag (simply swap them over when you get there). I can't emphasise enough how good exercise is for banishing cellulite. If you can't do this and you really aren't a gym-lover, just get active: wash the car, run up and down the stairs a few times (and never use an escalator), do your housework vigorously and do lots of gardening.
- Eat half a grapefruit half an hour before each meal you have. This not only speeds up your metabolism, which helps you to lose weight, but it also helps to plump out your wrinkles because of its high water content. If

you have it first thing in the morning it will detoxify your liver and cleanse your stomach.

- Believe it or not, stress can be a major cause of cellulite. When we're feeling anxious about something, we take short breaths and this encourages poor circulation, which can then lead to your skin not functioning properly and losing water. So try to chill out, whether it's by enjoying a relaxing bath, doing more exercise, going to the movies or simply taking in long, slow, deep breaths.

- A lack of shut-eye, whether it's because you're stressed out or out partying, is a major culprit of the unsightly dimples that get stuck to your derrière.

- Fake tan is great for camouflaging orange peel. It's a good solution if you're not tempted by the gym!

- Avoid taking long, hot showers or baths – they can greatly dehydrate your skin, which may result in cellulite.

- A good way to tell if you're dehydrated is to check if your lips feel dry. To send that cellulite packing, drink lots of water!

- For a cellulite-free body, eating the right foods is essential, especially raw foods (not meat, of course). Don't overcook everything. You can of course have a raw vegetable or raw fruit smoothie if you can't bear the thought of eating your way through a stack of carrots or apples. Some of my top foods are: pears (great for detoxifying); watermelon (great for combating water retention) and oats (excellent fat-buster).

- Make sure you include fibre in your diet every day to speed up the elimination of waste from your body and to stop the build-up of cellulite-causing toxins.

- To keep your fat little fingers out of the fridge and to make you feel guilty if you come within a hundred yards of it, stick a photo of Heidi Klum or Naomi Campbell in a bikini on the door.

- If your bum has a double dose (cellulite and spots), then the best thing to do is to put an egg cupful each of live yoghurt and honey in a bowl. Give it a swizzle, then apply it to your butt cheeks. Leave for 25–30 minutes, then rinse off in the shower. I find the best thing to do is to put a towel on the bathroom floor and lie on it first in case the mixture gets a life of its own and goes everywhere. Oh, and don't forget to put your favourite music on for while you're lying there, chilling.

- Shovel in that greenery like it's going out of fashion – kale, watercress and broccoli should be your best friends from now on. Avocado is also great for keeping cellulite at bay.

- Red berries, too, are amazing for warding off that horrible old pimply texture. Try eating blueberries and goji berries. They fight the free radicals that cause cellulite in the first place.

- Don't neglect your bum because it's behind you, you can't see it and because it spends most of its life locked up inside a pair of knickers! Give it the same attention as you do to your face. Once a month, combine a tablespoon of honey with the flesh of an avocado (mash the avocado first) in a bowl. Smear it all over your cheeky cheeks. Leave for 25–30 minutes and then rinse it off in the shower. (Don't forget to spread your towel on the bathroom floor to lie on first.)

- To banish that orange peel from your butt, cut down on your sugar intake. You may have to go through a cold turkey stage at first, but the cravings will subside after two weeks. By then, your body will be so used to it, it won't crave sugar any longer. To make things a little easier, try

sniffing vanilla oil – it will help you get over your cravings more quickly.

- OK, we all know how coffee can give you a blinder of a headache if you're used to having it every day and you then cut it out of your diet; also that coffee is one of the biggest causes of cellulite. So, to help you with those unbearable headaches and cravings, try eating chicory in your salad or drinking ginger and lemon tea. They not only stimulate your mind and body like coffee does, but you still get that feeling of having a lovely hot drink.

- Treat yourself to a little sauna next time you're in the gym. Research shows that, by having a sauna, the blood flow to your heart increases by 75%. The blood then transports the toxins to the surface of your skin. Then, when you start to sweat, the toxins will come out and leave your body feeling fresh and toxin-free.

- Having a regular massage is one of the most effective ways of banishing cellulite but, if you're strapped for cash, do your own DIY one at home. Many of us do it incorrectly because we think that sticking our needle-like fingers into our flesh and doing a sort of circular movement will do the trick, but it may do more harm than good, so use slow, gentle and long strokes that will stimulate the circulation flow – nothing too hard and fast. By having a massage you will boost poor circulation and get the oxygen flowing again. You could even get your loved one to help out with this activity.

- As we know, stress causes cellulite. If you are feeling stressed, try inhaling lavender essential oil. It's amazing for relaxation and will eliminate cellulite-causing stress. Put three drops onto a tissue and inhale deeply. Repeat five times.

Teeth – Perfect Pegs

A great, big, beaming smile says so many things – you're happy, you're approachable and up for a laugh, but a smile accessorised with yellow-stained teeth can be a very alarming experience for those who have to suffer it. It doesn't matter if you're the nicest person in the world – if your teeth look dreadful, the person you're talking to will look very uncomfortable. They'll be trying their hardest to steer you away from fun and giggly conversations onto more serious and even sad ones in a desperate attempt to try to encourage you to keep your mouth shut. Here's some tips to make you smile.

- Grated lemon zest is fantastic for making your teeth whiter – simply rub it over them.
- Cut strawberries in half and rub the flesh over your teeth to reduce stains. Don't forget to rinse them with water afterwards!
- Think about it: when we brush our teeth, we scrub away leftover food stuck in our mouth. Some of that food ends up living in our toothbrushes, as do lots of germs. So, make sure you rinse your toothbrush thoroughly under running water every time you use it. Plus change your brush every two months for ultimate hygiene.
- If you've got a throbbing toothache, drink a strong cup of fresh mint tea with the smallest pinch of salt. The mint will help to calm the pain down.
- Rub bicarbonate of soda over your teeth and then brush with a little bit of water. It acts like a natural bleaching agent and will leave your teeth sparkling like diamonds.
- If you do have yellowy teeth and want to brighten them instantly, wear a bold pink lipstick.

- Buy one of those pots with lots of little holes at the top to hold toothbrushes. Germs can transfer from one brush to the other, which could lead to infections and this kind of a pot will keep them separate.
- Don't be scared of your dentist – he or she is there to help you look beautiful and to save you from having to purchase a set of dentures just yet.

Banish Bog Breath

Bad breath is caused by so many things, including smoking, eating garlic and spicy foods, even hunger. So here's how to banish it. Believe me, your friends will thank you for it...

- Eat a handful of grapes to take a pungent smell away.
- Swizzle your mouth out with water and then scrape the white gunk from your tongue using a clean spoon or put toothpaste onto a brush and brush your tongue.
- Eat a small pot of live natural yoghurt.
- Chew fresh mint or a minty chewing gum. Ginger or watercress is also very good.
- Floss daily. Old food trapped between your teeth can turn pungent.
- Twice a year, you should visit your dentist or hygienist so that you can get your teeth and gums cleaned professionally. It's kind of like having your car professionally valeted.
- Chewing parsley is a good 'un for getting rid of garlic breath.
- Being partial to the odd glass of vino or ten can leave you dehydrated with a very dry mouth and therefore bad breath. To re-stimulate the saliva production in your mouth, chew some sugar-free gum.

- Chew a piece of fennel after you've eaten to cleanse the mouth.

- Smoking ciggies really dries your mouth out, leaving you with stinky, stale breath. Chop up a small lemon and squeeze the juice from it. Transfer to a glass and top up with water. Gargle the liquid, swizzle it round your mouth and spit it out into the sink.

C E L E B R I T Y   T I P !

Simon Cowell
Fresh minxy breath is the best compliment.

MINXY MITTS AND TOOTSIES

So many women walk out of the house with nicotine-stained, chewed nails and hands so rough they could be used to sand down the raw edges of a fresh cut of wood. To complete the look, there might even be a thin layer of little crusty bogies clinging on for dear life to what little shreds of nail are left!

They say your hair is your crowning glory, but I think your nails are even more so. They're one of the first things that people notice, and I'm sorry, but your little bobby-dazzler diamond rings don't deserve monster-like mitts. So arm yourself with a nail file, stop biting and do us all a favour – stop trying to look for a gold watch at the back of your nose. Just get a hanky and blow!

General Hand Care

- I always used to have dried flaky skin around my nails. To get rid of this, squeeze the tips of your fingers for ten seconds every day. What this does is to help stimulate the blood circulation. It can be a bit boring, so I do mine while I'm watching a bit of rubbish on TV!

- Use a face mask on chapped and dry hands – it will purify and regenerate dry skin.

- Always wear rubber gloves when doing the washing up, household cleaning or DIY as detergents and cleaning agents can be very harsh and may cause dried-out nails and hands.

- You'll be surprised how much dirt gets trapped under a ring! So every day, take it off (not above the sink), put it between your teeth (so you don't forget to put it back on), wash your hands and then put your ring back on.

- If you have green fingers, gardening gloves are a must – cut and bruised hands don't sit well with a beautiful French manicure.

- To re-nourish rough hands, smear them in Vaseline, put a pair of cotton gloves on, tuck yourself up in bed and go to sleep. When you wake up in the morning they'll feel as good as new. This is especially worth doing in winter.

- Your hands can be a big age giveaway and they're the one body part that you can't have surgery on, so don't neglect them. In the summer, apply sunscreen to protect them from the harmful rays that can cause premature ageing.

- While filming *60 Minute Makeover* for ITV, I must have got about a log's worth of wooden splinters stuck somewhere in my fingers, I joke you not. But some clever builder on the show gave me the best tip to get rid of them. Cover your fingers in either greasy hand cream or Vaseline and leave overnight. During the night, your skin will become mega-soft, which will eventually encourage the splinter to work its way out. Another way to remove splinters is to numb the area with an ice cube and then remove the darned thing using a pair of tweezers.

- If you've been out in the garden plucking and pruning bushes all day long, you may be left with hands that feel and look like sandpaper. To bring them back to their usual smooth self, get a handful of porridge oats, soak them with a dash of warm water from the tap, mix and lather up in the palms of your hands. Gently rub the mixture into every part of your mitts for a couple of minutes and then rinse off with warm water. Your hands will absorb the vitamin E from the oats, which will nourish your hands, and the fibre will help to remove the dead skin cells.

- Our hands are heaving with germs and most of the infections that enter our bodies are caused because we touch our eyes and mouth. Yuck! So wash your hands every hour. To prevent hands from drying out, keep a tube of moisturiser by the sink.

- If your nails have white polka dots on them (and I don't mean the fake nail extensions that you stick on), this could be because you are deficient in zinc so eat a small handful of pumpkin seeds or some sexy oysters as both of these contain loads of zinc.

- Do you know what? I wouldn't eat onions if they didn't taste so good as they make your eyes flood up with water, which then runs down your face and smudges your make-up; your hands will also stink to high heaven after preparing them. But there's a solution to these problems. When you cut the head and tail off the onion, rinse it immediately under running

water. This should take most of the toxic fumes away. To remove the stench from your mitts, rub the flesh of a lemon onto your hands for a few moments and rinse with water. You can do the same thing after handling garlic. Lemon is great for cleaning your hands and taking any bad smells away.

Nail Care

- Nicotine causes yellow stained nails. Try wiping your nails with lemon juice to get rid of the nasty colour. (Lemon juice is like a mild bleach and great for removing stains. In fact, it's the ultimate non-toxic cleaning product.)

- A high-maintenance French manicure has never been so easy. Buy a white nail pencil from a beauty desk and apply under the nail. It takes about 30 seconds, costs next to nothing and looks very, very convincing! How's that for ultra-lazy?

- If you wear dark nail varnish, always carry a pot around with you in your handbag to fill in chips. Always wear sheer nail varnish if you are a heavy-handed person because, if you chip them, no one will notice.

- Rub neat olive oil into your cuticles every night before you go to bed. This will encourage them to grow healthier and stronger.

- Try not to get nail varnish onto your cuticles; you'll not only dry them out but you'll also prevent them from growing properly.

- I used to bite my nails like mad when I was little. My mum even used to bribe me by promising that, if I stopped, she would buy me a new doll or give me extra pocket money, etc. For years, nothing worked and the only thing that did eventually make me stop was that disgusting varnish that you can buy in pharmacies – you paint it on and when you go to bite your nails it leaves the most revolting taste in your mouth for hours. It really does put you off and sooner or later your nails grow back to their full glory.

- Don't go back and forth when filing your nails – you'll only create split ends. Instead file in one direction only.
- There's nothing worse than chewed, bitten nails so try sticking false ones on. They not only stop you from biting them, but men will find them totally irresistible.
- Dark nail varnish can stain nails a horrid curry colour so buff them, then apply a layer of clear base varnish before you add your chosen colour. This can help prevent discoloration.
- If you have wide, stubby nails and want to make them appear longer and thinner, paint the coloured varnish only down the middle of the nail, leaving the sides bare. This will give a streamlined look.
- Freshly painted nails always take longer to dry on a hot day, so to speed up the process, run them under ice-cold running water for five minutes before you apply varnish. This helps to speed up the drying process.
- Buy ready-made pre-soaked pads so you don't have to carry round both cotton wool and nail polish remover. Ingenious!
- Cuticles are there for a reason – to prevent germs from entering our bodies. Never remove them completely, but don't let them grow over your nail too much either, as they will prevent your nails from growing. Use cuticle remover to keep them under control.
- Keep nail varnish in the fridge – it will last twice as long.
- Obvious as it might sound, always keep a nail file in your purse. If you get a little snag, you can prevent it from turning into a major breakage.

Because my purse is quite small, I chopped my nail file in half so that I could fit it inside.

- Don't use your nails as letter-openers or staple removers unless you want them to split. Instead, get the proper tools for these kinds of jobs!

TLC for Piggy-trotter Tootsies

- If you suffer from in-growing toenails, cut a V shape in the centre of the nail at the top to force the sides to grow inwards again, relieving the outer edge skin.

- If you're getting strange looks from people, your feet may just stink of cheese! If this is the case, fear not. Get yourself into the kitchen and sprinkle some baking soda onto them. This will help keep some of the smell at bay for a while. Oh, and don't forget to sprinkle some of this magic dust into your shoes, too. Leave it in overnight and vacuum it out in the morning.

- Another good way of attacking the cheesy-feet situation is to soak your feet in a lemon mix. Simply squeeze six lemons and add the juice to a big mug of warm water. Mix and then transfer to a shallow dish. Pop your feet in, turn on the TV, then sit back and relax for 20–30 minutes.

- If your tootsies feel like sandpaper, it's time to soften them before you wear through your shoes. Warm up a cup of olive oil in the microwave, on a low heat, until it's comfortably hot. Pour it into a shallow cooking dish or a plastic basin of some sort. Now pop in your trotters and leave for twenty minutes. Before you take them out, make sure you've rubbed in the oil over every part of your feet.

- To stop your toes from rubbing together after you've just painted them, roll up a long piece of cotton wool and quickly weave it in and out between each toe.

- If you stub your toe and it goes black, it will take roughly twelve weeks to grow out totally. The best thing to do to avoid your toe looking like it has a fungal disease is to paint your toenails in a dark colour to disguise it.

- If you suffer from athlete's foot, always keep your feet dry and wear clean cotton socks. Athlete's foot thrives in moist conditions, such as the warm atmosphere after a shower or bath. To dry out your feet thoroughly, blast them with your hairdryer, set to a medium heat. If the problem persists, consult your GP.

- If you're a city chick and you love to get your tootsies out in a pair of summer sandals, make sure you wash them before you go to bed. Your bare feet will have attracted hundreds of germs throughout the day. Yuck!

- For soft and sexy tootsies, soak them in warm skimmed milk in the washing-up bowl, which can be rested in the bath (sit on the edge of the bath). Rinse with water, exfoliate with a foot file, then moisturise with rich lotion and put your feet up.

- If you have cracked heels, here's a great remedy. Mush up a banana and massage it into the cracks. Leave for ten minutes, rinse off and then moisturise. To maintain your heels long term, squeeze the juice of six lemons into a washing-up bowl or roasting dish. Soak your feet in the lemon juice for 15 minutes and then rinse off. Do this on a weekly basis until the cracks have disappeared.

- If your feet sweat like crazy, spray an antiperspirant onto them before you put your shoes on.

- Blisters can be caused either by ill-fitting shoes or from the friction caused by hot, sweaty feet rubbing against a sock. To avoid blisters, wear shoes that fit properly, and keep your feet and socks as dry as you can. Leave an unpopped blister alone – it will re-absorb and disappear on its own.

C E L E B R I T Y   T I P !

Carole Malone – Journalist

Forget painting your toenails – which takes more time than a full face make-up and smudge if you put your shoes on within two hours of having them done (who's got that long to wait?) If you want your toenails looking fab in sandals, peep toes, in tatty old flip-flops and, yes, even in the bedroom for weeks at a time with no effort whatsoever, have gel and white tips put on them in exactly the same way you would on your fingernails. The difference is your fingernails need doing every two or three weeks, but for some reason the toenails last longer. Don't ask me why, but the nails must grow more slowly. Also there's this amazing gel called Pedique which comes in pinks and reds for toes and hands which lasts for weeks and just looks like nail varnish and doesn't chip. (In case you hadn't noticed, this is hand and foot care for the lazy cow but totally sophisticated obviously).

MAKE-UP

No one deliberately goes out looking like an orange transvestite with an oversized monobrow slapped across their forehead like a big slug but, you know what, it does happen – and, in my experience, far too often! Applying war paint to your face is rather like painting a picture: it has to be pleasing to the eye, something you hope people will look at and appreciate. So here's how to get lovely luscious lips and a killer stare without looking as if you've really tried.

Luscious Lips – Little Angelina Jolie Numbers

- To get plump minxy lips without having to resort to the old collagen, just rub raw chillies over them (but don't snog anyone too soon after or it will give a new meaning to 'hot lips'!). Or try rubbing pineapple juice on them, then add a layer of shiny lip gloss. The pineapple exfoliates the dead skin cells, the chillies stimulate your natural collagen and the lip gloss makes them appear larger – it's something definitely worth pouting about.
- Another good way to get plump and fuller lips is to use two different shades of lipstick. Apply the darker ones in the corners and the lighter one to the more fleshy part in the middle of your lips.
- If your lips are all scabby and chapped, the worst thing you could do is to keep licking them – this will dry them even more. You may be dehydrated and so you must drink lots of water. Also try applying a thick lip balm on an hourly basis. If your lips become severely cracked, go and seek medical advice.
- If you have thin lips and want the illusion of big ones, then use a light-coloured shiny gloss.
- Wearing a darker lip liner than your lipstick is the VPL of make-up. Always go for the same colour.
- Darker-coloured lipstick makes your lips look thinner and a light colour gives a fuller appearance.

- If you can't find the perfect lipstick shade for you, choose three or four different colours from the same brand. Mix them together using a lipstick brush on the back of your hand.
- No man enjoys kissing lips like sandpaper – you want to leave him wanting more! Using a toothbrush, gently scrub your lips to remove all of the dead skin, then apply a nice big thick layer of Vaseline just before you go to bed.

Eyes

- If you have little currant eyes and want them to look larger, apply white eyeliner to the bottom rim – it will really brighten and open them up.
- Put your eyeliner in the fridge for a few hours before you want to use it. It's easier to sharpen and you will have more control over where it goes. And if you keep your mascara in the fridge, it will last longer and prevent the germs that live in there from having a party! Store your perfume in the fridge, too, to extend its life.
- If you have heavy dark circles under your eyes, keep your eye make-up simple and light. Only apply mascara and pencil to the upper eyelid and leave the bottom naked for a refreshed look.
- Using eyelash curlers will make your eyes look bigger, but curl them before you add mascara otherwise you will pull them out.
- Before you put your eyeshadow on, apply a heavy dusting of loose powder directly below your eyes so that any loose eye-shadow particles that fall below can easily be brushed away with a big blending brush.
- If you're going for a vampy vixen look and want to create smoky eyes, pop your eye pencil under the hot water tap or onto a light bulb for a

few seconds before you apply it. You'll notice how much thicker and minxier it goes on.

How to Get Great Eyebrows

- To make eyebrow plucking less painful, place a warm flannel on your brows to open up the hair follicles and make it easier to pull out any stray hairs. When you have finished, hold ice cubes on your brows to close the pores and soothe them.
- To get the perfect arch, spray a little hairspray onto your fingers and quickly apply to your eyebrows. Brush them into shape using a dry toothbrush and leave to set. You can also do this by drawing a rough guideline on your brow using an eyebrow pencil for the shape and then pluck the unwanted hairs away from your pencilled lines.
- Always pluck from underneath and never above. And never pluck in the opposite direction to which the hair grows. Not only will it feel more painful but if you pluck in the direction of growth, it will grow back flat.
- Eyebrows give your face so much definition and character so don't take that away by overplucking. Never try to make each eyebrow appear identical – they don't naturally look that way.
- Brow tints are good news for those who have transparent eyebrows. They will last for about six weeks and help to give your eyes definition.
- To tame down your wild eyebrows, brush them up with an eyebrow comb or old dry toothbrush, then trim them with a mini pair of scissors. It will frame your eyes better.
- Plucking your eyebrows is so much easier if you do it by daylight rather than artificial light.

- Eyebrow plucking can really hurt sometimes, especially when you have your period. To reduce the pain, stretch your skin upwards with your fingers where you want to pluck and pull the hair out quickly. Or you could take a painkiller to reduce the painful sensation.

More Useful Tips

- Get fab features without cosmetic surgery by using a darker shade of blusher under your cheekbones and a lighter one on top to create high cheekbone shadows.
- Towards the end of a mascara's life it can become pretty dry, so to get those last few dregs out simply pop the bottle into a mug of hot water for two to three minutes to heat it up. It will become liquid again and ready to apply.
- Baby oil works a treat as a cheap and gentle make-up remover.
- If you use waterproof mascara, try to alternate it with a different kind. If used every day, waterproof mascara will dry your lashes out, leaving them weak and brittle.
- To get rid of a double chin, put a lighter shade of foundation under your chin.
- Like hair, eyelashes need feeding too, so rub Vaseline into them before you go to bed. This will keep them soft and nourished and prevent them from breaking.
- Go out with lashings of style in a pair of false eyelashes! They not only add depth and definition, but will also be the focus of everyone's attention – great if you have small eyes and want them to look larger.
- By wearing light-coloured clothing you will not only project light onto your face, making you look healthier, but it will also show off the colours in your make-up too.

- Eyeshadow creams can cost a fortune, so rather than chuck a couple of quid's worth down the toilet, save all the ends (make sure they're not out of date). Cut them in half, mix similar shades together and you've got yourself another month's worth.

- If you're out on the razzle and you have one of those ridiculous small handbags that fit nothing in them apart from one must-have item, then I suggest you choose a soft lipstick. It will not only go on your lips, but can also be used as a blusher (add a little dot to your cheeks and blend in).

- If you don't have a heated eyelash curler, stick your metal one under a hot hairdryer before curling. The heat will encourage the lashes to set better. A word of warning – make sure the curlers don't get too hot or you might scald your eyelid – they should be comfortably warm.

- If you have squeezed your spot and it's now open, the worst thing you could do is to immediately cake on cover-up. You'll only wake up the next day with an even bigger, infected spot. If you really must have a picking session and you want to wear make-up, then do it two or three hours before you go out so that it has time to rest and won't be so red.

- Natural daylight is the most honest light in which to do your make-up, so find a window away from harsh sunlight and apply your make-up there. If you're going to do your make-up at night, try to avoid doing it right under a spotlight. Choose somewhere where the light is even and won't give you that Count Dracula look.

- It's very tempting, I know, but try not to put fresh new make-up over old minging make-up that's been there all day! Though your face won't look like an old oil painting that's sliding South, it will clog up your pores and suffocate your skin, giving you spots.

- If you are going for minxy, smoky eyes then you need to protect the foundation that you have already carefully applied. To do this, all you need to do is gently press a little bit of loo roll under each eye when applying make-up and, when you're done, all the excess eyeshadow will have fallen onto the tissue, not your face.

- Applying make-up gradually to your face is the best way. Slapping it onto your face and trying to scrape it off in places where you've laid it on too thick will leave you looking like a Picasso painting!

- Before you try a lipstick sample in a shop, *always* ask an assistant if she can clean it with a tissue, so that you don't catch any infections from someone else that has tried it, but never bothered to clean it afterwards. This applies to all make-up samples, especially eye shadows too.

- I see it all the time... Women who trowel on foundation all over their face, stopping at their jawline and not blending it into their neck. I know it might feel a little bit grubby putting make-up on your neck and I know you might worry about getting foundation on the neckline of your favourite top, but really, girls, do you want to look like you're wearing an orange mask?

- You know those little net bags that you get with your washing tablets? Well, don't throw them out – they come in very handy not only for when you need to wash your delicate underwear and tights, but also for washing dirty make-up sponges in the washing machine.

- For cat-like eyes, always put more mascara on the outside of the upper eye and a light coating on the inside.

- If you don't wash your make-up brushes then your make-up will never look that fresh, plus your brushes will be loaded with germs. It's so easy – all you have to do is gently wash them in the palm of your hand with a dot of hair shampoo and then condition them. Dry somewhere flat, preferably on a little towel near a heater.

- If you have hard compact eyeshadows you can use both dry and wet (especially eyeliner), don't go dipping your brush in your mouth to moisten it. Believe it or not, your mouth is riddled with germs! Instead, put a dash of water into a glass and use this to dip your brush in.

- There's nothing quite like getting ready with the girls, is there? Cracking open the vino, blasting out Beyoncé and doing each other's make-up… There's only one problem with this, though. Sharing make-up brushes, eyeliners and mascara can be really unhealthy – cross-contamination can cause all sorts of problems such as the eye infection conjunctivitis.

- If you want to revamp your look and have absolutely no idea where to start, you can get make-up advice and have a practical demonstration at all major stores. They will show you all sorts of colours and combinations that you might not have thought about. You tend to have to pay for the

C E L E B R I T Y T I P !

Jamelia - Singer

The best two accessories a girl could ever wear are confidence and a big smile.

demo, but that's totally redeemable on a product that you buy from that particular brand.

- It's worth getting on all the mailing lists for your favourite brands and stores. They will let you know about all the future promotions and sales.

A HOST OF OTHER BEAUTY TIPS THAT EVERY GODDESS NEEDS

Stress – How to Chill

Your knickers are in a twist, you're tearing your hair out and you're so sensitive that, if any poor sod offers you a cup of tea instead of coffee, you fly off the handle, have a cry and end up on the floor in a dithering wreck. We've all been stressed. It's not a particularly great place to be and to be brutally honest you're neither use nor ornament. The best thing you can do to get back into serene siren mode is to reassess your life and learn how to relax and chill out.

- There's a reason why 'beauty sleep' (best miracle beauty product) is so-called. A good night's kip will prevent you from ageing prematurely and reduces unwanted dark circles from under your eyes. So you see, there's no need just yet to go for those collagen and botox injections high up on your 'to do' list.
- A thirty-minute walk every day rouses your immune system and cuts the risk of illness by half. You'll also notice how much more relaxed and happier you feel and your senses will be a lot sharper.
- After a hard day's work, turn your bathroom into a mini spa. Fill up the

bath, add some aromatherapy oils, put on some über chilled-out music, light a few candles, pour yourself a wee glass of vino, rest your head on your inflatable pillow and just melt down in it and dream away.

- A fifteen-minute power nap after lunch can do wonders for your stress levels. It's a quick intense sleep that really does improve alertness. Any longer and you'll feel groggy and grumpy, mind!

- Put five drops of lavender essential oil in your bath after a stressful day at work to chill you out and soothe your muscles. You can also add a little to your pillow to help you get a better night's sleep.

- Rub your temples if you can feel a headache coming. Remember, you might be dehydrated so drink a big glass of water, sit down and relax.

- If you have trouble sleeping, try to avoid anything that mentally stimulates your brain such as doing paperwork, watching TV and sometimes even reading before you go to bed.

- As I've already said, a good night's sleep is the best and most natural way to combat stress, so make sure your boudoir has black-out curtains or blinds to keep out the light. Or you could do what I do, and that is to have a black T-shirt by my pillow. When the light shines in, I stick it over my eyes. Beware, however – it's not the sexiest of looks!

- Now, this may sound a bit bonkers but it really works. If you suffer from mega-stress, it's time to schedule in a little Hannah remedy that's natural and fun – yep, it's time for a little countryside excursion. It's essential that you bring your camera as you will be taking pictures of sheep, bark and running water. Believe it or not, these elements of nature will really de-stress you. Choose your favourite image, the one that makes you feel happy and soothed (a sheep in a green field works wonders for me), get

it enlarged as much as possible and hang it on your wall. When you feel stressed, just sit back and daydream for a few moments and remember those relaxing times.

- Eating the wrong foods such as junky snacks only adds to your stress, so fill up your fruit bowl to the brim with every yummy fruit possible. This will entice you to eat it all; it will increase your energy and also make you feel more relaxed as you will be eating natural sugars.

- Being late for work or an appointment just gets you in a fluster so always leave fifteen minutes early to prevent this.

- A good way to get rid of a build-up of stress is to hang your rug outside on a railing and beat the crap out of it using a broom or tennis racket! If your neighbour passes by, you can quickly put on a smile and say you are just cleaning your rug. They don't need to know that you're clobbering the life out of it because you feel supertense.

- Although we think coffee is the answer when it comes to keeping alert, it can also make you feel more anxious, so cut down by swapping it for peppermint tea or caffeine-free coffee.

- Instead of pulling your hair out in despair, brush it instead! This not only massages several acupressure points but the repetitive movement is psychologically quite calming.

- Try wearing coloured clothes for the day. Colour is fashion's serotonin and always cheers people up.

- If you're constantly kept awake by the pneumatic-drill-like snore of your boyfriend, invest in a pair of earplugs – they will block it out completely. Disturbance and lack of sleep will leave you feeling grumpy and stressed the following day. You'll also find yourself in need of a severe munchie session of cake and other sugary goodies to keep your energy levels up.

- Always have a bunch of flowers with lots of foliage in the house. When you feel tense, sniff them. The more oxygen you inhale, the calmer you'll feel. Plants are good too, plus they will last longer than flowers.

- Do you turn into a raging road hog when faced with traffic and start effing and blinding at anything and everything? If so, keep a little pot of cinnamon in your car – when you feel the signs coming on, the scent will calm you.

- What you choose to eat really affects your mood. If you're feeling stressed, go for calming foods that are rich in B vitamins and starch, such as a boiled egg with wholewheat toast or porridge and chopped banana.

- Keep a pot of honey in your cupboard and, when you feel your brain's about to explode, dip your finger in it and suck the honey off. Honey is brilliant for making you feel less stressed and happy again because it releases the hormone serotonin after a few minutes.

- Don't play your banging hectic music as it will just make your mood go from bad to worse. Instead, try playing and even singing along to Christmas songs. 'Silent Night' is a good 'un!

- Do a headstand up against a wall or simply lie down on your back and put your legs and feet up against the wall. The sudden rush of blood to the head really does refresh the mind. Plus, I find a good old sauna session always helps to blow away the cobwebs – it's very relaxing.

- Sometimes a good old hug from someone you love can really do the trick if you're stressed.

- Have a day where you take off your watch, turn off your phone and

BlackBerry and go nowhere near your computer. Sometimes it's good to take a break and allow yourself to forget about your responsibilities.

- OK, sleeping on your desk while at work isn't a particularly good look, but having a sneaky little five-minute catnap can work wonders. Any longer and you may find your P45 slapped in front of your sleeping-beauty face!

- If you're going to go for a stress-busting run or brisk walk, then do it when the rush hour is over to reduce your intake of petrol fumes. And if you're taking the lazy option and driving somewhere, try to avoid putting the air conditioning on. Why? Because air conditioning systems take the air from the exhaust pipe of the car in front of you. Yuck! So always travel with your window open, where possible.

- Chilled-out spiritual music is great for relaxing a stressed-out mind and a screwed-up face. Choose tracks that have no words so that you can dreamily drift away and forget your troubles for a moment. Remember, if you're glowing on the inside, you will glow on the outside.

- Do you sometimes notice how dogs find a really weird place to snooze, whether it's on top of the back of the sofa, or with their heads hidden behind the bookcase, and how relaxed they always look? Well, take a leaf out of their book. Find a place in your house where you feel really, really relaxed. I love to lie under the kitchen table with a pillow and always have done since I was a little girl. Often I find my boyfriend in the airing cupboard because it's warm and cosy! So wherever this place might be, visit it when you feel like stress is really getting you down, and sit or lie there for ten minutes and let your thoughts just drift away.

- When your stress levels are at their max, you'll notice how your hands feel a little bit on the dead side as they go really cold. To bring your stress levels down, rub your mitts together until they warm up again.

- If you've been on your feet all day long and they're humming with pain, then it's time for a bit of tootsie TLC. Get your nightie on and fill up your washing-up bowl with hot water. Add a bunch of fresh thyme and a teaspoon of salt to the water. Now carry it into the living room, put on your favourite music, pop your feet into the bowl and rest. It's so therapeutic.

- Open up all the windows in the house for ten minutes every day – that whoosh of oxygen and fresh air around the house will get rid of any stuffiness. Fresh air always sorts out a foggy head so, whether you're in the office or going to bed, always have your window open a little bit to allow oxygen to flow in.

- When you're next in a shop, have a go at being really friendly and say something nice. By doing this, you are not only putting yourself in a more positive frame of mind but hopefully the sales person will respond with something really positive too, thereby creating a happy environment. If he or she doesn't, they're obviously just a miserable old sod – or having a bad day too.

- If you work in a windowless office and you arrive there in the dark and then leave in the dark during the winter months, then it's really important that you take a walk at lunchtime to get some sunlight. Natural light is so good for us as it provides our body with vitamin D, which is essential for our good health. Vitamin D helps to build and maintain strong bones – and our bones support everything else, so look after them!

- Whenever I'm feeling stressed, I seem to have two options: (i) to scream

so loudly my tonsils nearly fall out or (ii) to go for a massage (half-hour neck, back and shoulders isn't too expensive). A hard massage will get the circulation of the lymphatic system going, helping to rid your body of all those nasty old toxins. Make sure you get a male masseur or a massive shotput-throwing female to massage your stress away. I have an amazing one. She's like a butcher and she'll throw me onto the bed like a piece of meat. With her massive mitts, she'll pound me like a steak until I'm soft, tender – and bloody sore! Any pain and pressure soon disappears, though.

- When you get home from a stressful day's work, wash your face then soak a flannel in warm water. Now lie back on your sofa and place the flannel on your face. It will take away all that facial tension.

- Fake a huge smile – you never know, it might just turn into a real one!

- Turn on MTV and pretend you're one of Justin Timberlake's backing dancers. Make all the dance moves hot and totally over-exaggerated. This really will pop the stress bubble. Just make sure you've closed your curtains and locked the door properly. You don't want an ambulance turning up because somebody saw you and thought you were having some sort of fit, when all you were doing was de-stressing!

- A game of squash is a much better way to relieve stress than throwing your computer out of the office window.

- Grow your own herbs or some tomato plants on your windowsill. Taking care of something organic really does take your mind off other things. If you have problems sleeping at night, add rosemary, basil or sage to your evening meals. They are all great for inducing sleep.

- If you've got a hard day's work ahead of you and want to pep up your body, then get in the shower. Set it on your normal temperature to wash yourself then put it on cold. Freeze your arse off for one minute and get out. Now dry yourself off and notice how alert you feel.

- When you're next having a shower, massage your head with your shampoo and conditioner – you will be massaging all those worries away through your acupressure points.

- If you're one of those lovely people who always say 'yes' to everyone and everything, but don't have the time to do it all, then you really have to learn the art of how to say 'no' otherwise you'll get super-stressed and burn yourself out, and it's just not worth it.

- Sometimes you can walk into your office and be faced with a pile of paperwork that would give Mount Everest a run for its money. Rather than sitting down and getting totally stressed, spend twenty minutes sifting through it all the night before. Sort everything into sections and work out what needs to be done the following day in priority order. If you do this every day, you can just come in the next morning with a fresh head and get your teeth into it. You'll probably get twice the amount of work done, in less time and hopefully minus the stress.

- I find going on holiday so stressful – all the organising, the commuting there and back, planning what you're going to visit, where you're going to go and eat, etc... Sometimes it's a good idea just to take four days off and stay at home where you can get on top of all those nagging errands, see friends and catch up on sleep.

- Being stressed is bad enough, but not being able to sleep on top of that just makes the whole thing worse, so it's time to get back in the kitchen and prepare a little bedtime drink. Here's what you need: two big

courgettes (to chill you out), two Cos lettuces (they will make you feel sleepy) and some parsley (makes you feel less stressed). Now juice it all up and drink.

- Here's another recipe you can try: one ripe avocado (packed with B vitamins which help you sleep), one ripe banana (to de-stress) and 350ml (12fl oz) unsweetened soya milk. Blend all the ingredients together and drink.

- I always think your body is the best at informing you whether it's happy or not. If you've had enough sleep, you will wake up naturally but, if you wake up to the sound of your alarm all the time, maybe you should be going to bed a little earlier.

- Not getting your beauty sleep at night because you're stressed will make you look like one of those drugged-up rock stars whose flesh literally hangs off their face! So cut down on your caffeine intake. That means no fizzy drinks, coffees or tea after 1pm and instead try drinking a lovely mug of camomile tea before you go to bed. It will help calm the mind and promote sleep.

- Now we all know that a good night's sleep is a great stress-buster, but trying to do so when your mind's totally overactive is quite another thing, especially when you're trying to count sheep in the desperate hope that this will rock you off to sleep, but all you can actually count are all the emails you need to send. If this is the case then you need to start preparing yourself for bed about 2½ hours beforehand to relax your mind.

- Do you sometimes feel as if you're dragging your arms across the floor like a primate because you've been sitting at your desk in an awkward position all day? By hunching up your shoulders and neck, you'll develop backache and a whole lot more stress, so keep reminding yourself to relax the top half of your body. In addition, if you're hunched over your computer all day long, your tense muscles will clutch onto toxins such as lactic acid, so stretch for a couple of minutes – bend down, touch your toes or stretch up towards the ceiling. The more stretching you do, the more your muscles will relax and allow the toxins to go into your bloodstream for removal.

- If you're one of those people who practically lives in the office, constantly surrounded by computers, fax machines and printers, etc., then you're probably living in a very toxic environment. Before you become radioactive, ask your boss if you can put some dark green leaf and aloe vera plants in the office. They will clean the air and fill it with oxygen.

- Don't just lie there in the middle of the night thinking about your worries, they'll only seem worse. Instead, get up, go and make yourself a hot mug of milk, do a mindless chore, like unpacking the dishwasher, and then try going back to bed after half an hour. Alternatively, you could try writing your worries onto a piece of paper to get them off your chest. When you re-read them in the morning, hopefully they won't seem so bad.

- Now this is purely selfish, but if you're about to combust, phone your friend who has a dog and offer to take it for a walk. It's amazing how a little four-legged furry thing can totally alleviate tension, plus the doggie's quids in because he gets something out of it too!

- Ginseng tea in the morning is a great way to start the day as it makes you feel more energised and less anxious.

- An out-of-shape mattress can disturb your sleep. If this is the case, it's time to get a new one, which should soon have you sleeping like a baby

(see also page 120). Buy the best you can afford and you should only have to change it every 10 or 15 years.

- PMS can turn a lovely, bubbly girl into a venus-fly-trapping bitch. If this is the case and you are a fully packed, sugar-, coffee- and tea-guzzler, then you would do better to cut back on these as they all trigger mood swings. Instead try munching on carbohydrates to help stabilise your blood-sugar levels. Porridge oats, oat cookies, brown bread and sweet potatoes are all good carbs that will help to keep the beast locked away.

- I often get a headache when my sinuses are blocked and it can really be quite painful. A brilliant way to naturally get rid of the blockage is to eat a chilli – the heat will unblock the congested area.

- Alternatively, you could inhale over a bowl of eucalyptus oil. Add a teaspoon of the oil to hot water. Put your head over the bowl and chuck a tea towel over your head to keep the steam in. Breathe deeply over the vapours for about 8-10 minutes.

- A homemade fresh smoothie of pomegranate, carrots and grapes will give you the start you need to handle a hectic day.

- If all else fails, go somewhere private and have a bloody good cry! It's very soothing.

Quick Date Beauty – Emergency Tips

You're running seriously late after work, your greasy hair just got rained on because the weather forecast was wrong again and you left your brolly at home. You feel hot and bothered, your make-up has slid down off your face, and it's sod's law this happens on the very day when you've got yourself a hot date. Fear not, you dustbin impersonators!

- Always wear hot undies for your date – you don't have to take them off but I can tell you this for sure – you'll feel great and a lot more confident in them.

- If you haven't time to go home for a bath, wipe your armpits and private bits with body wipes and apply a fresh layer of deodorant. Finish off by spraying your favourite perfume all over your body.

- For skanky, chipped nails, just fill in the chips with the same colour nail polish or take it off altogether.

- If your date is straight after work and you have no time to re-do your make-up, don't panic. Just soak a cotton bud with eye make-up remover and clean away the old concealer from around your eyes and any spots, then rebuild these areas with new foundation for a fresher appearance. Lastly, apply a good old coat of lipgloss (having said that, go easy on the dark lipgloss if you're hoping for a smooch).

- For tired, red Dracula-type eyes, brighten them with a few eye drops.

- So many women apply a stunning and expensive perfume, only to ruin it by spraying on cheap and cheerful toxic-smelling BO-basher! Go for a neutral one that won't interfere with your lovely scent and will save your date from wanting to gag.

- If you can't clean your teeth, chew gum or fresh mint, or eat a handful of grapes with a glass of water.

- Sitting in front of the computer all day can leave you looking stressed and deathly white. For an instant tan, buy tinted body creams to rid you of that luminous glow within seconds. Also, allow yourself a few breaks in the day – it will do wonders for both your stress levels and your frown marks.

- If you've got really grubby hair, using your fingers, roughly gather it together into a ponytail. Don't use a brush – this highlights just how greasy it is. Alternatively, spray dry shampoo into it to soak up all the grease.
- To disguise your oil-slick hair and get instant night-time glamour, pop a few sparkly hair clips into your barnet.
- Dirty nails on a woman can mean 'dirty girl' to a man (and I don't mean the naughty Paris Hilton kind), so, if you suddenly realise you have grubby nails and you're at the table with your date, very nonchalantly take hold of the menu and very slowly, so as not to attract attention to what you are doing, bring the menu down on top of your lap and use a corner of it to pick your nails. Gross, I know, but you don't want to blow your chances with your hot date. Another alternative is to nab one of the toothpicks that you get at the table and do the same.
- Oily skin can make you look as if you've had your face stuck in the chip pan so always carry powdered blotting paper (mini sheets of paper coated in fine powder) in your bag. They will soak up all the grease.
- To transform daytime make-up into something a little more minxy, just add some smoky dark colours. He won't be able to keep his eyes off you.
- Always keep a pair of high-heeled shoes in your drawer at work – it's an instant glamour-fixer. Also have a supply of stockings and tights tucked away in there in case of emergencies.
- Another good tip to disguise your grubby hair is to take sections and wrap each one round your index finger, spray with a little hairspray and hold for a couple of seconds then drop. You will now have instant glammy Pammy curls.
- If all else fails and you really do look and feel like something that's stuck

on the bottom of someone's shoe, you can always tell him you're running half an hour late and to get the cocktails in. Hopefully by the time you get there he will be a little squiffy and you'll look as good as Claudia Schiffer in his eyes!

CELEBRITY TIP!

Stephanie Beacham – Actress

I never leave the house without wearing nail varnish and scent. Hey, I needn't look in a mirror. If I know my nails look good and I smell good, then I, too, feel really good!

Look Good Naked For Your New Man

Thank God light switches and blackout blinds were invented! One flick of the switch and he needn't be any the wiser about your cellulite, ghostly white skin or the big ugly spot on your bum. In actual fact there's nothing more attractive to a man than a woman who is confident about her body, and, yes, that does include the derrière view! So my advice here is that, even if you don't feel comfortable about your body, just pretend you do and he won't even notice your lumps or bumps. This section is all about how to accentuate the parts you love about your body and how to camouflage the ones you don't.

- If you are body-shy and not all that used to being naked full stop, then

close your curtains and walk about the house without any clothes. So as not to waste any time, you could even do the cooking or cleaning! Give it a few weeks and you'll notice how much more confident you are.

- To reduce the appearance of cellulite and to make you look thinner and more babe-alish, slap on a layer of fake tan the night before.

- Asparagus is a natural diuretic and therefore helps to get rid of a bloated stomach because it flushes out all of the toxins. It makes your skin glow too.

- Do lots of sits-ups on the floor before you go to work every day to tighten up those lazy stomach muscles.

- Like the interior of a house, it's the attention to detail that makes all the difference. So get rid of those nasty chipped nails and have some false ones applied, paint your toenails, get rid of your muff with hair-removal cream or wax, pluck your eyebrows, moisturise your body and put on some minxy make-up.

- Get those boobies looking hot! Fill up your garden spray bottle with cold water and spritz it onto your boobs for one minute every morning and evening. This will stimulate the circulation and make them pert.

- Another good way to get those baps looking North is to massage them every day to stimulate the circulation and to give them a healthy glow.

- Do a three-day detox. Cut out all carbohydrates after breakfast, eat loads of fish and vegetables and drink green tea. This is the route to a flat stomach.

- Good posture can transform your body. Push your shoulders back and stick your boobs out to make them look bigger, suck your stomach in and stand up straight to make yourself look taller.

- Avoid eating foods such as beans, pasta and bread before you go on your date as they will all give you a bloated stomach. Instead eat salads, chicken, fruit and nuts.
- Having a pre-soak in the bath is a great opportunity to chisel away those hard patches of skin on the bottom of your feet with a pumice stone. Afterwards, apply lots of moisturiser for ultra-soft feet.

Hot Holidays – Simple Seaside Solutions

You've got two choices when you hit the beach in your bikini: you can look like a lumpy lard-arse or babe it up, sun-kissed and super delicious as you strut down the beach looking like you own it! No competition, really. Here are some tips for all you beach babes out there.

- Sun cream goes off six months after it's been opened and it won't do its job properly. Leave your sunscreen in the fridge to prolong its life and make sure you replace it regularly.
- To keep those pest-like pubes from roaming out of their given environment, always carry a pair of tweezers in your bag to pluck the little blighters away.
- So you don't scare everyone off the beach with your Addams family skin, cheat a little and fake tan it a few nights before.
- To keep you cool by the pool, fill a little spray bottle with water and spritz your face every so often.
- Rub tea tree oil into your mosquito bites to stop them from becoming infected. Or, press ice cubes wrapped in a towel or a bag of frozen peas onto the bite and hold in place for eight minutes.

- Beach sand is a great natural exfoliator. Go for a lovely long walk along the beach to soften and smooth your feet (this is also very good exercise for your bum cheeks), then sit on the edge of the water and scrub your body with handfuls of sand to get rid of dead skin cells. If you're staying in a busy resort and don't want the entire beach watching you scrub away, take some sand to your hotel room in a cup and do this in private.

- Take your own green tea bags out with you to detox and make sure you do your stomach crunches daily for that washboard tummy.

- In summer your feet can develop a layer of hard skin that is ingrained with dirt from the pavements. To avoid this, wear cushioned sandals and use a foot exfoliator and pumice stone to smooth out the ridges.

- After swimming in the sea, your hair can become quite straw-like, all tangled and dry. A quick way to de-frizz it is to rub a little body lotion into it.

- Always carry baby wipes with you. They're so useful for cleaning sticky fingers before you eat, or sand from your sunscreen, or to get rid of running mascara – even to wipe away unwanted BO!

- I always pay a little visit to my hairdresser before I go on holiday for two reasons: first, if you have split ends, they'll only get worse in the heat and, second, if you leave your roots needing to be done, the sun won't bleach your hair in an all-over, even colour.

C E L E B R I T Y   T I P !

Richard Madeley - Television Presenter

If your dress shirt is looking horridly creased when you unpack it at your hotel, and you have no time to iron it, and the black tie event starts in half an hour, then just take it into the bathroom with you, hang it as close to the shower as possible (without it getting wet), leave it there whilst you have got the shower on full heat and then, when you come to put it on, all of the creases will have been steamed out.

2

Home, Sweet Home

'OOH IT'S A big job, it's going to cost ya,' says the tradesman, sucking through his teeth with an anxious look on his face, and, before you know it, you're writing out a hefty cheque, unsure of exactly what you've just paid for. This happens time and time again: women getting ripped off – they're easy prey for rogue tradesmen (plus, *all* men think women are dim when it comes to DIY!). On the other hand, there are also women with lazy, Alf Garnett-like husbands or boyfriends who, when asked to fix a shelf, reply, 'Yeah, yeah, later, love,' unable to prise themselves away from the footie.

Actually, on the subject of men, just because they're male, this doesn't mean they are automatically programmed with DIY knowledge from birth. Many modern-day men don't have the faintest idea how to change a fuse, let alone cope with a blocked toilet.

Well, we've had enough of rogue tradesmen and lazy partners, but let's be honest with ourselves here, girlies, who really wants to waste ten minutes of her precious day scraping away at stubborn toilet stains or washing out paint trays with her freshly painted nails? So that's why I've compiled this crucial chapter on handy home and DIY tips; little trusted tricks that will help you cut lots and lots of corners to prevent all those jobs piling up. You'll save yourself lots of dosh in the long run and, more importantly, keep yourself looking exceedingly gorgeous, no matter what.

Remember, one hour of DIY equals 300 calories. You can wave goodbye to those flabby old bingo wings at the backs of your arms and the muffin top hanging over your jeans, plus you'll no longer be dragging an extra set of bum cheeks around with you because you'll be giving your body the best all-over workout without the gym. Once you've read this chapter, ladies, put on your cutest flatties, jump into your car and get your trotters down to the DIY store!

FIRST THINGS FIRST: DIY FASHION & BEAUTY FOR A DIRTY GIRL'S WORK

Most women think they can get away with looking like a cross between a tramp and a burglar when doing a spot of DIY at home because they're hidden out of sight. Oh yes, it happens in every village and city every day, worldwide, as women rummage in a state of mania through the back of their wardrobes and reach for those ten-year-old and greying marquee-sized pants which only emphasise just how big your bum has grown since you last did some DIY! And it doesn't end there... You then have the boulder-holder bras, which trap and suffocate your precious man magnets as they desperately make a bid for freedom. And what's with those worn hipster trousers that reveal your builder's bum? Do us all a favour and throw the offenders out.

Just because you're doing a messy job it doesn't follow that you have to look unpolished or dress like a dog. Of course you're going to wear your old clothes, but why not look super-sexy and ravishingly tasty at the same time? You see, my philosophy is that, if you feel hot and minxy, this positive energy will filter through into your work, making your house look like it's straight out of the pages of a top interior magazine.

How to Look Like a DIY Diva

- Underwear is totally underestimated and it's one of the most important parts of your wardrobe. Remember, good underwear makes outerwear look better so there's absolutely no excuse for granny pants. Wearing fab lingerie day in, day out ensures that you always feel sexy and gorgeous the whole time.

- What's the point in looking gaunt and ghostly? Slap on a layer of fake tan first to give you that sun-kissed look.

- In a dire emergency you can use a bin liner as an overall to protect your clothes. Make a hole in the top for your head and one at either side to put your arms through. To stop it from billowing out and being dangerous, wrap some masking tape round your waist.

- Do wear stylish, flat, rubber-soled shoes – perfect for when you are doing electrical jobs as they're nice and grippy. Plus they are safe as the rubber soles will help prevent you getting shocks.

- Wear a minxy French apron with a pocket at the front. You'll not only look gorgeous but you can also carry your mobile and lipgloss with you at all times.

- Don't wear clothing with long hairs, such as fringes or mohair. You'll only end up brushing past your newly painted wall and leaving half of it stuck there.

- Make sure you wear fab hipster jeans (team with a long top if you have a jelly belly) or hardwearing tight trousers.

- This may seem obvious but never wear skirts, bangles, long neck-laces, dangly earrings or flared sleeves when decorating or working round the house – they can be very dangerous if they get caught in something.

- Because painting a ceiling can be a messy job, wear a scruffy hat or a plastic shower cap (the ones they give you in hotels) on your head to prevent your hair from getting caked in paint.

- Radiators are invariably placed quite low on the wall. So you don't end up with aching, black-and-blue knees, buy kneepads from a DIY store, or in an emergency unravel lots of toilet roll and place it in the middle of your kneecaps. Secure with masking tape and do the same with a plastic bag for each knee.

- If your clothes end up totally trashed, pour a can of cola over them then wash in the usual way with detergent in the washing machine.

- Make the glammest gloves ever to protect your hands and nails (you can create a second pair for doing the washing up). You will need one pair of rubber gloves, 1.2m (4ft) pink fur trim, two strings of fake pearls and one big plastic jewel. Measure the fur trim to fit the glove tops and sew onto them with running stitch. Repeat with the fake pearls, letting them hang a little looser. Glue the jewel onto one finger so it looks like you're wearing a ring. How Marilyn Monroe!

- This next tip comes from a jockey. Buy 'Healthy Hoof' by the tub-load over the Internet or from farming shops. In the equestrian world, it's used when horses' hooves have become dry and need some nourishment to make them strong again. And guess what? It's great for hands and it's also dirt cheap!

- To protect your nails, wear surgical rubber gloves (from all chemists) or, if you're naughty like me, take a little handful from the petrol pump when you're filling up your car. But before you put your gloves on back at home, heavily moisturise them in oily creams and then while you're sanding an old door, for example, those glorious oils will be working their way into your skin. So, when the job is done and it's time to whop your gloves off, your hands won't feel like sandpaper. Instead, you'll want to show them off!

- Always keep a tube of hand cream with you when you're working to prevent your hands from drying out. Have one by the sink too and so you don't lose your rings when you're washing your hands, clip them to a safety pin and attach to your clothing.

- Don't start stripping the wallpaper if you've just washed and styled your hair and are going out on the razzle later. When the windows are closed and that steamer starts to rumble, it will become like a sauna and you'll be sticky, hot and sweaty. On the flipside though, you're getting a free facial and will be able to get rid of all those nasty old blackheads once the job is done.

- Painting a room can be a very messy job. It's really worth moisturising Vaseline into your skin, all over your body, before you start (especially if you're using oil-based paints). When you take a shower later on, the paint will just fall off with ease.

- If you have painted your nails in a dark colour, always keep a pot of emergency matching polish in your toolbox in case you have to go out – there's nothing worse than scuzzy nails.

- You're best off filing down very long nails if you plan to do some heavy or fiddly work such as wallpapering (always carry a nail file in your tool belt for SOS repairs, too). Long nails will not only hinder what you're doing, they're also a nightmare if they break down to the cuticle. If you love your nails too much, call in the professionals for those hefty jobs!

C E L E B R I T Y   T I P !

Terri Dwyer - presenter of 60 Minute Makeover

I like to do my bit for the environment and I just love to create something new out of something old – you know, just getting arty and thinking in a creative way. An old pair of curtains could be dyed and given a new lease of life as the kids' playroom cushions or a bunch of leftover tiles could be used to cover an old table top. It's not only fun doing it, but you'll be saving a lot of money at the same time.

And When the Work is Done...

- If you bash yourself and you bruise easily, put a piece of uncooked onion over the bump for half an hour.

- Any leftover cement can be used to exfoliate your hands. Simply mix it in with a dash of olive oil and scrub. Rinse off with warm water.
- The dust and fumes of DIY can really clog up your skin, so blend some fresh mint in your kitchen blender and rub it into your skin before you go to bed.
- It's best to remove jewellery before you begin, but an old mascara wand can be very useful for removing unwanted dirt from your diamonds. Wash grubby silver with mint toothpaste and rinse in warm water. Your pearls can be cleaned with olive oil and a very soft cloth. For more tips, see page 221.
- To soothe aching muscles after a hard day's DIY, treat yourself to a relaxing bath with lavender oil and sip a lovely glass of vino. You've earned it!

GETTING STARTED

Your Must-have Toolbox

Going to the DIY store to stock up your first toolbox without doing your homework first is rather like hitting the supermarket for the weekly grocery run on an empty stomach. As we all know, going food shopping while peckish can be disastrous as you can end up filling your basket to the brim with lots of forbidden foods. By the time you get home you've not only consumed a large part of your shopping but you've also spent a load of dosh on rubbish. So, here are some guiding tips for when you're getting together all those odds and sods for your toolbox.

- Buy a toolbox on wheels – it will save you from getting a bad back.
- Do hunt around for the best tools to suit you. There's no point in buying a heavy hammer if it leaves your arm in agony after just two minutes'

work. There are female-friendly tools which are just a bit lighter than the normal ones but do the job just as well.

- Look for well-known brands that come with a guarantee. Study the quality of the tool: the more flexible the plastic or rubber, the better. If it's rigid, then avoid buying it and dull metal means it's a duff! Go for shiny. Also, if you buy a well-known brand, you know you are buying something that is safe and reliable. Cheap stuff can break and you could end up with an injury.

- Think before you buy – how many times will you use it? You may be better off hiring it instead. For example, a floor sander not only costs a bomb but is also a bugger to store. For the number of times you're going to use one in your life, you would be better off hiring it for a fraction of the price. The other plus side to hiring equipment is that the shop will test everything, so you know you won't be getting faulty goods.

- Do buy a tool belt – it's an absolute must-have! It prevents you from losing your tools every five minutes and it's very useful when you're stuck up a ladder.

Some Painting & Decorating Tips

- Before you paint behind a radiator, give it a little spring clean. Stick a sock on the end of a broom handle (secure with a bit of masking tape) and you'll then be able to reach those fiddly parts.

- Never paint a radiator when hot – not only for safety reasons but also because the paint will crack when dry.

- Use a special radiator roller. It has a very long handle with a small roller at the end and will do a much neater job.

- Forget dirt-cheap brushes: they only shed their bristles, leaving them stuck to the wall when the paint has dried. Go for the man made fibre – they're easy to use and clean (and they won't moult).

- After you've stuffed your face with your Chinese takeaway, don't chuck your chopsticks away – they are very useful for stirring paint.
- To save yourself having to wash the paint tray every time you use it, cover it with a plastic carrier bag (secure in place with masking tape). When you've finished painting for the day, simply remove the bag and dispose of it.
- Invest in a pair of kneepads (see also page 70) to protect your knees from getting all bruised and sore. You'll be scrabbling round on the floor a lot, so buy a good pair.
- A dust mask will prevent you from getting a sore throat, clogged-up lungs plus a collection of crumbly bogies up your nose from all the paint and dust flying around the place. Protect your eyes with a pair of goggles, too.
- If you find yourself staring at the hideous floral wallpaper in your new house (teamed naturally, of course, with smoke-stained ceilings and swirly brown carpets) and you don't have the foggiest where to start, empty the room completely. Give the walls and ceiling a good old lick of white paint – this will create a fresh blank canvas for you to project your ideas onto.
- Always paint from the top of the room down: ceilings, walls, woodwork, radiators and then floor.
- If you don't intend to paint your doors when you're painting the rest of a room, cover them in an old bed sheet or plastic door covers.
- Lay dustsheets down on wooden floors and use masking tape to secure the corners. If you have a carpet, lay down sticky plastic dustsheets (they lightly stick to the carpet so that they don't move around everywhere).
- If you can't move really big and/or heavy pieces of furniture out of a

room when you're decorating, try putting tinfoil pie dishes on each of the legs so you can easily scoot the furniture around.

- Make sure your paint roller is completely coated in paint before applying to the ceiling or wall to prevent patchy stroke marks from appearing. Be careful not to overload it with paint – it'll splash everywhere and you'll be covered.

- Don't totally immerse your brush in paint either – it'll drip everywhere. For a neater job, cover it one third of the way up the bristles.

- Paint kettles are small and fitted with a handle. They are useful for carrying smaller amounts of paint instead of having to lug round full pots. So you don't have to clean the pot afterwards, line it with aluminium foil from the kitchen and, when you want to put tools down at the end of the day, all you have to do is to remove the foil and throw it away.

- To prevent your rollers, paint trays and brushes from drying out when you take a break, wrap them in clingfilm or a plastic bag (secure with a rubber band) to make them airtight.

- Always open the window when painting to avoid paint toxification, and leave it open for at least 12 hours. You can, of course, buy VOC (Volatile Organic Compound)-free paints – B&Q have a great range which are totally non-toxic.

- When you first open a can of paint, give it a good old stir with a stick so you get an even colour throughout.

- Applying one coat of matt emulsion on your walls just shows up all the imperfections. Ideally, you want to apply two or three coats. Alternatively, you could buy a really thick emulsion and one coat of this would probably do.

- Painting one colour next to another can be a tricky business if they meet in a corner or on an edge, e.g. ceiling to wall. To get an über-straight line if you don't have the best eye or a steady hand, masking tape is the answer. Stick it down the side of one edge of the wall and paint the different colour on the other edge. When you peel it off, you'll have a straight line. Do the same on the other side.

- If you're painting over a wallpapered wall and there are lots of gaps between the lengths of paper, sand down each edge a little and no one will know.

- When painting a door, you can learn the hard way like I did and get yourself locked in the room (and hope that somebody comes to your rescue), or do it the easy way and put all the door furniture (handles, locks and hinges) into a plastic carrier bag and tie it to your belt until you've finished painting the door and it's time to put it all back on.

- Cover door hinges in masking tape to prevent them being covered in unwanted paint and wedge the door open with a piece of cardboard.

- Unless you want a heavily textured surface, then I suggest you don't drag your brush across the surface in a forceful way. Instead, work in smooth strokes for an even surface that's free of brush marks.

- Put masking tape around the edge of each window pane to avoid getting paint onto them – it can be a real bugger to try to get off!

- To temporarily disguise a scratch on wood, rub cod liver oil into it.

- If your wall has an uneven surface, use a sponging technique. This not only disguises the flaws but also makes a potentially boring wall look exciting.

- There's a golden rule with brushes: clean them once you've finished with them. Look after them, and they'll look after you. Really cheap brushes can be thrown away at the end of the day, but expensive professional brushes are high maintenance and need serious TLC. Water-based paints can be removed with soapy water and oil-based paint can be removed with white spirit – soak the brushes for as long as you need to.

- To store your brushes, wrap them in newspaper and tie an elastic band round the tops. This will help keep their shape. You could drill a hole in the handles and hang them on a nail on the back of a utility door.
- Never throw away leftover paint. Instead, store it in a cool, dry place as you never know when you might need it to repaint a chip or a stain. Chuck it after 18 months, though.

C E L E B R I T Y   T I P !

Brian Friedman - choreographer/artistic director

The simplest things are what truly take your home from beautiful to livable. I have two tips that will keep people feeling welcome. Always make sure that there are great smelling candles in every room, and that you light them daily. The next is to use fresh floral arrangements. The smell of the candles and flowers make people feel at home. It works for me... I practically have to kick everyone out of my house!

Wallpapering Tips

Wallpaper can be a nightmare to hang so if you have a seriously wobbly hand, a dodgy eye or are a bit partial to the odd glass of vino then I suggest you save up and call in the professionals. Hanging wallpaper incorrectly can be a timely and expensive mistake. However, if you still want to have a go, here are some guidelines.

- If you're a wallpapering virgin, then it's advisable to start with a wall that doesn't have any windows and doors.
- Wallpaper with a big pattern is much easier to match up when hanging than paper with a small pattern.
- If your walls are in a really bad state, covering them in wallpaper hides and disguises a multitude of sins. Hang lining paper first to smooth out the bumps.
- If you have walls with *really* bad lumps and bumps, then I'm afraid it's time to call in the professionals and get them replastered. Papering on an uneven wall is to the interior design world what the VPL is to the fashion world – a huge faux pas.
- When wallpapering a room, keep the windows closed. The hotter the room gets, the easier the paper will come away, especially if you are using a wallpaper remover which is hot and steamy anyway.
- After you've measured your length of wallpaper, always add an extra 3cm (1½in) to the top and the bottom of your measurement – this will act as your safety net in case you make any mistakes when cutting.
- When buying wallpaper, always get one extra roll in case you need to do repairs later down the line. Make sure it's from the same batch so the colours are exactly the same.
- If you have a focal point in the room – for example, a fireplace – start above it so that the pattern over it is symmetrical.

- When you are pasting short lengths, put biggish pebbles in each of the corners to prevent them from curling up.

- Some lengths may be longer than the pasting table. If so, paste one end, fold it up like a concertina and place at one end off the table. Then paste the rest of the length, concertina it up and set aside to soak up the paste.

- If air bubbles form from trapped air that hasn't been brushed out properly, don't start to over-work the paper with the brush to try to smooth them out because you may rip the paper. Instead, leave it to dry and using a sharp craft knife cut a little slit, put a tiny bit of paste inside and smooth down using a damp clean rag.

- If you've made a mini bodge-up with the wallpapering at the top, where the wall meets the ceiling join, don't get in a stew. This is where that clever invention – the 'border' – comes in handy. It will disguise all those imperfections that you don't want anyone to notice.

- Wallpaper can be very expensive so, if you see a design that you love and it's way out of your price bracket, buy enough to cover one feature wall and then paint the other walls in a complementary colour.

- A very busy and complicated design only makes a room appear smaller in size. Use vertical-striped wallpaper in a low-ceilinged room to give the impression of height. This is a great visual trick (it's the same with fashion). Avoid horizontal-lined wallpaper if your room is small and claustrophobic; the same goes for dado rails and borders. If you have low ceilings and want to give the illusion that they're higher then hang your dado rail (wood or paper) 10cm (4in) lower than normal (usually 1m/3½ft).

- Wash wallpaper paste out of your brushes with hot, soapy water. Rinse them and, using the hole in the handle, hang them from a nail inside your DIY cupboard.

C E L E B R I T Y   T I P !

Craig Phillips - first Big Brother *winner and*

handyman on 60 Minute Makeover
There are always odd jobs around the house for your good old trusty drill. Drilling into ceramic tiles can be a slippery business. So, to stop this from happening, try sticking a clear plaster up on the tile where you want to drill and this will keep the drill head in the right place and you don't have to worry about it sliding off.

If you are drilling into a wall, attach a paper envelope using sticky tape just under where you want to drill, and this will catch all of that heavy dust and stop it from ruining your wall below – and of course it will save you another vacuuming job!

INTERIOR DESIGN

Colour

When you're at home, do you sometimes find yourself with the right old hump, extremely edgy or grumbling at anyone who dares comes near you? Asked why you were in such a bad mood, you probably wouldn't have a clue – you just are. Well, strange as this may seem, it could be down to the colours and textures that you have chosen to use throughout your home.

Maybe the colour of your sofa entices out the crabby and irritable witch within you, or perhaps the bedroom wallpaper subconsciously makes you feel uneasy and irritable. I understand that people choose different textures and colours to determine the atmosphere and style of their home, but they can also have a huge psychological effect. Your home should be an extension of your personality, somewhere that makes you feel happy, safe and relaxed, somewhere that stimulates your senses and creates a feeling of harmony. Below is a list of different colours and how they affect you.

- *Red* is the colour of love. Feng shui experts advise that a dash of red in the boudoir works wonders for the love life – it's a very stimulating colour. It also does well in the dining room as it's an appetite stimulant.
- *Yellow* is a cheerful colour. Strange, really, because, although it's a sunny, happy shade that looks great in entrance halls because it's so welcoming, people also tend to lose their temper more often in a yellow room and it makes babies want to cry!
- *Green* makes you think about the outdoors. It's a fresh and invigorating colour. Because green symbolises nature, it calms us down psychologically into a peaceful mood.
- *Blue* is a fresh colour that can make you think of water, perhaps the seaside. It therefore stimulates our senses and makes us feel chilled out.
- *White* is also fresh. It's clean and airy and gives us the feeling of space. Because it's a great light reflector, it helps to breathe life into a room.
- *Black and gold* are dark and mysterious. They are very stimulating colours and can make us feel sexy and, strangely enough, very creative.
- *Brown* is taken from nature and also food. It makes us feel safe and comfortable so try it out in your living room or bedroom if you want that cosy, homely ambiance.

Colour Tips

- Be careful which colour you choose — it can change the size and shape of a room.
- Paint a ceiling white and the room will appear taller and, if you paint it in a dark colour, the room seems a lot shorter.
- Warm colours (pinks, oranges, reds) make a room feel smaller, while cool colours (blue, green, white) give a sense of space.
- A good way to make a room look taller is to paint the skirting board in the same colour as the walls.
- If you have a small home and want it to appear bigger, then paint the walls in the same colour tones. This gives a feeling of continuity — one room just flows into the next.
- The size of your rooms has a major influence on what colours you should choose. It tends to be that, if you have lots of small rooms, you are better off sticking to a paler/lighter colour palette and, if you have a large spacious place, then you can use darker colours in the spectrum, if you wish.
- Natural light can really alter colour depending on whether it's a warm, sunny light or a dull, miserable one. If there's a constant, cold light when entering a room and you want to paint your walls, opt for a warm cosy white rather than a cold stark shade — this will make it a more inviting place to live in.
- Rather than painting a whole wall dark red and then waking up the next day and hating it, buy a tester pot, paint five or six pieces of A4 paper in your chosen colour and blu-tack them to the walls. Watch how the light affects them during the day and night and think about how they may alter the perspective of the space.

- Replace standard light bulbs in the bedroom with tinted bulbs to create a rosy glow.

- When choosing your colours, think about the relationship between the room and the external environment. For example, my kitchen at home has a very rustic Provençal feel to it and is made up of country creams, olive green and natural woods, and, because my garden leads off my kitchen, I wanted one to flow into the other, making my kitchen look twice as big as I brought the outdoors inside.

- There's a vast array of whites out there: you have creamy whites, contemporary whites, cool and warm whites, lime whites and antique whites, so choose one that will blend in with the rest of your colour palette. For example, if you're going to use a cool blue, pick a cool white to go alongside it – a warm white would clash and look disharmonious.

LIGHTING

Artificial Lighting

What's one of the worst things that could happen when you invite your hot new date home for a coffee? You open the door, throw your keys on the side table, kick off your little stilettos, put the light on... and argh! Shock, horror, the down-lighters have just revealed not only the big, crusty spot that you tried to conceal earlier with make-up (which has now slid off), but also a rather drunken-looking face, too! To prevent this disastrous scenario ever happening, install dimmer switches. They really are a girl's best friend – low lighting will keep you looking mysteriously minxy even if you really resemble a drunken old trog!

Artificial lighting can be a very powerful tool. It conceals unsightly points in a room (by angling the light elsewhere to leave the ugly part in the shade) and also accentuates the good points such as highlighting an unusual architectural design. Layering different types of lighting can also change your mood and the atmosphere in the room.

Natural Light

Pull back the curtains, roll up the blinds and flood your home with natural light. It has the ability to make us feel happy and, because natural light is forever changing, it will totally alter the feeling of a room and is therefore one thing to bear in mind when you choose the colour palette for your scheme. A room that doesn't receive much sunlight would benefit from the added help of some artificial light.

If your bathroom has an ugly view and struggles to receive light, a great way of disguising and solving the problem is to cut out frosted adhesive glass to fit the window. This not only keeps it a private place for splashing around in, but also ensures the room is not deprived of any natural light and adds a lovely softness. It's very quick and very cheap. Clean your windows regularly with vinegar and newspaper to allow more light to enter the room too. And I'm a massive fan of mirrors – hang them opposite a window to reflect even more natural light around the place.

FLOORING

If there's one thing you don't want to scrimp and save on, it's the flooring because of constant wear and tear. Do this cheaply and you'll be replacing it before you know it. You should buy the best you can afford.

Choosing the correct type of flooring is one of the most important decisions you will ever have to make about your décor and you want something that's both comfortable and practical. Here are some things to bear in mind:

- Take into account the period of your house – a stainless steel studded floor would look ridiculous in a Victorian house, as would a thick granny carpet in an ultra-modern apartment with clean lines. What activities will be going on in each of the rooms? Keep this in mind.
- In the bathroom opt for stone tiles or good-quality vinyl. Both withstand steam and are easy to clean and maintain.
- Carpet is a no-no in the kitchen. Choose easy-to-clean surfaces such as stone tiles, good-quality vinyl or gorgeous varnished floorboards.
- In the hallway flooring needs to be hard-wearing such as sea-grass, stone tiles or wooden floorboards.
- Keep wooden and vinyl flooring swept and vacuumed at all times, to prevent a build-up of dirt that will eventually ingrain itself into the flooring. When cleaning your chosen type of flooring, use a cleaner recommended by the manufacturer for the finish of that particular floor. When mopping vinyl or tiles, use a mild detergent and don't apply too much water to the surface. Always rinse so as not to leave any detergent behind. In addition, make sure you don't use an alkaline product on vinyl or linoleum as these can give the floor a yellow appearance.
- To clean ceramic tiles, use a mild detergent and rinse well with water afterwards. For unfinished concrete, vacuum and sweep as necessary, wash with a mild detergent and then rinse.
- For the living room/dining room, go for more luxurious and cosy

textured carpets or how about painted floorboards? Paint them black for a dramatic look or whitewash for an airy, spacious feel.

- You can, of course, opt for cheaper carpets in rooms you don't use that often – spare rooms, for example, where carpets don't suffer as much wear and tear as they do in other parts of the house.

- A good hardwearing carpet is the best option for stairs. You'll be going up and down it every day, so it needs to be durable.

- Do you want the flooring to be understated (neutral) or would you prefer a feature such as a rich pattern or parquet? If you are unsure about colours, then you are better off choosing something neutral. Neutrals pretty much go with any scheme, never date and save you having to replace it – you could easily become bored of a strong colour or pattern.

- Check underneath manky old carpets – you may find hidden floorboards that you could paint or varnish back to their original gorgeous glory.

- As a rule, flooring should always be darker than the ceiling, never the other way around (unless you like the feeling of claustrophobia).

- Rugs can be used to divide off different areas of a room. For example, if you have a dining area at one end of your living room, putting a rug down in that space creates the illusion that it is another area. To stop your rug from constantly slipping on a wooden floor, fit rug grips underneath.

- When laying a wooden floor, make sure the boards run the length of the room rather than its breadth. The room will appear bigger and it will give a cleaner look.

- Buy and fit your flooring before you choose your curtains and cushions, etc. It's easier to match fabrics to the flooring than the other way around.

- It's vital that you vacuum a carpet regularly as trapped dirt will become so embedded after a while that it will eventually become part of the design. Dirt attracts more dirt!

C E L E B R I T Y   T I P !

Nick Knowles - Television Presenter and Handyman

Spend twice as much time on lighting design as anything else, read all the magazines, watch design programmes on TV and, with luck, you'll never get round to doing anything and will spend the money on a decent holiday instead.

WINDOWS

Do your windows overlook ugly views such as a car park full of wheelie bins overflowing with rotten food and beer bottles? Are you comfortable taking a shower? And do your windows create an un-homely feeling when unflattering light spills in from the outside and draughts push their way through the old cracks so it's freezing even when the heating's on full blast? If the answer's yes, then it's about time you changed your window treatments. Below are some things to consider when you're deciding how to dress your windows.

- Are the curtains going to be a feature and hold a lot of colour or pattern, or will they simply blend into the background?
- Take into account the period of your home. Thick, rich, opulent curtains

would look ridiculous in a minimalist apartment, while sleek blinds could work wonders.

- Will the curtain or blind fabric be appropriate for its surroundings? You need easy-to-clean fabrics in a kitchen and fabric that can withstand steam in the bathroom, such as wipe-clean PVC.

- If you hate being woken up early, choose something that contains blackout and is of a slightly heavier material.

- Do you want your window dressing to be an extension of the outside view? For example, I chose gorgeous cream textured linen to dress my French windows – I wanted to link them with my garden, which is old and rustic. Had I put up a pair of dotty Art Deco curtains, the eye would have stopped at the curtain because the flow would have been obstructed. On the other hand, in certain situations you may want them to do just that!

More Window Treatment Tips

- Before you chuck out the chintz, have a think about whether you can recycle your curtains in any way. For example, you could make cushions, dye them, use part of the material to edge new material for a blind/curtain, run up a skirt, make a tablecloth or even create a lampshade.

- If you have a narrow window and want to give the illusion of it being a lot wider, choose a curtain rail and curtains that are wider and extend past the window.

- To give the impression that the room is higher than it is, choose long, vertical-striped curtains and hang them from ceiling to floor.

- Your curtain pole has to match the style of your chosen fabric. Plain, contemporary material would look good with a modern pole while rich extravagant material is great with an OTT-style pole.

- If your window looks out onto a beautiful view without any neighbouring windows peering into yours, how about leaving your window bare? Instead, arrange some white church candles on the sill. This would look really stunning and create such an impact. Never leave them unattended, though!

- Never skimp on fabric for your curtains – the ones that hang flat when pulled together look really cheap and nasty. For fab-looking curtains buy fabric two or three times the width of the window. The ideal length for curtains is either to the windowsill or to the floor, never midway.

- Use café clips – mini clips to hang lightweight fabric such as muslin, voile or organza to a thin, lightweight pole. Try hanging coloured sheer panels.

- Make your own tie-backs: you could use neutral-coloured rope if you are dressing a beach-themed room, or string brightly coloured beads together for a Moroccan theme. Or weave ribbon in and out of a lightweight chain.

- Mix old and new: if you have a small piece of gorgeous patterned antique material, consider using it as a border for the top and bottom of a new pair of plain curtains.

- Choosing a different lining to the actual curtain fabric looks super-stylish and adds a funky twist. For example, plain blue curtain fabric lined with blue-and-white stripes.

- If your house is at street level, but you want lots of light to filter in while having some privacy, consider putting up half-height wooden shutters. Very stylish!

- If you have patterned wallpaper, then you are better off going for plain blinds and vice versa.
- I once made a pair of curtains for a house in Mexico – I collected lots of brightly coloured napkins and sewed them together. They looked so unique!
- To make your house more private without having to hang curtains, which can often swallow up space, try sticking opaque panels to the windows. They'll keep you out of view from the outside world while letting lots of light filter in.
- Never hang your curtains or blinds until all the decorating is done.
- If you put a coin in the hem of the bottom of a curtain it will hang better and straighter.
- Rub the curtain pole with a plain waxed candle and you'll be able to open and close the curtains with ease.
- Keep fabric patterns in proportion to the size of the window and room. Large prints look fab in spacious rooms and small patterns are good in tiny spaces.
- Try dyeing voiles and muslins with Dylon and add sequin bead detail around the edges.
- You can reuse an old broom before you send it to the knackers' yard – simply remove the brush and turn the handle into a curtain pole.
- Dry pieces of fruit, such as slices of orange (cut in circles), and thread leather through them to create curtain ties.
- To clean, vacuum your curtains and blinds. Or you could send your curtains to the dry cleaners.
- When plain curtains fade, just re-dye them if you can.

ACCESSORISE, ACCESSORISE

Oh my God, what was she thinking? She was wearing a beautiful dress, had a great hairdo, perfectly manicured nails and, wait for it... socks and sandals! WHAT? An atrocious mistake such as this is known to us fashionistas as a 'fashion faux pas'. It's a look so breathtakingly bad it leaves passers-by gasping for air as they cry with laughter or just stand there, jaws on the floor in pure shock that someone could actually go out thinking that they genuinely looked good like that.

Ladies, this shouldn't happen in fashion and it shouldn't happen in interiors either – but it does! Accessories may (and can be) small, but they bring a wealth of colour, texture, shape and character to a room. They give the eye something to focus on and can finish off the whole look with professional style. There are rules to accessorising successfully: the colours of the accessories need to echo the general theme of the interior and you need to display them against the right background. There's no point in putting a red bowl on a red tablecloth – it would just disappear. Instead, display a cream bowl that would stand out while still fitting with your overall scheme. You need to work out whether you want your accessory to stand alone or grouped with other similar pieces such as jugs or pictures. Think about whether you want a focal point or if it should melt into the background. So, as you can see, every accessory has a very important role to play and if you display them well, you will not only be creating maximum impact but, also a lot of 'oohs' and 'ahs' from your family and friends.

- Think of a scheme as a whole, not just individual items. Ask yourself if each item flows comfortably into the other. If something lacks harmony, take it out of the scheme.

- For complete co-ordination, cover old books in the same wallpaper as you have used on the walls.
- To make an instant piece of modern art, stretch a piece of material or a length of wallpaper with a bold print on it over a piece of MDF and display it on the wall.
- Pictures can often look lost on a wall, so try grouping them together. Practise on the floor first and then you won't make any mistakes when you bang the nails in. Or hang them symmetrically either side of a window, door or mirror.
- Don't just pile your books in a heap inside a cupboard or up on the bookcase in any shape or form, make a feature of them. Arrange them in different height patterns. What looks really stylish is painting the back of the bookcase in the same shade as one of the dominant colours in your scheme. Books also look superb framing a door or a window by building a shelf all the way round the edge. A floor-to-ceiling bookshelf in a wide corridor can look quite arty, too.
- Don't overclutter accessories: you are better off displaying three of your favourite jugs than all twenty-three!
- You can find lots of goodies in antique shops, on eBay and at car-boot sales.
- To disguise ugly dining-room chairs, simply pop a swathe of material over the back of each one, tie it in place with a long piece of ribbon and tuck a little flower inside.
- Make your own candles. Melt down old candle stubs, removing the wicks.

Pop in a little candle dye to match your scheme, if you want, and then pour into a mould with the wick. I use leftover milk cartons as moulds for the wax.

- To tie in plain, boring-looking candles to your scheme, tie a piece of ribbon around the middle and into a bow (the ribbon has to match the scheme).

- Arrange a collection of jugs or vases of the same colour but in different shapes on a shelf.

- Sheer coloured glass looks great on a windowsill as it lets the light through.

- Revamp old picture frames. You can decorate them with little pieces of driftwood and sea shells for a beachy feel and try mosaic glass squares for a Moroccan look. Or replace the glass with a mirror and attach a candle to the front like a mirrored sconce reflecting a soft light everywhere.

- You could also cover old picture frames in leftover wallpaper or fabric. Pretty much anything can be covered to tie in with your scheme.

- Old jam jars make great hurricane lamps for outdoors. Fill the bottom of the jar with sand, to about 2cm (¾ in) high and then wedge your candle firmly into the sand, making sure it won't fall over.

- Do buy matching kitchen appliances. For a modern kitchen, invest in stainless steel and if you have a simple Shaker-style kitchen choose creams and pinks, or whites and blues.

- There are so many door handles available these days, so replace those that don't fit your theme with some that do. Good fittings also make a room more expensive-looking.

- If you are going to display something on one side of a mirror or fireplace surround, then you have to make it symmetrical and do the same on the other side.
- Using fruit can be a cheap and fun way of adding a hint of colour to your room. If you have red in your scheme, you could use red and green apples. You can always eat them and then replace them!
- Cushions and throws can really inject colour into a lifeless-looking sofa or chair. They can be swapped regularly, too.
- You can handpaint your glassware to tie in with your kitchen.
- When your flowers are looking a bit sorry for themselves, how about drying them and making homemade pot-pourri? Or put them in a hand-painted jar? You could paint delicate little flowers on to the side, for example.
- You can make your own napkin rings out of pretty much anything. Try a string of beads, shreds of material, ribbon, leaves, wire or raffia or string. Tie raffia straw around each napkin and tuck a flower into it.
- Echo various patterns and textures throughout a scheme – e.g. wood, floral or stripes, mirrors, metallic, stony textures, plants, etc.
- Frame old vintage posters for a modern apartment.
- If a wall has an unsightly lump or a rough patch, a quick and easy solution is to hang something over it, such as a picture. Or hang a beautiful piece of material or even a favourite vintage dress over it.
- To make an unusual doorstop, paint a pebble with a marble effect in colours to match your scheme, of course!
- Always consider your budget – you are better off splashing out on one or two really eye-catching pieces than trying to compromise everywhere.

- Plants are really important in the home – they look good, they purify the air and they signify growth and development.

- I have scented candles and joss sticks everywhere – they can really uplift an environment and stimulate and relax your senses. They have the ability to make you feel positive and happy.

- Don't go splashing the cash when there's no need. Your home can still look a million dollars on a tight budget – just get creative! Shop in the sales, eBay, salvage yards, junk shops or on your travels.

C E L E B R I T Y   T I P !

Carole Malone - Journalist

I love fresh flowers and used to have them all over my house. The problem is, they're expensive, the flowers start smelling and looking grubby after a few days and dirty water looks – well, dirty.

Solution – silk flowers from Sally Burr. No, don't say, 'I hate them,' because I used to hate them until I discovered Sally's. She supplies some of the best addresses in London (I know who they are but I'm not allowed to say). And, yes, they're a bit more expensive but they're the best I've ever seen (I buy huge white amaryllis and white orchids). The trick is to mix them with real greenery and no one will ever guess.

- Be an ambassador for individual style – don't blindly follow others and end up looking like a complete fashion victim!

- If your fish have died, you could reuse the bowl. Fill it with something fun.

It could be feathers, fairy lights or little shampoos to put into the bathroom for your guests.

- I love trailing around markets for cheap hidden treasures such as stunning vases and antique bed linen.

STORAGE

I used to be a magpie, collecting anything and everything from spare plastic bags, clothes that I hated but thought I might like again one day to keys that no longer had any use and, well, basically any old paraphernalia! Believe you me it wasn't easy trying to find space for it all. It seems you can never have too much storage and making use of forgotten spaces such as under the stairs, below the bed, above and behind the door will transform your home into an organised haven rather than a whirlwind of destruction – which is what my bedroom used to look like!

Storage Solutions

- Before you try to house all your bits and pieces have a little de-cluttering session first. Go through your house room by room with a fine-tooth comb and cull. Be ruthless. Do you really need 400 Tupperware boxes? Collect all of the good stuff that you no longer need and drop it off at your local charity shop. Not only are you doing your bit for charity and helping others across the world, but you will get a warm fuzzy feeling inside – well worth it.

- Most people dump their suitcases up in the attic or cupboard and leave them empty, not realising they are wasting valuable storage space. When you're not on holiday, fill them up with things that need to be stored away.

- Divide your odds and sods into groups – what things do you need to access regularly and which ones are only needed every so often?
- Use the redundant space under the stairs – a great place to store vacuum cleaners, etc.
- If your hallway is wide, use this area to build shelving on either one or both sides and stick your books there. This will not only give you more room in your living room it'll also make a real feature of the hallway too.
- Washing-up bottles can make a pretty kitchen look ugly so decant the liquid into a cute little bottle and pop it by the sink. (You can do the same with olive oil.)
- Concealed storage has huge amounts of appeal. For example, a window seat in a bay window not only looks good, but also gives you additional seating and another storage space. Footstools, trunks and coffee tables can all do the same – they serve a purpose and often have a cavity in the middle under the lid to store things.
- Building a shelf above and around a doorway is a great way to store or display books and ornaments.
- Rather than just ramming your tinfoil, greaseproof paper and clingfilm into the bottom drawer, blocking everything up, have a designated space. Get an old vase, arrange them all in there for easy access and display it somewhere on your work surface.
- Wicker baskets dotted around the house look stylish and also hold lots of bits and pieces.
- A thin box-room would be great transformed into a walk-in wardrobe, leaving your bedroom clutter-free. Install hanging rails, shoe racks, open and closed shelving.

- If you have a small bedroom with not much space for other pieces of furniture, buy a bed that is slightly higher than average, then you can fit loads of storage boxes underneath. You can also buy drawers on wheels that fit below beds.

- If you have a tiny bedroom and want to create some floor space for the day, then you may wish to install one of those beds that reftract up and back into the wall.

- Us girlies love our make-up and beauty products, but having them scattered all over every single surface not only attracts dirt but also looks and feels a mess. So buy a specially designed cabinet to put above the loo and provide shelves for all your clutter.

- Being able to get to an organised make-up stash when you're in a hurry is essential for those doing a quick beauty booster fix-up job. Being super-organised prevents you from getting stressed and being late. So, get one of those magnetic strips that come with five little metal pots that are actually intended for storing herbs. They are brilliant for holding your make-up. Simply fill them up and stick them onto the strips. The other good thing about using these magnetic pots is that you can again use dead space on the back of your bathroom cabinet, allowing you to keep your make-up out of the way.

- Buy a magazine rack to house all your favourite weeklies, but, if your house is beginning to look like a bit of a newsagents' yet you can't bear to throw out your magazines, go through every single one and tear out the articles that interest you. Put them into an organised and labelled box then throw out the rest.

- Never throw away shoeboxes – they really come in handy for storing odds and sods and it's more eco-friendly too. Just write the contents on the shoebox. If you go to Muji you can get clear boxes, which allow you to see what you have in there, especially if they're wedged under the bed. They are especially good for shoes.

- I'm not a violent person at all, but there's one thing that did get a lot of abuse from my foot and that was my pots and pans cupboard! It used to be mayhem, with everything just spilling out each time I opened the door. It was only when I went down to my friend's house in the country and saw how she stored her cooking stuff that my pots and pans abuse came to an end. She hung her pots and pans on a rail plus hooks above the cooker, cleverly using the dead space and leaving more room in her cupboards for other things.

- This little tip is one I used on my CBBC series *Clutter Nutters*. Get five old jam jars and nail the lids to the underside of a shelf and then screw the jars back on. This is a great storage idea for anything (nails, screws, sweets, cotton wool, etc.) and, once again, you're making good use of dead space.

- Paint the tops of old jam jars with white paint. You can then write on them what you have stored in there. Every time you change the contents, re-paint and re-label them. Of course, you can use sticky labels as an alternative.

- If you store your pots and pans in a cupboard and have limited space, flip the lids upside down and place on top of the pots then stack each one on top of the other.

- No one really needs to be reminded that you are on your period! So stuff your tampons into a sweet pot with a lid or a cute little box.

- If you're one of those people who cover your loo roll in a hideous knittted doll, you need to be locked away and they should be burned!

Instead, try putting them in a little basket on the floor right by the loo.

- My dad takes pride in his beautiful collection of glasses. He has collected them for years and only gets them out on very special occasions such as when he got his MBE for his services to Cornwall in 2007. So as not to get any chips on them, he always stores them upside down (this prevents them from collecting dust) on a piece of felt, which stops them slipping or becoming chipped.

CELEBRITY TIP!

Poppy Delevigne - Model

I try to keep my closet super organised. Everything from a pair of jeans to a pair of shoes has its own home. All my bags and clutches are kept in their original soft bags and all my shoes are stored in the boxes that they came in. This means I always know where everything is and, as I'm always in a rush, this is very useful. It also means that they stay in pristine condition which cuts down on the maintenance side of things!

QUIRKY HOUSEHOLD CLEANING TIPS

I absolutely hate cleaning with a vengeance, yet I loathe even more the thought of living in a grubby old pigsty! So to help me get through one of life's most hated jobs, I have this magic rule: I do fifteen minutes' tidying up every day and then I do the odd jobs such as cleaning the worktops and toilet seats, or cleaning the oven hob – basically dealing with the small jobs before they turn into big ones. So, girlies, get that little minxy French apron on, pick up your feather duster and crack on your favourite CD so that you can dance and dust away while sprucing up your house.

In General...

- When doing the housework, wear a pinny or a dustbin bag to protect your clothes. Also, wear rubber gloves to protect your hands.
- Rather than trying to juggle your cleaning tools and products up and down the stairs and around the house, put them all in a bucket with a handle.
- Freshen up manky old cloths by dumping them in the dishwasher or the washing machine.
- To remove grease from your hands, rub them in washing-up liquid.
- Be green and recycle whatever you can. Old toothbrushes can be used to clean awkward nooks and crannies or even little bobby-dazzler diamond rings. Old bed linen (cut into pieces), clothes, socks and tights make excellent little dusters. Use newspapers to dry and buff windows, as an emergency dustpan, to wrap up and store glass, to dry out sodden shoes and to catch dripping varnish.
- Use plastic bottles to store liquids such as homemade soups or salad dressings and various cleaning and decorating solutions.
- Reuse the lids from plastic yoghurt pots and other tubs to cover opened tins of smelly cat or dog food in your fridge.
- Pop a little cinnamon stick into your vacuum cleaner bag: when you turn it on, it will give off a lovely sweet smell. Incidentally, professional cleaners always vacuum before they dust. If you start off vacuuming, you'll pick up

the dust that has settled on various surfaces – job done! If you dust beforehand, the dust only wafts up into the air for an hour and settles somewhere else after you've vacuumed and you'll have to start again. What a waste of time, hey?

- Dab vanilla essence onto a light bulb. When the light is on, the room will smell delicious.
- Wipe the surface of a hot radiator with fabric softener for a fresh smell.
- Spray furniture polish behind a hot radiator – it will give people the impression that you have been busy cleaning the house!
- Sometimes when dusting, all you are actually doing is moving the dust around rather than taking it away. Use a very slightly damp cloth (or a scented cleaning wipe) and the dust will stick to it instead.
- Shattered glass can be picked up with a hunk of dry bread. Always dispose of it carefully.
- Empty the contents of your vacuum cleaner onto damp newspaper – this will prevent any of the dirt from becoming airborne.
- If you can't find your dustpan, lay a sheet of newspaper on the floor (secure it in place by wetting the edges), then sweep the dirt onto it.
- Over time, patches of carpet fade and discolour. To re-match with the rest, paint over the patch with fabric dye in the same colour.
- Never pour water- or oil-based paint down the drain. Always put it into a container, such as an empty plastic milk carton, and then put it in the dustbin.
- Nail polish remover is superb for removing roving paint on glass. Use a cotton bud for the really awkward bits.
- Greasy hands are easily cleaned – try rubbing them in a little sawdust.

- Because cleaning is sooooooooooooooooooooooo boring, distract yourself by putting on your favourite CD at full blast and sing your head off even louder. Try not to upset the neighbours, though!

- A good cleaning session uses up lots of energy. Brew yourself one mega-sized coffee before you start. A true builder always has a thermos flask close at hand. To keep yours fresh, fill it up with hot water, add five indigestion tablets, leave to work for an hour and then rinse.

- The one rule when cleaning a stain on a carpet is to press the sponge into the stain, rinse the sponge and repeat the process. Do not keep re-pressing the stain without rinsing – you'll only make it worse by spreading it.

- If you've had a dinner party and used lots of wine glasses, rather than putting them into the dishwasher which only leaves them looking smeary and gloomy, place them in a bowl of warm soapy water and leave overnight. The next morning, all you have to do is rinse them with warm water. A word of warning, though: if you are using hot water, don't rinse them in cold water immediately – they will crack due to the change in temperature.

- Treating your carpet to a professional clean every two to three years not only prolongs its life but also removes deep in-ground dirt and stinky odours.

- While the carpet is drying thoroughly, stick drink coasters or jam-jar lids under each furniture leg. This will prevent the carpet from getting permanent dents.

- To stop your chimney from clogging up and getting all skanky, sprinkle a little bit of table salt onto the fire.

- If lily pollen falls on your carpet, use sticky tape to remove it.

- To clean leather furniture, rub with saddle soap to re-nourish it – leave to dry, then shine.
- Remove cigarette stains from the walls by rubbing them down with a pair of old tights dipped in water and washing-up liquid.
- Squeeze a whole lemon into the hot water before you clean the windows. You can also rub lemon juice over brass handles to clean them.
- Wipe down a grimy glass table with lemon juice, then buff with crumpled-up newspaper when dry.
- To wipe a glass coffee table clean and dry, try using paper coffee filters.
- Tempting as it is, don't clean your windows on a sunny day. The heat will dry the windows too quickly, leaving visible smudge marks. Don't clean them on a bitterly cold day either because they may shatter. An overcast day is best!
- Wooden floors come up a treat if you clean them down with soapy water and two tablespoons tea granules.
- Use an old soft toothbrush to clean engraved silverware. The brush will get right into all those nooks and crannies. Any really valuable stuff should be professionally cleaned, though!
- To remove dog or cat hair from your furniture or even your car seat, use a sticky clothes roller (from dry cleaners) or a length of masking tape.
- Remove cobwebs from cornicing in the ceiling: get a bicycle pump and blast them off, or use a hairdryer to dislodge them.
- Put a pair of thick old socks over the ends of a ladder top so that it doesn't scuff the walls.
- To remove the dust from really heavy velvet curtains, lightly wet a chamois cloth in water and gently wipe from top to bottom.

- If you want a greener approach to cleaning the house and your hands are starting to look like those of a witch, try some homemade remedies which are just as good as those toxic chemical ones that you can buy in the shops.

- To clean your wooden furniture, simply mix a cup of lemon juice and a cup of vegetable oil together, put it onto the cloth (not the actual furniture) and clean away. Always test a patch first before you do the whole thing.

- When you want to remove grimy marks from the floor, fill your bucket with 5 litres (9 pints) hot water then add a small cup of vinegar. Dip your mop in it and away you go!

- Vinegar is amazing for removing marks, germs and revolting smells from your toilet! So chuck a cup of the stuff down, leave for 15 minutes to do its job and then flush away.

- There are many other uses for vinegar: it is brilliant for getting rid of rust; it removes bad smells (good if you have dogs and cats); it is superb for getting stubborn stickers off a wall; it gives copper a real gleam; dabbed on a cloth, it will remove carpet stains and both ants and cats hate the smell of it, so put it in areas you don't want them mooching around. It's also great for removing hard water marks and superb for disinfecting kitchen utensils and making fine crockery gleam, as well as cleaning grubby marks off stainless steel.

- To clean a leather chair or sofa, heat up a solution of half-vinegar, half-linseed oil, leave to cool and then dip a cloth into the solution and rub over the furniture.

- Every time you walk off the streets and into your house you'll be bringing in lots of germs. Most of them can be vacuumed up and cleaned away, but a lot can't. So bear this in mind next time you drop your boiled sweet out of your mouth onto the floor and put it back into your mouth! Why not avoid the problem altogether and do as they do in Thailand and remove your shoes at the door? To encourage those who don't seem to have the vital word 'tidy' in their vocabulary, put a basket by the door so that all they have to do is take their shoes off and lob them in!

- To dust lightweight curtains, put them in the tumble dryer for fifteen minutes on a no-heat setting (cold).

- Vacuum your curtains every two to three weeks with the soft bristle attachment. For heavier curtains, attach a soft brush attachment to the end of your vacuum cleaner and work from top to bottom.

- To spruce up old discoloured net curtains, dissolve a denture tablet in hot water and soak them in it for about an hour.

- Vacuum your cushions once a week to keep them fresh.

- To rid your chairs and sofas of the smell of ciggies, sprinkle bicarbonate of soda on top, leave for twenty-five minutes and vacuum it all up. You can also freshen up smelly carpets, especially if you have pets, in the same way.

- Candles are one of my favourite things in life – they are about the only thing that genuinely makes me feel chilled out, but, because I'm constantly burning them, I'm always left with the problem of getting the wax out of the bottom of the glass votives. To get them sparkling again, just dump your votives into a bowl of really hot water, let the wax warm up and come loose and then remove. Don't pour the waxy water down your sink – you will block it up. Instead, run cold water into the bowl, let the wax become hard, scoop it out and chuck in the bin. The water can then go down the sink.

- If you get a stain on your sink, rub it with half a raw potato.

- When cleaning a window, first vacuum up any dust, then wipe off any excess dust using a damp cloth. Clean with soapy water. Clean the frames and sills first, then the window panes. Do the outside panes with vertical strokes and use horizontal strokes for the inside. This will indicate whether any marks or streaks left are on the inside or the outside.

- Dust just loves to park itself above wardrobes, kitchen units and bookcases! For easy cleaning, lay newspapers on these surfaces and remove and replace every two weeks.

- Spray water onto a wood burner or fireplace before you brush up the ashes so they don't go everywhere.

- Clean curry stains from a carpet by washing the affected area with lemon juice and water.

- Plants that live on a carpeted area should really stand on plastic trays that fit the bottom of the pot. This will not only prevent a permanent dent in the carpet but will also stop mildew forming when you water them.

- To clean a glass lampshade, fill the sink with warm water and add a cup of laundry detergent. Lay a towel in the bottom and lay the lampshade gently on the towel in the sink. Wash it, then empty the sink and rinse with warm water. Leave to dry on a clean, dry towel.

- When you want to get rid of the dust in a pleated lampshade you can either use a shaving brush, getting into all the nooks and crannies, or blast away the dirt with a hairdryer.

- Crayons aren't just for kids, you know. They come in handy for disguising small scratches on wooden furniture. Get a wax crayon in the same colour as the wood and rub it over the surface.

- When you've had a house party, there's nothing worse than coming down the stairs in the morning and being confronted with last night's rubbish – beer bottles filled with fag ends, old lager-drenched cocktail sausages and half-eaten pizzas. This is one good thing that I learned from my student days – always do the big clear-up before you go to bed. You don't have to get the vacuum out or wash the sideboards – just bag up the bottles, cans and tired old quiches, etc. and dump them outside in the dustbin. Believe me, you're much better off doing this while you're merry than when your're miserable and hungover.

- I had the worst Saturday job in the universe: I had to clean my dad's copper pot collection. He taught me to rub tomato ketchup all over the pots, leave for ten minutes and then rinse with warm water. They sparkled like mad.

- Everybody has one, a goofy friend who constantly knocks over their glass of red wine. So either ban them from drinking the stuff in your house or, to remove red wine spillages on a carpet, pour white wine, soda water or lots of salt onto it. Or dab white loo roll or a white tea towel into the soda, then dab onto the carpet (or clothing). Keep changing the cloth so you don't spread the wine around.

- To remove a dent from wooden furniture, wet a cloth slightly, put it over the top and then with an iron set on medium heat, gently work over the area until the dent swells back to its original state.

- Put your doormat in a bin bag and shake it. The dust will detach itself and stay in the bag.

- So that you don't vacuum up tassles on a carpet's fringing, put a pair of thin tights on the end of the vacuum-cleaner head, secure with an elastic band and vacuum. Dirt will be the only thing going up the tube.

- To remove scuffmarks from a wall, rub toothpaste on to them with a toothbrush. Afterwards, wipe with a clean cloth.
- Getting clear wax out of a tablecloth is easy. You just put a piece of brown paper over the top and iron over it using a low heat. But if you're trying to mop up red or any other colour wax from your pristine white linen, I'm afraid there's not much you can do about it as the dye will have stained the cloth.
- When you want to lift candle wax from a carpet, put a piece of soft cloth on top of the wax, iron over it (low setting) and the wax will re-melt and cling to the piece of cloth. If there's a little bit left, sprinkle baking soda on top, leave for twenty minutes and then vacuum it away.
- To clean the armrests on a leather chair or sofa free of grubby fingerprints etc., squidge stale bread over them to remove the dirt. Remove grubby fingerprints from around a light switch with a rubber.
- Pop a couple of tablespoons of white distilled vinegar into your washing-up bottle when you are nearing the end of it and give it a good old shake. This will increase the amount that you have in there and vinegar is amazing for getting rid of grease.
- I have to wear glasses because I'm shortsighted. When I'm doing messy work around the house, I always protect my glasses by putting clingfilm tightly over them and then all I have to do is replace the clingfilm every so often, saving my glasses from ruin.
- Always puff up your cushions and make your sofa look nice before you go to bed. An untidy sofa starts your day off with a cluttered brain.
- If your lazy cat's favourite place to snooze or moult is on your smart

furniture, then, to put him or her off, lay some tinfoil on top of each surface. They hate the noise under their tootsies.

- When getting rid of a stain, always work from the outside in with the cloth or sponge. Why? It starts to dry from the outside first.

- If your tablecloth is stained/dirty and you don't have time to wash it before your unexpected dinner-party guests arrive, sprinkle glitter and flower petals over the top to disguise the stains, or simply ditch the overhead lighting, which will show up all signs of laziness with regards to the house cleaning, and go for a low lighting option such as candles that make everything look good.

- If God didn't bless you with lovely long legs here's the solution to washing tiled walls in the kitchen or bathroom that go from floor to ceiling. Use wet wipes. Put them onto the end of your broom and clean away.

- Use a toothbrush to clean carved wood.

- To remove a beer stain from a carpet, pour a little soda water over it.

- If you have a scratch or marks on your white walls or skirting boards, then you can use a white correction fluid (such as Tippex) to disguise them.

- Before you wash a wooden floor, sweep it then wash with a solution of 3½ tablespoons vinegar, 1 tablespoon liquid furniture polish and 2 litres (3½ pints) water. But don't wash a wooden floor too often or it will warp.

- I love sitting on my stairs to work, which inevitably ends up with me stupidly getting ink onto the walls. To get rid of this, simply take a cotton bud, dip it into a tiny bit of bleach and gently clean the offending area.

- Don't chuck out old paintbrushes – they can come in very handy for cleaning your lampshades. Make sure your brush is superclean, though.

- When I was a little girl, living in Cornwall, my parents had beehives and so I've always had fresh honey. We put it on everything from meats and cereals to salad dressings. But I also know how hard it is to remove it from spoons, cups or jars, etc. Dunk a bit of kitchen roll in olive oil, let it absorb into the paper, then rub over the spoon or jar. When you dip the spoon into the honey it will roll off really easily.

- If you are buying a new sofa, then consider buying one that has removable covers. This will make life a lot easier and you will get many more clean years out of it.

- Dust can be so difficult to remove from the tops of books, so rather than bashing them around the place to tease the dust out or just leaving them to die slowly, buried under a mound of fluffy dead skin, get a hunk of fresh bread flesh, crumble and gently squeeze it into and onto the top of the books to shift the dust.

CELEBRITY TIP!

Chris Rogers - ITV News Correspondent

A tidy house equals a tidy mind – Alexis and I spend every Saturday at some point cleaning the house. I do downstairs and she does the upstairs. We don't see it as a chore, but rather something that is really satisfying. When you have blasted through the house, you can both sit down, pour yourself a nice glass of wine and relax in your lovely, organised house.

- If you live in a Joan Collins-style house and you've got a gorgeous chandelier that needs cleaning, then do so with a pair of cotton gloves. That way, you won't leave your grimy little fingerprints on the glass.

Bathroom Cleaning Tips

- To make cleaning the bathroom quicker and easier, close the door, put the taps onto superhot, wait for the room to steam up and then clean.
- When cleaning a bathroom, always vacuum all surfaces first and then wash (see also page 101).
- To remove a ring stain from the bottom of the toilet, coat the inside of the loo with a can of cola. Leave to work for two hours, then flush the loo.
- Another way to clean your toilet: put 300ml (½ pint) white wine vinegar down the loo, leave for five minutes, then flush. You could also drop three indigestion tablets into the water for half an hour as an alternative.
- I always have a little stash of those bathroom cleaning wipes tucked away in my cabinet by the sink in each of my bathrooms. Every night before I go to bed, I give the sink a little five-second wipe. There are two reasons for doing this: it means I wake up to a gleaming sink and cleaning the sink never builds up into a massive big job.
- To make a shower door sparkle for longer, give it a little clean with furniture polish. If it has soap marks, rub a sheet of fabric conditioner over it.
- Get rid of limescale from taps or the showerhead: fill a freezer bag with warm vinegar, secure the bag to the head using a rubber band, leave for eight hours and then rinse.
- If your shower curtain dips into the bath then wipe baby oil on the end of it to prevent mildew and mould from growing.

- You can remove mildew elsewhere by wiping concentrated lemon juice over it.

- If you have mould in the sealant around the sink and bath, dip a toothbrush into bleach and scrub.

- I'm all for a bit of colour co-ordination but, when it comes to bathroom towels, only white will do. You see, if you have dark blue or dark red, for example, then you don't know when they are truly grubby. So lob out the old dark ones (or save them for when your dirty dog needs a shower) and replace with white.

- Bars of soap can be very messy indeed. So put the last dregs into the kitchen blender with some water and a dash of glycerine then blitz until you get a lovely liquid soap (clean thoroughly afterwards!). The other reason for using a liquid pump soap (whether you make or buy it) is that it's actually quite unhygienic to leave a soap sitting in a little pool of dirty water; it's also easier.

- To clean chrome taps, rub them down with plain flour, then rinse off.

- To prevent plugholes from blocking up, put a mug of baking soda down the drain hole and then a mug of white wine vinegar; leave for an hour and rinse. Repeat every six weeks.

- To keep your laundry basket sweet-smelling, vacuum it and put a fabric softener sheet into the bottom every week.

- To bring discoloured bathroom tiles back to life, mix half bleach and bicarbonate of soda together and rub over the surface. Rinse when stains have gone. You can also clean them with half hot water and half lemon juice.

- If you can't be bothered to iron, put your clothes on hangers and place in the bathroom. When you take a hot steamy shower, the steam will get rid of all the creases.

- To remove heavy stains from a bath, fill it with hot water, then add ½ cup of biological washing powder. Leave for eight hours and then rinse.

- A little bit of decent pot-pourri in the bathroom can do wonders for disguising any bad smells. Every couple of months you can put 'reviver oil' on it as it will lose its scent with time. Give it a little stir every week to stop the dust from settling too.

- To make mirrors sparkle, spray air-freshener on to them.

- You can also wipe shaving foam over bathroom mirrors to prevent them from steaming up so quickly. To de-fog a steamed-up mirror, blast hot air at it using a hairdryer.

- Remove drip stains from your sink and bath by rubbing salt and lemon into them.

- Don't forget to clean all the handles in the bathroom, especially the one on your toilet as they will be heaving with germs and bacteria.

- I wear my socks to death, but I also give them a second lease of life by ramming them with soap to use as an exfoliating soap cleaner. Don't forget to wash the sock every day!

- To clean away black mould on top of a damp patch, scrub with a toothbrush soaked in half water and half bleach.

- If you have to clean under a cupboard, but you can't get your hand anywhere near the wall at the back, then secure a cleaning wipe on the top of a broom handle with an elastic band. Now get down onto your tummy and away you clean!

C E L E B R I T Y   T I P !

Rick Parfitt of Status Quo

If you've got a ciggie burn on the carpet, rather than replacing the whole lot or having to rearrange your furniture to try to hide it, get a pair of scissors and cut away the burnt bits. Don't use regular scissors, you'll only end up skinning your carpet. Instead use small nail scissors and you will have more control over it.

Kitchen Cleaning Tips

- To clean the inside of sticky kitchen cupboards, wear rubber gloves to protect your hands (incidentally, this applies to all cleaning jobs). First, empty the contents, wipe with a damp cloth and sprinkle baking soda everywhere. Leave for twenty-five minutes, then wipe clean.

- Clean your wooden chopping board regularly to remove bacteria and smells. Make a thick mixture of warm water and baking soda, smear it on and leave for twenty-five minutes, then rinse. I have three chopping boards: one for fruit and veg, one for meat and fish and one for cheese. Each one is a different colour, so I don't mix them up and risk cross-contamination between foods.

- Cover half a lemon in salt and rub over the surface of a wooden chopping board to remove stains.

- To freshen up a stinky old oven, heat it up to 200°C/400°F/Gas 6, then put some orange peel into an ovenproof dish. Close the door and leave for seven minutes.

- Clean glass kitchen cupboard doors with a mixture of half vinegar and half water. To clean vinyl and plastic cupboard doors, use a sponge with warm soapy water. Rinse with clean warm water and a non-soapy sponge.

- Brighten up the kitchen blender: put 3 cups water, 5 ice cubes and a dash of dishwashing liquid into it. Blend for one minute, rinse and dry.

- To unblock the kitchen sink, put ⅓ cup of baking soda down the drain, then ⅓ cup of vinegar. Wait for two to three minutes and then pour boiling water down to rinse.

- Always store your wine glasses upright – if you store them upside down they'll trap cooking smells and alter the taste of your wine.

- To clean behind the kitchen taps, use a toothbrush.

- Wash a grimy old hob with a solution of white wine vinegar and warm water.

- Coffee stains can make drinking out of the cup a non-pleasurable experience, so soak them in white wine vinegar overnight. Stained coffee and tea cups can also be cleaned using whitening toothpaste – simply rub it into the cup and then wash up as usual.

- Rub half a lemon sprinkled with salt onto a stained glass coffee pot, then rinse away the residue with hot water.

- To clean the fridge, first turn it off and wash with warm soapy water. Then put a cup of bicarbonate of soda inside and leave for about six hours – this will remove all stale smells. Alternatively, put some vanilla extract onto a piece of tissue on a plate and leave in the fridge.

- Although granite work surfaces are highly desirable, they need to be treated carefully because they won't withstand harsh cleaning products. Simply wash them down with hot water and a sponge.

- When you are doing a full load of washing in the dishwasher, add one or two tablespoons vinegar to the detergent. It's excellent for breaking down stubborn grime.

- Washing machines always seem to get scratches on them, so rub car wax all over to hide them – it'll look as good as new.

- When cooking, put tin foil at the bottom of the oven. This will reduce cleaning time as any dripping fat or loose crumbs will fall onto the foil, ready for you to chuck out.

- To remove stubborn hard food from glass oven doors, soak kitchen paper in brown vinegar and stick it to the glass. Leave for twenty minutes or until the hard food has come loose, then wipe with hot water.

- A simple way to clean a microwave is to put two tablespoons lemon juice into a cup of water in a dish and boil for five minutes in the microwave. Leave to cool, then give the inside of the microwave a good old scrub. The lemon juice will have already loosened the dirt inside.

- Another way to clean a microwave is to fill a dish with 2cm (¾in) water and 1cm (½in) white wine vinegar. Boil for three to four minutes until the food starts to loosen, remove the dish, then clean the inside with soapy water.

- Cleaning under a fridge can be very tricky due to it being a tight space. So, put an old sock on the end of a broom handle and drag the dirt towards you, then sweep into the dustpan.

- Put fresh herbs, such as rosemary or mint, or a sheet of fabric conditioner at the bottom of the dustbin to stop it smelling.

- To remove hardened stubborn food from cutlery, soak in fizzy water then wash as normal.

- If your stainless steel sink/work surface is beginning to rust in areas, rub it with lighter fluid to remove the rust. Thoroughly clean the area afterwards with a regular kitchen cleaner, especially if this is where you prepare food — if the food gets contaminated, you could poison yourself.

- Give your mop some TLC. Trim it down an inch — it will make it easier to use. When you want to wash the mop head, put it into a pillowcase and pop in the washing machine.

- The best way to clean a white sink is to soak paper towels in bleach and stick them to the walls of the sink. Leave for a few hours and then rinse.

- If you are lucky enough to have beautiful slate floors, when cleaning them add ⅓ cup milk to a fresh bucket of water for the rinse.

- To clean a dishwasher, empty it, then put a bowl of white wine vinegar in the bottom and set on a normal wash.

- Herbs are absolutely essential in cooking and, like flowers, they need to be kept in water in the fridge otherwise they will soon die. You can, of course, buy the potted versions, which last a lot longer or grow them in your window box. I have a big selection including thyme, basil, mint, coriander, dill and parsley.

- Newspapers can double up as extremely good plate scrapers. Crumple the paper up into a ball and then scrape the food off the plate into the bin. You will be able to remove more and won't scratch a lovely pattern.

- If for some reason you have to move your heavy fridge, to make life a lot easier, put on your washing-up gloves or your fake tan gloves. This will give you the good grip that you need to move the monster around. If that fails, ask a strong friend to give you a helping hand.

The Lazy Goddess

Steve Strange - Singer and Former Front Man of Pop Group Visage
Put everything to one side until your cleaner comes on Tuesday!

Bedroom Cleaning Tips

- Because we sweat at night, leave your bed to air in the morning: (a) it will smell nicer and (b) your bed bugs will move on elsewhere as they hate the cold!

- I'm all up for going to auction houses and markets to look for old bits of furniture to revamp, but if you see a bed that you love and it would be perfect for your bedroom, then leave the mattress behind! It's just not hygienic.

- Every couple of months, flip your mattress over so that it gets even wear and tear. Buy one of those mattress protectors (a kind of cover) that you place directly on top of your mattress to prolong its life. Remove and wash every couple of weeks.

- Vacuum your mattress once a month to remove mites, dead skin cells and dust. To get rid of odours from a tired old mattress, scatter baking soda over it. Leave for three hours and then vacuum it up.

- If you use the space under your bed to store things, don't neglect this area and allow dust to build up. Put your bits and bobs into drawers that slide out easily from underneath it and then vacuum up all of that dead skin dust.

- To shine brass knobs on the bed, rub with lemon oil on a damp cloth.
- If there's a short-cut to take when it comes to cleaning, my mum's the first one there. That's why she never irons her sheets on the ironing board, she does it directly on the bed. How lazy, but brilliant is that!
- It's not a particularly attractive sight, but we all do it – dribbling in our sleep! We may also go to bed with last night's make-up on and a greasy barnet. Of course, this all ends up on our pillows so, rather than risk getting spots as a result of it, change your pillowcase every two or three days. Or, if you're like me, change it every day – it feels so lovely and fresh.
- I'm a fake-tan fanatic – I always look like I've been on holiday and yet the furthest I've been away in the last two years was Manchester! Now we already know how a fake tan can make you appear thinner and how it hides the dreaded cellulite, but this can sometimes come at a cost. Yep, after a few months of going to bed wearing fake tan, your lovely white sheets soon become yellowy and dirty-looking so bring them back to their full glory. Fill your bath up with hot water and add a little cup full of biological washing powder. Dunk in your sheets (use a wooden spoon to get them right in under the water) and leave to soak overnight. When you wake up, take them out and put them through a washing cycle as normal. I guarantee they will be glowing white again.
- Remember to vacuum your curtains. Oh yes, dust and grub loves to hide here too.
- If you have one of those lovely old dark leather chairs just to dump your

clothes onto, then to prevent it from cracking, rub it down and feed it with castor oil twice a year.

- Cleaning slatted blinds is a tricky old job at the best of times and dusting with a feather duster means all you are doing is spreading the dust around. So, get a wad of kitchen towels. Take one of them and wrap it around your index finger, dampen it a little and then run it along the slat. The dust will stick to the damp towel.

- To check if you have bed bugs, flip back your duvet and look for little spots of blood on your bottom bed sheet. If you do, a great way to tackle them is to vacuum all the creases, nooks and crannies in your mattress and even your duvet and pillow. Next, treat the affected areas with a low-odour bug spray – this should remove both bugs and eggs.

- If you have one of those wonderful old beds with not so wonderful creaky bed springs, then rub a thin layer of Vaseline onto them. Next time

C E L E B R I T Y   T I P !

Duncan James - formerly of Blue

One of my greatest treasures is my piano – my grandfather (who was a pianist) passed it down to me. I have a great tip to keep the ivory keys in pristine condition – put a small amount of fluoride toothpaste onto a damp scrap of material and work it into the keys. When all the dirt has been removed, rub it again with a clean piece of material to bring it back to its former glory.

you're jumping around on your bed, your neighbours won't need to know about it.

Cleaning Electrical Objects

- To clean a computer keyboard, use cotton buds to get in between each key.
- Use a sheet of fabric conditioner to wipe down the TV screen. This both cleans it and prevents dust from settling.
- To clean around light switches, cut a template with thick card, place around the switch and clean it. The template will protect the surrounding paint or wallpaper.
- Hand sanitisers are good for so many reasons. The obvious one is to keep your hands clean, but they are also brilliant for cleaning stainless steel appliances such as toasters and kettles – plus they kill all germs.
- To give your vacuum cleaner the best life possible, change the bag once a month. This not only prevents bacteria from growing and causing disgusting odours every time you vacuum, but you will also stop it from getting over-heated due to being clogged up. But, if you like all the mod cons, then treat your house to a bag-free Dyson; they're expensive but worth every penny in the long run.
- Keep your toaster crumb-free to prevent the crumbs from catching fire. Simply tip it upside down over a dustbin and tap it.
- To clean a kettle, fill it up with a solution of half water and half white wine vinegar. Bring to the boil, leave for ten hours and then rinse with hot water.
- To clean and un-clog a coffee grinder, put some white rice through it instead of coffee. This will not only clean it, but also sharpen the blades.

- If your steam iron is looking a little sorry for itself, then give it a clean especially if it has become blocked. Pop some clear distilled vinegar into the section that holds the water, turn the iron on and leave it for a couple of minutes to steam away by itself. Leave it to cool down then rinse it through with cold water.
- Telephones are crawling with germs! Give them a good clean every few weeks with a soft cloth dampened with white wine vinegar.
- Every few months, put your washing machine on a normal wash, but leave it empty. This allows it to have a good old clean by itself. Do not use any detergent, instead add a descaling tablet.

Clothes Maintenance

- To freshen up smelly trainers, put baking soda into a thin sock, pop it into the shoe and leave for eight hours, preferably overnight.
- You can clean dirty trainers with baby wipes. To dry wet trainers, scrumple up some newspaper and stuff them with it.
- To remove ink stains from clothing, dab and rub alcohol into the affected area then put through a normal wash.
- If I have to wash one of my beautiful delicate cashmere jumpers I use cold water and lie it flat on a light-coloured towel (I have some old ones especially for this job). After this, I roll it up into a big sausage shape, pushing down on it to help absorb excess water. I then get another dry, old, light-coloured towel, lob it on the floor so that it's flat (tiled or lino floors are the best) and lay the jumper on top, making sure that it has no creases in it, and leave it there until it is dry. The reason for doing it this way is that, if you hang it up to dry, it will stretch out of shape and will

be ruined. (But of course if you have long arms and you need your jumper to fit, then ignore what I've said and hang your cashmere jumpers up!)

* If you get paint on an item of clothing and can't get it out, then deliberately splatter a little more to just one side of the mark, cut the label out and tell everyone it's designer.

* To remove black grease from your clothes, apply margarine to the stain, then put the item of clothing through a normal cycle.

* A great way to de-bobble a jumper is to get one of those 'de-bobbling' gadgets. I got mine in John Lewis and it is brilliant!

* If you are a jim-jam lover then make sure you put on a clean pair every two days, if not every day. When you are sleeping they will rise right up into your crotch, which will make them smelly! If you are unsure, then have a little whiff of them to see for yourself if they need changing.

* To waterproof and seal your shoes, rub floor wax into them or treat with a water-resistant spray.

* When you are next on a walk where there are horse chestnut trees, gather some of the conkers from the ground and take them home. Put them into your drawers, or wherever you keep your woollen jumpers – moths hate them!

* Before washing my jeans or any other clothes I always turn them inside out – this will help them to keep their colour. It's also a good habit to get into when washing jumpers in the machine as this will stop them bobbling up so much.

* Before you put a top with heavy deodorant marks into the wash, rub vinegar into the stains and then put on to a normal cycle.

* If you look after your bras, they will look after your boobies. So don't just go

dumping your underwired bap-boosters in the washing machine – they will start to fall apart in no time. Instead, wash them by hand or place in a little mesh bag and put through a gentle wash. Hang up to dry, don't tumble-dry.

- You'll know when a bra is about to kick the bucket: it will go grey and will start fraying. This is when it's time to stock up with some lovely new boulder-holders.
- Always iron clothes inside out. This prevents you from scorching the visible side.
- Don't go throwing away old sheets. They come in very handy for all sorts of things – dusters and dust sheets; also cloths that will protect clothes from the heat when you're ironing them.
- Never use hot water to try to remove blood from fabric, you'll only make it solidify and become permanent. Instead, use cold water and a little liquid detergent.
- If you spill coffee, then you must act immediately. Mix up an egg yolk and glycerine and apply to the stain. Rinse with warm water.
- To resolve water marks on suede shoes or bags, gently rub an emery board over them.
- If you want to check to see whether a certain item of clothing may run, put it in the wash on its own with a piece of white cloth or a hanky. If the hanky comes out white, you know you're safe to wash it with other things.
- When you think that a bit of action is on the cards, get those knickers of yours smelling like a good old appetiser! Spray a tiny bit of your favourite perfume onto them and the rest is history.
- To remove rust marks from cotton, rub in salt and lemon juice and leave to dry.

- If you need to wash something that's mega-dirty, then, before you put it into the washing machine, dab a little bit of washing detergent onto the area. Leave to soak in for a couple of minutes, then wash as normal.

- When you're vacuuming the house don't forget your shoe rack and your shoes. Stick the nozzle right into every trainer and boot.

- To freshen up stinky shoes, stick a sheet of fabric conditioner into each one and leave for eight hours.

- To clean really dirty clothes, soak them in a bottle of cola, along with ½ cup of liquid detergent before you wash them. Now wash in the washing machine as usual.

- If you iron bone-dry clothes, I guarantee you will be there for a long time. To halve it, always iron your togs when they're just a little bit damp. If they are bone-dry, then, using your garden water sprayer, spray a little bit of water onto them and iron away.

- Always do up zips, hooks and buttons before you wash clothes as they can damage other items in the washing machine.

- I always used to get grubby neck marks on the inside of my shirt collars until I washed them with a strong shampoo.

- If your underwear goes grey, boil it in a pot of water and lemon juice for five minutes and it'll come out white again.

- From time to time, wash your clothes pegs in soapy water so they don't mark clean clothes with grub. This also goes for the washing line and peg bag.

- What a waste of money buying tights can be! You wear them once, put them in the wash and they come out laddered. To prevent them laddering and ending up in a big ball when you wash them, spray a little starch on them and put them in the delicates bag. Alternatively, put them in a pillowcase.

- To reduce drying time, roll your wet clothes in a towel, squeeze to remove excess water and then pop into the tumble dryer.

- Don't wedge too much into the washing machine at once or your clothes won't wash properly. You might also damage your machine.

- If you only have a small washing line in the garden but lots of washing to hang, clip your socks and knickers onto a hanger to save space.

- Hanging up wet washing is enough to send you to sleep! But if you leave your coloured clothes in the machine for too long because you can't be bothered to get them, then you run the risk of the colours bleeding into each other for a very permanent hippy tie-dye effect.

- To get rid of cigarette smoke from clothes, pop them into the tumble dryer with a sheet of fabric conditioner for five minutes.

- To freshen up a stinky over-filled washing basket, dust a wee bit of baking soda into the bottom of the barrel once a month (no one is going to do it more as it's such a boring job, let's face it!). Leave overnight and vacuum up any residue.

- I would love to be able to eat like my dad – he's like a hamster! He shoves in food till his mouth is filled and then chews away for the next twenty minutes. So for him, dinner lasts about one and a half hours. I know I'm a fast eater – I can spend ages preparing something from start to finish only for it to disappear in about three minutes, as if food is going out of fashion or like I'm in some sort of speed-eating competition. But this competitive streak comes at a cost as I invariably end up with half my dinner down my front, like the Twits! So, if you're a mucky pup like me and get oily foods down your front, pop the item of clothing into a bowl of warm water and washing-up liquid and leave it to soak so that the oil can wiggle its way out. If it happens too often, you can always hang a tea towel off your necklace or even better eat in the nude and then you'll never have to worry about getting food stains on your clothes.

- How many times have we done it? Sat on a seat on the bus or train and got stuck to it, just because some goof was too lazy to put their chewing gum in the bin – and now it's stuck to your gorgeous black pencil skirt. Annoying as this is, don't try to pick it off right there and then – you'll only make the problem worse by spreading the gum further and deeper into the fibres. Instead, wait till you get home and put it in a freezer bag or some clingfilm and then chuck it in the freezer. Leave until it's rock solid, then pick it off.

CELEBRITY TIP!

Jenni Falconer - GMTV *Presenter*

I once had the most beautiful pair of cream suede Vivienne Westwood shoes that ended up getting a big black mark on because somebody stood on my foot. A model friend of mine came up with the best piece of advice, and that is to dip a cotton bud into some nail polish remover and gently dab it onto the area where the mark is. Don't go using loads, though, as you will end up discolouring the suede.

3

Dating & Love Life

HOW MANY TIMES have you wanted to be a fly on the wall when a bunch of guys are talking about us chicks after a date? I mean, do they gossip like girlies? You know what we're like – we share every little detail from what car he picked you up in (an Aston Martin or a rubbish dump on wheels) to the first kiss, which could have been totally delicious and leaving you wanting more or so horrific you can only imagine what it felt like kissing a cat's arse! And were those pecs under his disgusting Hawaiian shirt in actual fact a pair of very well-camouflaged man boobs that would give yours a run for their money? We have a good old giggle about it, and no harm done, but with men it's an entirely different case.

Through my own experience, and from asking my girlfriends, I've come to realise there are two types of men: those who brag about their dates, saying that all the chicks they meet and get lucky with are serious superbabes, hoping this will make them look like a huge stud in front of the boys in the office. They forget to mention that the same girls had hairy armpits, grubby toes, corned beef hash-like skin and daggy clothes. Mad as it may seem, we kind of like these guys because, if we do get asked out on a last-minute date and don't have time to wax our legs, we know that it won't be broadcast to the entire male population the next day because information like that wouldn't do the man's status any good!

Then there are those men who can be very dangerous indeed in damaging our reputation, thus we cannot afford to make a single mistake. Like us girls, they love to dish the dirt – not only all the good, but the bad bits too. Here's what I heard one guy telling his friends about a girl he had just met and it really did shock the living daylights out of me. 'Nah, nah, mate. She was more like a doner kebab – a bit fatty, a bit smelly, always a great idea after a few beers, but something you really regret in the morning.' It was at that point that I realised I had to do some hardcore groundwork and research how us chicks might avoid being involved in that kind of chat!

Here's my survival guide on how to flirt like a good old tart but with class, how to spot a loser from a mile away and, once you've found your knight in shining armour, how to keep your sticky mitts on him!

How to Detect a Complete Tosser

First things first: if a man ever approaches you and cracks out any of the chat-up lines that you're about to read, take my advice and RUN!

- All right, darling, get your coat, you've just pulled!
- There's a party going on in my pants tonight and you're the only one invited!

- If I was the one who had come up with the idea of the alphabet, I would have put U and I together.

- Hey, baby, I'm ready for some fun. I already have the F and the N, now all I need is U.

- I've lost that loving feeling – will you help me find it?

- Congratulations: you have been voted the most beautiful woman in the room and the grand prize is a night with me.

- How do you like your eggs in the morning – fried, scrambled or fertilised?

- They call me summer – I'm a long time coming, but when I come I'm hot.

- Do you want a dance? Yes! Go on then so I can talk to your pretty friend.

- Your lips look so sweet, just one kiss and I swear I will give up sugar for life.

- Can I buy you your last drink? You say, 'Why will it be my last drink?' and he says, 'Because after that one I'm taking you home.'

- As you're leaving, he says, 'Hey, aren't you forgetting something?' You say, 'What?' and he says, 'Me.'

- Excuse me, do you mind if I stare at your face for a minute? I want to remember it for my dreams.

- I like maths. Do you want to go to my room, add the bed, subtract your clothes, divide your legs and multiply?

- You might not be the most beautiful girl in this room, but beauty is only a light switch away.

- Do you believe in love at first sight or do I have to walk away and walk past you again?

- I'm a great swimmer, please can I demonstrate my breast stroke?

- Hey, I've lost my phone number, so can I have yours?

- Why don't you come on over here and sit on my lap and we can talk about the first thing that pops up?
- That dress looks great on you, but it would look better in a pile on my bedroom floor tomorrow morning.
- Just wondered what you wanted for breakfast tomorrow morning?
- My friends said you would definitely turn me down if I came over here and offered to buy you a drink. Would you help me prove them wrong, please?
- Do you have the number for heaven? It seems to me they lost an angel.
- The word of the day is 'legs', so let's go back to my place and spread the word!
- Your dad must have been a baker because you really do have a great set of buns!

What Makes a Rotten Old Apple of a Man?

- If he spends more time than you getting ready to go out, then you might have trouble trying to convince him that he may fancy you more than he does himself. Watch out for these self-lovers.
- Don't bother dating someone who is more interested in himself. You'll only end up being their audience, date after date.
- If you're looking to be in a relationship, don't date someone who has no intention of being in one – you'll only get hurt when they dump you to move onto their new bit of totty.
- If your conquest treats you like a sponge, offloading all his problems on your first date, then get out of there quick!
- Your date should make you feel good about yourself and inspire, not constantly criticise you. If they do, it's time to see who else is out there.

Having said that, a little bit of constructive criticism is OK – you want your date to have an opinion, after all.

- Never go out on a date with someone who won't tell you where they live. They may be a complete weirdo, pretending to be somebody they're not or, worse still, they might have a girlfriend or wife and kids at home.
- The same goes for someone who after a few dates won't give you their home number, just their mobile. They may be worried their girlfriend or wife will pick up the phone.
- I'd be very wary of a man who rocked up to every date drunk – is he doing it because he can't handle conversation? Or he might not like you that much, or he could even be an alcoholic.
- If he takes you out with his friends and leaves you alone all night, it spells trouble. He simply isn't that interested.
- If you are out on a date and he rudely keeps texting, from my experience it could be another one of his many women.
- Keep away from those men who are forever looking over your shoulder to see if anything better comes along.
- Never date a man who is already in a relationship. He's bad news and will probably treat you the same.
- If you want to be in a relationship and all he wants is sex, then I'd stay clear. You're only going to get hurt.
- Let a man chase you. If it's always you doing the organising and putting in all the effort and he can't be bothered, then move on to the next.
- If your date starts chatting up other women in front of you, make an excuse and leave.
- If he passes the bill to you or gasps at the price, then this isn't a very

manly sign, especially on the first or second date. Once you've been seeing each other a little while, you can definitely go 'even Stevens'.

- Never play second fiddle when it comes to football, rugby or any other sport. It's not cool if a guy puts watching the footie before you all the time. It'll only get worse if you end up going out with him. There are exceptions to this rule, such as if it's a really important World Cup match – then let him go off and hang with his mates to watch it. If the sport starts to take over, you need to set some hard and fast rules, girls – you're too good to watch the back of his head day in and day out!

- If a man constantly talks about his mother, then I'd do a runner and call it a day! A protective mother-in-law can make your life hell.

- Watch out for men who send you a million messages a day and flatter you like never before and whose hands seem to be a permanent fixture on your body, even on the first date. Those guys generally tend to be the ones who like to play a game: chase you, flatter you, get you into bed and then dump you.

- Also, I'd be a little suspicious of a man who acts all sneaky on the phone when it rings. It could well be another girl that he is dating.

- Give up if he says he'll phone and he never does. If he hasn't phoned within five days, then he's a loser. Move on – his loss.

- Do you remember that film called *Sleeping with the Enemy*, where Julia Roberts led a life of imprisonment due to her husband controlling her every move? Well, I can only imagine that's a life you'd rather avoid. Here are some control freak signs to look out for: he has a go at you because you are talking to other men – not even flirting, just chatting; he starts to tell you what you should and shouldn't wear; he doesn't ask you what you'd like to eat, just goes ahead and orders; and he's jealous of your relationships with your friends and tries to stop you from seeing them. My advice is to dump him now!

What Makes a Man a Good 'Un?

- He treats you like an equal and he even puts you before football.
- Manners cost nothing. If he has George Clooney's manners, then he's a good 'un.
- He's someone who makes you feel special and that really enjoys spending time with you.
- He's a good listener and loves to hear about your life as he wants to learn about you.
- He phones when he said he'd phone and doesn't play stupid games.
- He's also punctual and arrives at places before you.

CELEBRITY TIP!

Francis Rossi of Status Quo

If you are interested in a guy, then send out the signals: lick your lips, flick your hair back or hold his gaze for a few seconds longer.

- He's there to support you through both good and bad.
- He's an independent guy and has his own life, job and friends.

- He doesn't always bring his work problems home.
- He knows how to romance you and surprise you occasionally.
- He respects your space.
- He wants to introduce you to his friends and, eventually, his family.

Where to Find a Date & What to Do Once You've Met Him

- First, you'll never meet anyone moping around at home in your ten-year-old threadbare pyjamas. So motivate yourself to phone a friend, hit the town and start meeting new people.
- Start going to naturally sociable places such as cafés and bars. The more you go, the friendlier you will become with the staff and eventually you'll get talking to the other regulars.
- If you go to a function by yourself rather than with a group of pals, you'll be surprised how many people will come up and talk to you.
- Trying to muster up a conversation with a stranger can be really scary, especially if he takes your fancy. Practise on little old ladies by opening doors for them and chatting to them about anything (they always love a good old gossip!).
- Who on earth will want to approach you if you've got a face of thunder on you? Look friendly and put a smile on your face.
- When you're introduced to a person that takes your fancy, make sure you hold their gaze for a moment longer than you normally would, preferably giving them a cheeky smile.
- To ooze confidence, walk into a venue like you own the place and smile, even if you feel quite shy inside.
- When you enter a party, don't make a beeline for somebody you

know straightaway. Instead, stop, glance round the room to check out possible fitties to talk to later, then go and chat to your friends.

- There's no point sitting in the corner at a party because no one will see you and you won't be able to check out the talent. Stand as close as you can to the entrance so you spot who comes in.
- How about getting an evening job in a restaurant or bar – you will encounter loads of people and may just meet a potential partner.
- On an evening out, don't rule out the bar or restaurant staff – that barman might just be the one.
- To send out the message of success and confidence without saying a word, stand straight, look well groomed and look people directly in the eye.
- You'll exude confidence if you feel comfortable in your own skin, so take some time out to focus on yourself rather than trying to be someone else.
- If you feel really nervous when chatting to a possible date, imagine you are with your best male friend, having a giggle. This should relax you, allowing you to enjoy being chatted up.
- Being relaxed on a date can be very contagious and makes the other person feel comfortable too. The same goes for being nervous.
- If you've just split up from someone and are feeling hurt and very vulnerable, maybe now isn't the time to be looking for a new man. You'll only end up becoming needy and might just drive them away, leaving you feeling worse. The best thing is to build yourself back up and feel confident with who you are again. Only then will you be ready to get back out there on the dating scene.
- WARNING: Fast passions can fizzle out quickly.

- Don't fall into the trap of being someone he wants you to be. It spells danger as you'll only have to live up to that image day in, day out.

- Try to go to places with lots of atmosphere so that if there are any awkward silences the music or general banter in the place will fill them up. Having said that, avoid venues where the music is so loud that you can't hear each other.

- We usually attract people who have similar personalities and characters to ourselves, so work on being the type of person that you would like to attract.

- Try to be attractive on the inside as this will make you a lot more attractive on the outside.

- If you feel too nervous to smile, then fake it. Eventually it will turn into a real one.

- Listen to the other person's language and try to incorporate it into yours. This will make him feel more relaxed.

- Think carefully about whether you really like the guy before you accept any date.

- Do tell your friends that you are single so they can invite you to lots of dos where you may meet Mr Perfect.

- Interesting people attract other interesting people, so start up a hobby or two.

- Joining a gym is not only really good for you, mentally and physically – it's also a great place to meet men.

- Supermarkets are also fantastic spots to meet a possible date. Check out what he has in his basket. If he has lots of meals for one, then you know he could be single, so start fluttering those eyelashes!

- Ask your friends to do a bit of matchmaking and have them send you on a blind date with one of their other single friends.
- If you have been set up on a blind date, then make sure a couple of your friends know where you are. Always take money in case you need an emergency escape taxi (licensed cabs only, girls) and always keep your mobile switched on. It's always best to be on the safe side.
- If you're out on the town and want to meet a man, then you're better off going out with just two other girls. A whole big group of giggling gals can often look like a hen party, the number one deterrent for a bloke. So don't expect him to come over – he'll be terrified!
- If you're not very good at flirting, watch and learn from other people.
- When you see a man that you quite fancy and you want to get this message across, start preening!
- If you want to meet a compatible man, then start doing activities that he would also enjoy, such as walking, joining a book club, etc. You are more likely to be suited because you already have something in common.
- If you meet a guy in a club and the barman has been a wee bit generous with the vodka servings, whatever you do don't let a stranger take you home. Get his number, phone him and find out what he's like when the alcohol isn't talking.
- Keep an open mind when it comes to finding love. You may meet your future man in the strangest of places: the bus stop, your local DIY store, waiting for your meat at the deli counter – he could even be your gas man!
- Making new friends is a good way of meeting a whole set of new people, one of whom could be a possible date.
- If you have a friend who is well connected and has loads of friends, get

them on the case to look out for a potential hottie and to get you hooked up on lots of dates.

- My good friend Jackie Michaelsen gave me this next tip, which we have played on numerous occasions in restaurants and it's such a giggle! If you have a paper tablecloth (or you can ask the waiter for some paper), then rip off a small square of paper, write a little minxy note on it, fold it up and ask the waiter to take it to a person you like the look of. It's hilarious watching them scour the room to see who sent it. But of course you mustn't give the game away by staring back. Instead, take a sneaky look out of the side of your eye. This is not only great for practising your flirting skills but it also gives somebody a real happy boost.

- If you've swapped numbers with a man, don't torture yourself by hanging around by the phone, or staring at your mobile, waiting for it to ring. Go out and do something fun with your friends, and if he phones, it's a bonus.

The Signs: How to Flirt Like a Good Old Tart, But With Class

Now if he licks his lips, does this mean he's cleaning the spaghetti bolognese he had for lunch off his face, or is he giving you the come-on by teasingly trying to tantalise your taste buds? Watching somebody's body language is a brilliant way of detecting whether or not that person fancies you. And if you've spotted a hunky man from across the other side of the room you may find yourself automatically twizzling your locks around your finger or pointing your little piggy trotter toes in his direction, or even licking your lips all seductively too. Before you know it, you've lured him into your naughty little Venus flytrap without having to utter a word due to your irresistible man-magnet techniques!

The Lazy Goddess

USE BODY LANGUAGE TO LURE A DELISH MAN

- Preen like an animal – caress your hair, toss it over your shoulder or twizzle it around your fingertips.
- Maintain a fixed stare for about three seconds.
- Licking your lips will leave him quivering.
- Point your body in his direction.
- If you don't like champagne, get into it now! Why? Because it's generally served in long glasses, meaning you can caress your glass to mimic a bit of hanky panky, if you know what I mean...
- Don't cross your arms – it will make you appear unapproachable.
- Being tactile is a great little tell-tale sign. So gently touch his arm or brush past him, etc. Basically use any excuse to get your sticky mitts on him!
- When you sit cross-legged, point your knees towards him, not away from him.
- Flutter your eyelashes.
- Give him a gentle smile from the corner of your mouth.
- Put your finger into your mouth and lick it. I don't mean in the way that you would devour a lollipop, but so sexily undercover that nobody notices except you and him.
- Get that little index finger working! Lick your finger indiscreetly and move it down towards your boobies, thus tempting him to have a quick sneaky look at what fun he might find himself involved with later on!
- Being in a noisy place is a great opportunity to close the space between the both of you and for you to allow your faces to touch so you can hear him properly.
- Don't bite your nails, twitch or swing your leg up and down when

crossed — it will make you look very nervous indeed. Aim to ooze confidence and look like a woman in control.

- Having good posture (bum in, shoulders back and tits out) not only makes your clothes look better, but you also look much more confident and cool.
- If there are sparks between you, you will notice that you are mirroring your movements subconsciously.
- Apply lipgloss onto your lips while gazing at your prey.
- If he's getting a bit tactile, i.e. he guides you through a crowd of people wedging himself up close to you while doing so, you're in, girl!

HOW TO DETECT WHETHER HE'S INTERESTED IN YOU

- He winks or smiles at you.
- He notices you, then moves his body to face yours.
- He starts to play suggestively with his tie while looking at you.
- He looks at you while he's talking to someone else.
- He stands tall to show off his manliness.
- He finds an excuse to walk past you and accidentally knocks into you.
- He offers to buy you a drink.
- He stands with a very open posture.

AND WHEN HE'S NOT INTERESTED IN YOU...

- He doesn't make any eye contact or hold your gaze.
- He's constantly trying to create space between your bodies rather than getting all cosy.
- His arms are crossed.
- He always looks over your shoulder when he's talking to you to see if

there's any other talent that might be better. If this happens, move on and forget about him.

- He doesn't turn his body towards you.
- His eyes have a dull look about them.
- His mouth stays closed.
- He's eyeing up somebody else.

C E L E B R I T Y   T I P !

John Barrowman - Actor

Flirting is like window shopping and I love to do both. I stroll slowly past, a quick glance of interest, a step closer for a better look, a small gesture, maybe a word or two . . . but no sale. The pleasure is in the process.

The Big First Date: What to Wear, Beauty Tips & Nerve-busters

- Three days before you go out on your date, do a detox. Eat lots of fruit and vegetables and cut out coffee, tea, alcohol, all sweets and starchy foods that will bloat your stomach. Drink lots of water and herbal tea instead. Your skin will glow as it flushes out the toxins.

- Get plenty of early nights for a whole week before your date. It will make you look younger (reduces lines), fresher-faced, more alert and reduce tired, red-looking eyes and any bags underneath them.

- Ask your date beforehand what the dress code is so that you don't turn up looking like a fish out of water. It'll really knock your confidence otherwise.

Dating & Love Life

- Have a thirty-minute power nap before your date. It'll relax you and is a nice little energy boost. Having said that, if you sleep for any longer you might feel groggy and not want to go out at all!
- Before you leave home, drink a fruit smoothie. Blend a banana, some strawberries, honey and a raw egg together. It will line the stomach if you are going to be drinking alcohol and is something you will really appreciate the next morning!
- Make sure you leave yourself enough time to get ready so that you don't end up rushing and getting your knickers in a twist whilst working up a lovely old sweat, leaving you feeling all stressed out.
- Put on your favourite CD so that you can sing away while applying your make-up, to get you into a positive frame of mind.
- While having your relaxing soak in the bath pre-date, think about what topics you might want to talk about, in case you get stuck for something to say. Also, have a quick flick through the newspaper so that your current affairs knowledge is up-to-date and listen to the radio news for any interesting stories.
- Presentation is so important – have your hair done, get yourself a manicure and pedicure, and apply some gorgeous minxy make-up.
- Have a small glass of wine before you head out the door. It will not only calm your nerves, taking the edge off your inhibitions, but also dilates your pupils making you look even sexier. Only one, mind!
- When on your date, don't let the other person think that you have just spent the entire day getting ready. Give them the impression that it all comes very naturally and that you always look this fab.
- Try to avoid eating garlic, onions and anything else that can give you bad

breath on the day of your date. No one wants to snog a dustbin! Brush your teeth and always carry mint chewing gum in your handbag.

- We tend to tighten our shoulders when stressed, so, to avoid this, clear your head of negative thoughts. Instead, think of happy times such as a great holiday or a friend's outrageous birthday party.

- Girlies, only wear one sexy piece of clothing at a time! Don't wear a top that shows off your boobs at the same time as a pelmet mini skirt. Be mysterious, tantalising and harder to get.

- Wear something that not only suits your personality but also makes you feel comfortable and super-sexy. If you don't, you will only focus on what feels uncomfortable while pulling and tugging away at whatever it is, rather than concentrating on your date.

- It's always better to underdress than overdress. If you feel like a twerp throughout your date it will affect the way that you come across.

- Putting your waistline in the spotlight will help to attract the pheromone-oozing male species. But don't worry if you have a trunk-like waist – through clever dressing you can create one. All you have to do is wear a belt to give your waist some definition.

- Another clever little trick to create and define your waist is to stuff your bra with some fake jelly fillets (you can get them from a lingerie shop) so that you appear bigger on top, making your waist look more shapely.

What Turns a Man On

- Women who have their own lives – whether it's a job, hobby or friends, basically not just sitting around waiting for a man to give her a life and therefore coming across as totally desperate.

- A woman who feels comfortable in her own skin and is not always giving her man a list of what she's eaten that day.

- Don't let your new date know you're totally blown away by him. Keep him guessing and you'll keep the sexual tension and challenge alive. This is what men love.

- Don't be predictable. Keep those boys guessing where you are on the odd occasion. It's not playing games and it keeps them on their tippy toes.

- Don't try too hard or your date will take you for granted and won't put in any effort.

- Men find it very attractive if a girl receives a compliment happily. It shows you are a strong and confident woman. They might even be offended if you throw it back in their face. And like us girlies, all men love to be given compliments, whether it's about his outfit, choice of restaurant or his aftershave.

- Women who have a sense of humour and aren't too precious always appeal, as does a woman who enjoys tucking into her grub when she's out to dinner.

- A woman who says kind things about other people rather than a sour grapes who keeps bitching.

- Always be the first to end a telephone conversation – it will leave him wanting so much more.

- A woman who doesn't give a detailed list of what she has just been up to – i.e. you've just been to the supermarket to get some washing powder or you've plucked your eyebrows. If it's not interesting, don't bother saying it! Leave him wondering what you were just doing. It's all about being a mysterious little bee.

- It's far cooler not to change your already fixed plans to accommodate him. He'll respect you so much more as it makes you appear a strong, confident woman whose life doesn't revolve around men.

What Turns a Man Off

- Saying 'I love you' before he does. He may not be ready to hear this and it could freak him out.
- Women who are lettuce-leaf pickers: what I mean by this is women who push their food around the plate rather than eating it.
- Drunken Bridget Jones-style phone calls late at night, telling him how much you love him and you've only been dating for a week. If you are especially prone to this, then write his phone number down at home and delete it from your mobile.
- Talking about your ex a lot is an absolute no-no (he'll assume you are still hung up on him), as is trying to squeeze information out of him about his ex-girlfriends.
- Don't suffocate someone – let him breathe. Give him lots of space to do his own thing and, in the meantime, get on with yours. This will result in him wanting to spend more time with you.
- Constantly asking a man what he's thinking will eventually start to annoy him.
- Let a man have his independence and do his own thing. Don't try to change him into what you want him to be; love him for who he is.
- Don't get absolutely trashed on booze when out on a date. Not only will you look haggard and rough, but you'll start to say things you'll regret afterwards.

- Don't babble or giggle like a little girl.
- Men hate needy women who are always fishing for compliments.
- Let the man be the first to talk about babies. If you constantly talk about them and he hasn't even thought about a family yet, you may frighten him off.
- Trowelling heavy make-up onto your face rather like a builder uses cement in the hope of getting that air-brushed magazine look can be very unattractive. Men want to see your natural face with some minxy make-up on, not an entire make-up counter stuck to it.
- Don't nag a man to death if he's done something that you don't agree with. He's big enough and old enough to realise he's done wrong, so let him work it out for himself.
- Women completely underestimate how important it is to have nice feet. So if yours look like, and indeed are, the perfect breeding ground for growing mushrooms, men will only assume that all your other body parts will be the same.
- Never discuss your sexual encounters on your first few dates – he'll just see you as one big s**g. Plus, never tell him how many people you've slept with – keep this kind of info locked up.
- Don't rabble on about what you look for in a man on the first few dates. It'll just make you look mega-desperate and way too needy.
- An indecisive woman, one who doesn't know what she wants to do, can be a real turn-off.
- Being overly tactile may look a bit desperate and needy, yet being as cold as stone and/or shy can be equally off-putting.
- A woman who constantly looks in her mirror and re-touches her make-up in front of him.

- Don't be too predictable. On the odd occasion, don't pick up the phone. If it was him calling, call him back three hours later and tell him you were busy doing something cool.
- We all love a little flirting, don't we? But don't take it too far and start talking about full-on sex on your first few dates – it just makes you sound like a tart.
- If you have a volume control problem and your voice pretty much drowns out everything around you, then it may be worth lowering it a bit.
- Whatever you do in the bathroom should be kept private. The top of the list has to be not letting a man ever see you on the toilet, even when you're married. It just isn't sexy! Next has to be shaving your armpits or plucking unwanted long hairs from your nipples and, lastly, squeezing your spots.
- Most men find high-maintenance women very off-putting. That includes constantly wanting attention and for the focus to be on them, a continuous flow of presents and to be taken to expensive restaurants all the time.
- Don't even try to compete with his mum or to come between them – she'll only make your life hell! Similarly, men hate to be mothered and don't tell him to grow up.

CELEBRITY TIP!

Amanda Ross - Owner of Cactus TV

Because I go out a lot after work, I keep a stock of things in my office that will give me a day-to-night transition such as glam heels, evening bags and glitzy tops.

Dating & Love Life

The First Date

- Being really late just isn't a 'cool' thing to do. Always aim to be about ten minutes late, no more. Early or on time just makes you look too keen.

- For obvious reasons, never order spaghetti bolognese. Tomato sauce round your chops is never a good look!

- If you are worried that you may have a little piece of food stuck in your teeth, angle your shiny knife or spoon so that you can check your reflection.

- If the date isn't going too well, don't worry – just look on it as a learning experience for what you do and don't want, and you'll know what to avoid next time.

- If you find the conversation drying up, then a good thing to do is to ask him a question about himself. Invariably people quite like to talk about themselves.

- Men always like a little encouragement and to have their egos massaged. So, if the date went well, tell them. And you're always better off ending the date on a high, so dangle a carrot and leave him wanting more!

- If you are in a club, always leave before the lights go on at the end. You'd rather he went home with the memory of your gorgeous fresh face from the restaurant rather than later when you're looking less than your best, wouldn't you?

- Always be the one to say goodbye first and, if the date went well, take control and get in that driving seat by deciding when the next one will be. Tell him you'll give him a bell.

- Starting up a fresh conversation with a complete stranger can be really scary at the best of times, so arrange to meet your date in a place where they do really unusual dishes or fabulous cocktails that you can discuss and giggle about.

- If you are a bit of a shy girlie and are worried you may run out of conversation halfway through the evening, write down some subjects that you love to talk about and stuff the list into your handbag. You can always run to the bathroom to swot up!

- Never give the impression that you get so trashed on alcohol that your poor date will start to wonder whether he may have to get that gym membership after all – to build up the muscles he needs to carry you out of the restaurant!

- Isn't it funny how the closer you get to the bottom of your wine bottle, the more attractive the guy becomes? So, if you have given him your phone number and he asks you out on a date and you can't remember for the life of you what he looked like or whether he was cool or not, suggest to him that you should go on a daytime date rather than a night-time one. You will feel less pressured into kissing him and, because it's during the day, you can always have an excuse to get away by saying that you have a meeting.

- If you are unsure about your first date, have one glass of wine and bring your car with you so that you have a getaway vehicle at any time.

- Just in case your date goes hideously wrong and you desperately need an excuse to get the hell out, have a friend phone you at a certain time and then pretend to your date that your friend is in trouble and that you have to go to her rescue!

- You can mention your ex-boyfriend only once. Any more and you will really do his head in!

- Keep the conversation light and fun, rather than heavy. Don't delve into his personal life by asking really personal questions unless he talks about something first.

- If you accidentally knock some red wine onto either of you, soak a napkin in a little white wine and apply to the stained area. Or rub salt into it as an alternative option. If nothing else, it's a good way to get tactile! Don't forget that it's only polite to apologise and offer to pay for his dry-cleaning bill, although he will most likely decline your offer.

- If you suffer badly from BO, then I strongly recommend that you avoid any garlicky or spicy foods – they can cause body odour to increase.

- If you have arrived at the place where you agreed to meet your date but you got caught in a rainstorm, quickly run into the bathroom and stick your head under the hand-dryer. The same goes, within reason, for wet clothes: take them off and shake under the heat.

- Never have sex on the first date. You are worth more than that, so let that boy work for you! He'll respect and appreciate you more in the long run.

- If you are one of those girls who is absolutely fine when she's had one wee cocktail, but any more and your skirt and knickers end up around your ankles, then I'd strongly advise you to go easy on the booze. Have one non-alcoholic drink for every alcoholic one.

- He's an absolute no-no if he so much as brings out a calculator and starts working out who pays for what! If he's that stingy on the first date when he's supposed to be impressing you, then he's really missing out on the chance to show you how much he could, or can, look after you. Run a mile and delete his number!

- If you have a weird interest (such as dressing up in nappies or loving to be pinned up against a wall and having knives thrown at you), keep it under wraps until at least the second or third date. Otherwise, you may scare him off because he thinks you are a complete psycho.

- Men tend to like confident chicks and the more confident you are, the more you double your chances of dating success. So if you are lacking in the confidence section, fake it. Eventually it will come naturally.

- Unless you're a teenager and saving up for your first flat, if he says he's still living with his parents and he's over the age of 30, then I would definitely cross this one off your list too. He has obviously got very cosy at his rent-free home and is being waited on hand and foot by a doting mother. But you know what's coming next? If you do end up dating him and then moving in with him, guess who's going to be the mug tied to the sink and forever clutching the laundry bag for the rest of her life?

The Naughty Girl's Sleepover Essentials (Keep In Your Bag When Going On a Date)

- Condoms: you can never be too careful – never risk STIs.

- We've all done the walk of shame in the morning in our glammy Pammy numbers while everyone's going to work, haven't we? You may as well just walk around with a sign stuck to your head. What a tart, hey? To avoid this humiliation, take a pair of flat foldable ballet slippers with you so that you can put them on the next morning and put your sexy stilettos in a plastic bag (keep one in your handbag). Also, take a thin T-shirt with you to swap with your busty sparkly top.

- Chewing gum is a must. It will get rid of that wheelie-bin-like breath no man wants when you give him his goodbye kiss.

- If you have forgotten to take off your make-up the night before, you may wake up looking like a cross between an abstract Picasso and the exterior of an old suitcase! First, try to get up before him so that you can scrape off some of the old make-up and replace it with a fresh layer. Remember that, when he last looked at your face, your make-up was in all the right places. Always carry an emergency make-up kit with you: a lipstick that doubles up as a blusher, a mini mascara (you know the freebie types that you can get over the counter in department stores) and a mini bottle of light foundation or concealer.

- Decant your perfume into a tiny bottle. This is a real life-saver: first, it's great for getting rid of unwanted morning BO and, second, if you find yourself in the awkward situation of needing to do a poo in his flat then it comes in very handy for disguising aromas that would otherwise leave his bathroom smelling like a rat had just died in there!

- A dental floss G-string. Walking the path of shame is bad enough, but doing it in a pair of day-old knickers just makes it that bit more awful!

How to Leave His Flat In Style

Rule One: Follow all the advice above and leave the house looking as gorgeous as you arrived so that he can lie there in his bed and have a good old morning dream about you.

Rule Two: Don't hang around, overstaying your welcome. Give him a minxy peck on the cheek and leave the house Danielle Steele-style, with him wanting more.

Rule Three: Whatever you do, DON'T leave your necklace or earrings there to have an excuse to go back and see him. First, he may not want to see you again and, second, he'll see right through your plan, resulting in you looking a little desperate not to mention totally transparent.

Revving Things Up in the Boudoir

We all have them, don't we? Days from hell, that is; days when the bags under your eyes are so big you could carry your groceries home in them, you look bald because your hair is so greasy and stuck to your head and you have so much work to do that you don't even have time to leave the office at lunchtime to get a bite to eat.

So what do you do instead? You bulldoze your way through the chocolate and crisp vending machine, you stalk the lady with the cake trolley, bite your nails and the skin around them nervously and your eyes become so red you start to resemble the Devil. You leave the office tired, with zero energy, practically hallucinating from the combination of stress and sugar overload. On the way home, you drag yourself along the pavement and dream of a cup of cocoa and your lovely bed. You fall through the front door, wanting to collapse from exhaustion… but, rather than seeing your boyfriend there, open-armed with a cup of hot choc in his hand, all ready for a big stress-busting hug, he's in the doorway, leaning up against the wall and thinking he's the missing link to the next James Bond film, all ready for a bit of action!

WHAT? Meanwhile, you've been busting a gut at work, ramming a never-ending stream of coffee, cakes and chocolate down your throat and the last thing on your mind is to whip off your kit, transform yourself into a man-eating, hot luscious lips and get down to some dirty business. And that's where the problem lies. He doesn't see that you are tired. You really love him, but you really need to stare at white walls and space out for a bit so to make yourself feel a little human again. He sees this as neglect and so the awkward atmosphere starts to build up. And the more it builds up, the more tension enters the relationship, and the more stressed out you become.

You're not alone in this one. There are so many couples out there just too tired to have a bit of leg-over and can go for weeks without seeing each other's boobies and bum cheeks. High stress levels, exhaustion, eating the wrong kinds of food, even being in a long-term relationship can really affect your libido. So if you feel like a freak for not wanting nookie, or at a dead end when it comes to making love, it's time to clear out the cobwebs and rev up your sex drive...

- If you think that you might get lucky tonight, lay off the big full-fat, four-course dinner. Stuffing your face will kill your libido and leave you looking (and feeling) a bit of a beached whale. All that food will just sit in your stomach and you'll feel far too bloated and sluggish to get laid. But you can still have a romantic dinner and enjoy it. Order lighter options such as fish, vegetables and salad rather than car-wheel-sized pizzas and stodgy, creamy pasta dishes.

- To spice things up well before you get anywhere near the bed, eat foods that look sexy and make you feel sexy while you're eating them. Try strawberries dipped in chocolate or cream, spicy prawns with chillies (the heat of the chilli on your lips makes you feel aroused), oysters or asparagus drizzled in hot butter and ice cream (share a spoon). All these guarantee lots of fun and giggly mouth bites.

- A bit of romance goes a long way on the odd occasion, so leave your loved one something really sweet or minxy on top of his pillow as a little surprise. It could be a packet of Love Hearts, a little handwritten note or even a lipstick kiss on a piece of paper.

- If either of your bodies smell of BO or fish, sex is definitely off the menu! Our sense of smell is the most powerful of all the senses. So do each other a favour: lose the fishy fragrance and put something yummy and sensual on.

- Having nookie in the bath is almost impossible and because it's so awkward you run the risk of slipping, knocking yourself out and falling in a really unattractive position. But I'll tell you what does really work and is so much fun: having a bath together and taking a bottle of champers in with you. Forget the whole washing each other thing, it's so naff.

- Give each other a massage. Body contact is very intimate and tends to lead to a little more.

- Sharing from the same dish or using the same fork or spoon can be really intimate and sexy. I'm talking about cute little dishes such as tapas here, not a big Sunday roast or cheese-filled jacket potato.

- Fun and games in bed can be great for getting the energy in bed going, even something as little as tickling. You'll be screaming with laughter as you try to fight each other off.

- I know the gym can be a bore, but it will make your sex life a whole lot better. Exercise increases your testosterone, which will in turn boost your flagging libido.

- Some couples set their alarm to a really early time so that they can squeeze in some cheeky time before they go to work. This is a bad idea because you will both feel exhausted for the rest of the day. Instead, get naughty during the night when you're half-asleep. It may only last three minutes, but at least you can go back to sleep and enjoy happy dreams!

- Create a sexy environment. There's no easier way to kill the ambience than by putting on harsh spotlights. You don't want to be reminded of the doctor's waiting room, do you? Get hot! Light loads and loads of candles so the mood is seductive and flattering.

- If your love life is about as exciting as watching paint dry, don't just reach for the Viagra to try to rev things up, try Horny Goat Weed. It's a herbal aphrodisiac that's supposed to make you feel very frisky indeed.

- Lavender oil is great for making you feel relaxed and helps to reduce the stress, which often puts us off sex. So either put some in a burner or ask your loved one to give you a soothing massage.

- Oysters, I can't bear them! They look like giant bogies and are an acquired taste but they're amazing for getting you in the mood for a bit of hot hanky-panky under the sheets. Oysters are rich in zinc, the magic recipe for increasing blood flow. For him, the blood only seems to go to one place, and it gives you great energy and gets you all minxed up and in the mood for all sorts of unmentionable things! But if you don't want to bust your budget on expensive oysters, or you like them as much as I do, try other foods that are rich in zinc, such as strawberries (dipped in a bit of dark chocolate with a high cocoa percentage), cod, spinach and brown rice.

- Being able to laugh together is one of the biggest bonds in a relationship. So, when it comes to the summer, have a barbecue (you can buy one of those disposable ones if you don't have a proper barbecue already). Don't invite anyone around – this is a barbecue with a twist. Do it only wearing an apron and nothing else. It's so much fun! If your house is overlooked by a million others though, give this one a miss and keep the neighbours happy. Alternatively, you could do a bare-bum barbie in your kitchen!

- I don't know what it is about sleeping in hotels that turns us girls into wannabe prostitutes! If this is you, then you and your man should book yourselves into a lovely hotel every couple of months and act out all of your fantasies.

- If you're both out at a really boring or very corporate dinner together, spice things up a bit. When you're dying with boredom halfway through the evening, whisper to him that you aren't wearing any knickers. It will drive him wild!

- If your boyfriend's birthday is coming up and you want to do something really thoughtful and hot, then get a friend to take some steamy boudoir pictures of part of your body that only your boyfriend would recognise. This could be the curve of your back or a faded-out profile of the side of one of your boobies, nothing full on. Keep it classy and creative, not Page 3! Oh, and black and white is always more flattering.

- A little cocktail may get the party in your pants going at the beginning, but it will soon wear off. Alcohol is a depressant and a de-stimulator. It can make a girl feel less sensitive and you just wake up looking rough anyway.

- Watch a hot sizzling film (or a porn!) together and eat some sexy food (see above). That should get you in the mood.

- The bad side to watching a horror movie is that you have to go to bed with the lights on because you're too scared to go to bed in the dark. But the good side is that it gets your adrenalin rushing, which also encourages your sex drive to get going too. And it means you'll be glued together in bed in case the bogeyman comes to get you!

- Come on, be honest, who goes to bed in their hundred-year-old, yellowing pyjamas? They might be incredibly comfortable, but are they really going to rev things up in the bedroom? Of course you may be lying next to a pair of dishcloth-looking Y-fronts in bed. Take a little trip down to Marks & Spencer to load up on hot undies for both of you and I guarantee this will help spice things up.

- Watching mindless rubbish on the TV is very addictive and can kill a couple's sex life. Why? Because you both sit there like two zombies! When it's time to go to bed at midnight, you are far too tired to think about getting jiggy and just want to go to sleep. So make a plan. Have a yummy dinner together at the dining table (no TV), then go to bed mega-early. Lie there gossiping and giggling, telling each other funny stories and what you've been up to for the day, etc. You'll have nothing to distract you from each other's company, and it's good quality time. Also, because it's early, you won't feel tired so, if something hot happens under the sheets, it's because the mood is right and not just because you feel like you ought to.

- If your bedroom looks really clinical and unsexy, of course this isn't going to get you in the mood for a bit of loving. It's time to get yourself down to B&Q, load up on sexy paint colours, candles and cushions, etc. Buy a bottle of vino and take yourselves off to bed for an early night after you've done your re-decorating. You've earned it!

CELEBRITY TIP!

Chad White - Male Model
Give and take – being selfish is a vice.

4

Fashion

FASHION – YOU CAN either do it the super-glam SJP way or the super-scruffy Vicky Pollard way. It's your choice. You have to ask yourself whether you want people to move aside when they pass you in the street so that they can grab a glimpse of your breathtakingly beautiful ensemble whilst drooling with pure jealousy, or whether you are happy to spend the rest of your life having litter lobbed at you because people have mistaken you for a rubbish bin.

The way we look can totally affect our confidence, our personality and the way others treat us. If you look like crap, you may well get treated like crap. It's harsh, but it's reality...

Does My Bum Look Big in This? Cacks for Your Cracks

Do you sometimes treat your rump and spend more than £30 on a hot pair of sexy knickers hoping they'll make your arse look more like Heidi Klum's and less like a pimply, bald-headed man? And do you find that out of that £30, twenty quid's worth is gobbled up by your crack every time you wear them? Well, if your bum has more chins than a Chinese phone directory, maybe it's time to invest in a selection of sausage casings – a.k.a. body-sculpting underwear.

- First things first, you need a good stock of knickers to see you through every occasion. VPLs are an absolute no-no, the ultimate fashion crime so invest in G-strings in white, beige and black – brilliant for below figure-hugging tight clothes. Every girl needs a couple of pairs that match their skin colour exactly for wearing under light or sheer clothing. If you have a good stomach and no added chicken wings to your hips, and you're going to wear low-rise trousers, make sure you wear low-rise knickers so they don't poke out over the top. If all else fails, go commando. But please... don't do a Britney getting out of the car!

- Good underwear makes outerwear look better, so treat your undies with respect. If you have wooden drawers, line them with some paper to prevent them from tearing or catching.

- I love to open my drawers and smell something yummy – it always puts me in a good mood. So I pop in lavender bags.

- Never dump your delicate tights and stockings in with the rest of your bras and panties – they will only snag. Store them in little tiny silky bags and this will protect them from becoming laddered and all tangled up.

- Drying your pants in the tumble-dryer is like sending them to the slaughterhouse – it makes the elastic really stringy. So to give them a long life and keep them in shape, dry them on the neck of a hanger and attach it to the end of the clothes horse.

- Every so often, detox your underwear drawer and chuck anything way past its sell-by date. While you are doing this, give your drawers a good old vacuum too.

- Try to avoid big pockets on the backs of your trousers. You're just adding another layer of bulk to your bum.

- To prevent your backside from morphing into a hot-air balloon, avoid wearing any dresses and skirts that are cut on the bias.

- Magic knickers that hold you in like a sausage skin are brilliant for smoothing out lumps and bumps, especially if the material of your outfit isn't that forgiving to start with. Also, they can magically make your bum look half its size. So, girls, go and invest in a pair! But beware – although you can just stuff your wobbly bits into tailored pants, if you buy a pair that is too small for you, then your flab isn't going to just magically disappear, is it? It has to go somewhere and that tends to be higher up your tummy, or wherever it can escape outside the pants. Believe you me, it's not a pretty sight!

- Floaty material does nothing for a big bum as it offers it no support at all. You're better off going for a more structured fabric that holds all the wobbly bits in.

- Thin white material is a beacon for cellulite so either wear double-layered material (loose-fitting) that hides and disguises the orange peel effect or opt for a darker colour.

- G-strings are disastrous if you have a big bottom – they will make it seem even bigger. Instead, treat your peachy cheeks to some fifties-style shorts. Trust me, you'll feel great in them.

- Whatever you do, Lycra is a no-no if you've got a big bum that's covered in cellulite as it will cling to every little bump possible, making it look like a big old blancmange (this especially applies to gymwear).

- Wearing a massive great baggy tent-like dress that completely drowns your figure isn't going to hide your big bum and make it look smaller – it will actually make it bigger. You're so much better off going for something fitted, structured and lined that will flatter your shape.

- There's only one person who can get away with displaying a thong while wearing a shell-suit combo and that's Vicky Pollard from *Little Britain*. Everybody else, leave the look well alone! So keep your pants firmly locked away, please.

- It's really important that your pants have a cotton crotch to allow your front flower to breathe.

- I always keep the plastic packaging that my tights come in as they're very handy for storing your tights so they don't become laddered.

- When I've finished with my old little washing powder boxes, I cut off the lids and I put them in my underwear drawer to use as dividers. I separate my light and dark knickers into boxes and my socks go in another box. It means my drawers are always organised, which comes in very handy when you're half-asleep in the morning and in a rush.

- Tights can be so expensive in the long run. It doesn't matter how much you spend on them, they all have the potential to ladder during the first wear, so for that reason I wouldn't go spending a fortune on them.

- If you have little twiggy legs like Gwen Stefani, then skinny jeans (or tapered trousers of any sort) are so for you. On the other hand, if you've got turkey drumsticks for legs, be über-careful wearing trousers that are literally sprayed onto your pins – they will accentuate your shape and make your calves look thin and your bum will seem enormous. Instead, you need to balance out your shape and the best way to do that is by wearing wide-legged trousers.

- The all-in-one body slip is a must-have if your stomach and bum have a mind of their own. It will slim your size down, control the wobbly bits and give your boobs a bit of a lift, too.

- Remember, wearing small patterns in a dark colour is always more flattering than big patterns in a dark colour.

- If you have got a flabby tummy, opt for a swimming costume with ruching across the stomach. This will help to camouflage the rolls.

- Patterns can disguise cellulite – always a helpful little trick.

- Pencil skirts are great – they act like a corset to hold everything in where it should be.

C E L E B R I T Y   T I P !

Jenny Packham, Fashion Designer

Become a glamorous goddess by focusing on the less-is-more philosophy. Look to the runway and the red carpet for inspiration. With dewy make-up, glossy hair, the perfect pair of vertiginous Christian Louboutins and an unusual piece of vintage jewellery, you can look effortlessly glamorous from head to toe in seconds!

Revenge Dressing: Make Your Sorry Ex Gutted

The last time you saw your ex you were probably in your 'I've known you far too long' Vicky Pollard tracksuit with a greasy chip-pan hairdo. But then you got dumped as he thought the grass was greener… But do you know what? You can go out there and show that pile of rotting compost that, if you deadhead the pretty rose in the garden, her thorns will come out and remind you of what you're missing. So, if there's even a mini chance of you bumping into him on any occasion, make sure you look mouthwateringly delicious. Go and draw blood with your thorns, girls!

- Never look like you've tried too hard to look good: let him think this is the new and improved, gorgeous you. He doesn't need to know that you spent almost five hours deciding what to wear and then a further three doing your hair and make-up.

- A big, super-happy smile and being the centre of attention will eat away at him, even if you feel as depressed as anything and want to cry your eyes out.

- Get some new HOT underwear! Not only will you feel really confident and hot within yourself, if you deliberately have a little bit showing, he won't be able to take his eyes off you.

- Get your trotters down to that gym and make sure your body looks sizzling, then wear a sexy secretary skirt suit and make him jealous.

- Don't go loading on the make-up – you don't want him to think you're hiding behind a mask of insecurities (even if you are).

- Be a temptress like sexy Angelina Jolie and wear killer heels. No man can help himself when he sees them.

- Get your boobies looking like big cream buns and put a couple of gel chicken fillets into your bra.
- Don't under-dress but don't overdress either. Under-dressing will make him think he's missing out on nothing, while overdressing gives the impression that you're feeling insecure and trying to capture his attention. Keep that bit of mystery going.
- Make your lips look more kissable than ever. Rub fresh chilli flesh onto them and then apply a hot, glossy red lipstick. They will look so big and scrummy.

CELEBRITY TIP!

Eugen Bauder - Male Model

An unusual pair of shoes is what sets you out from the crowds and totally transforms a potentially boring outfit.

Shop Till You Drop

If there's one thing us girls have perfected over the years, it's shopping. Shopping till we literally drop to the floor. In fact, I reckon shopping is exactly like racing old bangers. We will zoom round the shops like we're competing against each other on a dirt track, deliberately trying to wreck the opposing vehicles until we've smashed up every car in sight to be the winner. It's true, though, isn't it? We do burn it around the shops in a haphazard way, pushing and shoving off all of the competition until we've got what we want. We're ruthless, but then that's what shopping is all about!

As with banger racing there are absolutely no rules or regulations to shopping, just get out there and win! Here are a few little helping tips to get you to the chequered till point... first!

- Now it depends on whether you're shopping for just a cheeky, quick pick-me-up to add a little something to your wardrobe, or if you're going to do serious damage to your credit card, whether you completely empty all of your clothes and accessories onto your bed for a stock take or not.
- If you're in dire need of quenching your mega-thirst for retail therapy, then I suggest you empty the entire contents of your wardrobe onto your bed. Start to put together all the outfits that you love and then work out what's missing and what you need to buy.
- Unless you're loaded and money isn't an issue, I suggest you set yourself a budget and stick to it. It's so easy to get tempted by all the gorgeous things waved right under our noses when we're out and about in the shops. Willpower, that's all I need to say.
- Store cards – there are good and bad things about them. On the plus side, if you have a store card, you get to hear about special offers, events and promotions before the general public do. Conversely, spending on a store card can easily get out of hand and they usually have higher interest rates which means your debt can mount up very rapidly. Keep store cards to a minimum and write down what you spend so that you know how much money will be leaving your bank account.
- It's worth putting on some make-up that makes you feel glam when shopping for a hot little glitzy number. A blotchy, greasy face is just going to put you off whatever you try on.

- Similarly, never go shopping with greasy hair – it will always make you feel ugly, no matter how lovely the outfit.

- Wear the right type of shoes for shopping. High heels are a no-no – your achy feet will slow you down and make the whole experience a tough one. Glam trainers, ballet shoes or tiny kitten heels that slip on and off easily will do the job.

- Handbag essentials – take water, healthy snacks, your mobile and cash.

- If you are going by car, then make sure you have a bag of change with you to feed the meter and don't forget to set the alarm on your mobile for just before it runs out so you don't get a ticket.

- Never take boyfriends shopping. They only sit there huffing and puffing, looking miserable, and tell you everything looks good just so they can get you out of the shop as quickly as possible. Take a good friend who has a great eye for fashion, or go on your own. You can always take it home and then get a second opinion.

- Before you purchase something, have a little peek at the washing label inside. It may say dry clean only, which in the long run can actually end up costing more than the item of clothing, especially if it's white and needs constant cleaning.

- Eating porridge for breakfast will keep your energy levels high. Having a heavy calorie-laden lunch only makes you feel sluggish and bloated when trying things on. Let's face it, everybody hates the sight of their figures in those wretched changing rooms that seem to have a hundred mega-watt light bulbs shining down and highlighting your cellulite, so don't make it any worse by overeating at lunchtime. Instead, choose a protein-filled salad (such as tuna or chicken) that is light and delicious

and won't leave you feeling like a walrus while you are trying on clothes.

- In case you have to try your clothes on in a communal changing room, make sure you wear underwear that you don't mind other people seeing. Perhaps leave the half-nipple-baring bras at home?

- Make sure you wear clothes that slip on and off with ease. You don't want to be fighting with a zillion buttons and laces – it will drive you up the wall and make you super-aggravated, which will only result in mistake purchases.

- Just because you've seen Kate Moss wearing something in a glossy, it doesn't mean it's going to look amazing on you. Don't buy just for the sake of fashion.

- Planning to hit the vintage boutiques à la Sienna Miller? Don't overdo the lace and wear it from head to toe, dressing like a Victorian, instead mix it in with some denim for a modern take. If it smells really musty, there's a chance the smell may never come out, so you'll end up whiffing like a family heirloom!

- If you're shopping for a winter coat and we're having a hot September, then it's paramount that you try it on with a jumper. There's no point in you wearing a tiny summer dress only to discover the coat doesn't fit when the harsh weather kicks in and you need to layer up.

- I love long coats – they can look so elegant. But if you're really short then a long coat will make you look like a midget because you'll more than likely be dragging it around with you, forever lifting it off the floor. If this is the case, opt for a three-quarter-length coat instead.

- An overcoat is a very hard thing to alter, unlike a dress or a pair of trousers. So if it doesn't look totally amazing the first time you try it on, don't even contemplate it.

- When you're shopping for a bikini, make sure you're wearing non-bulky underwear that won't interfere with the line of the bikini to get a true idea of what it will look like.

- If you want to get a fuss-free tan on your holiday, then go for a bandeau-style bikini.

- Don't give yourself a cardio attack when trying on bikinis and swimming costumes. Yes, most wretched, unkind changing rooms do have dreadful light that shows up every lump of cellulite, but don't let that stop you from buying a potentially great bikini. All I can say is, when you're on that beach, the lovely sunlight will blast out any imperfections on your body. Hurrah!

- If you have to buy a bikini in a size bigger, then do so. Don't bother what the label says, worry about the fit instead.

- For many of us, trying on a bikini in a harshly lit changing room can be utter hell. But instead you can order a whole bunch of bikinis online from a website and have them delivered to your home, then try them on in your own home in front of your trusty old mirror. When you have chosen what you want, you can send the rest back.

- It's really important that you do a bit of jumping around in a new bikini to see how it sits on your body. If it disappears right up your crack after only a couple of jumps, then it's not right for you. You don't want to be playing volleyball on the beach with half your ass on show for the world to giggle and gawp at, do you?

- Should you spot an item of clothing that you can't live without, but which

doesn't quite fit you properly, ask an assistant whether they have an in-house seamstress who could alter it to fit you.

- Buy a cheap shirt but make it look more unique and expensive by removing the buttons. Sew on some funkier ones instead.

- If I really like something that would be a good staple item for my wardrobe then sometimes I will buy two of it. Finding a fab pair of trousers or a skirt that fits really well and makes your figure look even better is worth investing in, plus you can alternate so they don't wear out quite so quickly.

- When trying on new shoes, it's really important that you take a walk around the store to get an idea of how they feel to walk in. Do they pinch, force you to change your posture (which could affect your knees and back) or make your legs look chunky?

- When you're looking to buy a pair of slingbacks, go for a pair with elastic at the back. The reason for this is because they can then fit to your feet at all times, whether your feet are hot and puffed up, or cold and smaller.

- How many times during the summer have you seen a woman who is unaware that she is wearing a transparent skirt? It's probably because she has tried it on in a changing room with no backlight, only above-lighting, so just be aware! You may want to take it home and try it on in front of a mirror where you can have a source of backlight (either a window during the day or a lamp).

- If you do find yourself with a see-through skirt, one solution is to wear a flesh-coloured slip.

- If you are trying on a garment while wearing lots of make-up, ask the sales assistant if she has a silk scarf that you could cover your face with while you try on the item. This will prevent getting make-up on the outfit as you pull it over your head.

- I always go and check out the kids' section when I'm in a department store for fun pieces of jewellery that are cheaper than adult ranges. Plus, you don't pay VAT on kids' clothing and accessories.

- When buying a dress, let's say for a black-tie do, where you know you'll have to stand, sit and dance in it all night long, it's worth doing all those activities in the shop so that you know it actually does what it says on the label. If it feels uncomfortable at any time or ruches up when you sit down, don't get it – it's not going to get any better and it could even ruin your night.

- If you're buying for a dressy event, sheer fabric is always acceptable (with the right undergarments, of course). See also page 163.

- If you're going out to buy a dress, then wear suitable underwear and take the right heels so you can get the whole feeling of it.

- If you are on the 'boot' hunt, there's absolutely no point in your going to the shop to try them on when you are wearing a pair of jeans. You won't get an honest fit. Wear a skirt or dress instead.

- A coffee or tea break is great for taking the weight off your feet and recharging the batteries. And a glass of champagne break is just fine (in fact, it's a must in my mum's school of thought) as long as you stop at the one. Otherwise you may wake up with not only a cocktail hangover, but a bank-balance hangover too having blown all your money in the shoe department at Selfridges.

- You know, sometimes we'll buy something because we love it, only to realise later that we don't have a thing to go with it – because it's a tricky

colour, let's say. So, rather than consigning a garment to the back of the wardrobe, take it back out with you to the shops to see if you can match it up. Don't try to buy something without taking it with you – it's a massive gamble. If it's really not right, you may get a refund or a credit note (check the store's policy when you buy).

CELEBRITY TIP!

Mario – R&B singer

Firstly never go shopping with a woman, as a guy always go by yourself. It's really important you make the time to try everything on that you are thinking of buying to make sure it fits, so that when you leave that store you are feeling amazing and shining like a star.

Drop a Dress Size in an Instant: Clever Styling

Wouldn't it be lovely to look a dress size smaller without having to tie yourself to the treadmill, or bypass the cake shop because you're frightened you might be tempted by a cream horn? Well, you know what, girls? Now you can! You can fool the whole world that you're a size smaller, simply by learning some sneaky snippets of clever camouflaging. So, here's how to do it!

- Don't worry about what's in fashion, only wear clothes that make you look truly amazing.
- If you're worried about showing off your bingo-wings, cover up your arms with a little cape or a shawl.

- Yes, black can be very slimming but it can also drain the colour from your complexion if your skin is on the pale and pasty side to begin with. Browns are more warming and have a similar effect, but, if you love black, just make sure you add a zest of colour around your face to liven things up a bit.

- An empire dress is one of the most flattering styles if you want to look taller and thinner. Because the drop starts from just underneath the bust it gives the illusion that this is where your legs start.

- Don't wear shiny fabrics in the areas you're trying to conceal – this will only highlight them instead.

- Hanging around the house in huge clothes that are out of shape will actually make you eat more because your body already looks massive. Wear comfortable clothes that show off your shape and build your confidence so you won't be tempted to order a pizza for eight!

- If your bum is already the size of a giant pumpkin, why make it look any bigger by wearing high-waisted trousers? All they do is make your butt look twice as big and long.

- Look out for tights that have elastic in them. They will sculpt and hold your figure in place, dramatically changing your shape and size in an instant.

- Avoid patterned tights especially if they are a large scale and you have thunderous legs. Black opaque tights, however, are very flattering on the leg.

- If you have fat legs or calves, then avoid wearing knitted tights – they will make them look even bigger.

- The smaller the pattern, the smaller you will look. The bigger the pattern, the bigger you will look.

- If your SJP pleated skirt doesn't lie flat, then I'm afraid you are too big for it. Give it to a friend or head for the gym!

- Wear the same colour from head to toe. The darker the colour, the more flattering the outfit will look on you – and vice versa, of course.

- Getting the right fit is so important. A big billowing outfit will only drown your body (and won't disguise your big belly); it'll also make you look twice as big.

- Also, an outfit that's just a little bit of a squeeze to get into and slightly on the tight side makes you humungous. You should really be opting for something that has structure and sculpts your body in all the right places.

- A three-quarter-length coat that fits perfectly over your body has a more streamlined effect.

- If your thighs have a life of their own, invest in a pair of slightly flared trousers and they will balance out the whole of your legs. An A-line skirt will also balance out a big bum.

- A wrap dress can be a saviour for women with big boobs, tummies and waists. The eye is directed in the way that the folds go, which takes the focus off your tummy and boobs. Also, the wrap effect helps to break up and separate your boobs so you look less like you've got two melons stuck to your chest!

- If you have chunky-monkey calf muscles, avoid wearing boots that stop halfway up the calf – they will only accentuate the enormity of them. Instead, go for knee-length boots or shoes.

- Magic underwear (ie undies that hold all your wobbly bits in the right places) is always going to give that much-needed and appreciated helping hand when it comes to taming those rolls of flab, which will of course always make your outerwear look a darn sight better!

- Beading and sequins are great for disguising lumps and bumps. High heels are always going to make you look taller and thinner, too.
- A trouser suit is much more flattering than a skirt suit – it helps to stretch out and streamline your body.
- Avoid horizontal stripes and go for vertical.
- In some shops I'm a size 6 and in others I'm a 12, when in actual fact, I'm a size 8–10. It's ridiculous! But to be honest, I wouldn't rule out buying a top because it's labelled size 12. If it fits and I like it, I'll get it. But so many people out there will squeeze themselves into a top that's far too small for them as it makes them feel better, but they don't realise they just look bigger.

Bags of Fun or Bag Lady?

You can cruise around looking outrageously cool, Sarah Jessica Parker style, as if you've just raided *Sex and the City*'s prop box, or you can simply look like you live on the pavement, tramp style, surrounded by fading, broken-handled plastic carrier bags filled to the brim with your worldly goods. The choice is yours.

Now I know where the 'kitchen sink' phrase comes from: once upon a time, I used to be that bag lady. I had such a collection, carrying at least eight around with me at any one time. In fact, I even kept the nicer-looking ones for best and used to co-ordinate them with what I was wearing! How shocking is that? And the worst thing is, I used to have hippy dreads too, so I really did look like a crusty old tramp! Well, thankfully times have changed and these days I'd rather run the risk of getting caught red-handed in SJP's prop box!

- A scruffy bag can ruin a beautifully put-together outfit.

- When buying a handbag it's really important that you try it on in front of a mirror to see whether it suits you. If you are Kylie Minogue tiny, then an oversized bag is just going to make you look like you're carrying a suitcase around with you.

- Make sure you see what a summer bag feels like. A scratchy fabric or a basket weave may irritate your skin when you're wearing your lovely summer dress.

- If you are wearing a gorgeous silk or satin dress, then don't wear a beaded bag – it will snag your frock.

- When you're not using your handbags, stuff them with old tops or towels so that they keep their shape.

- Looking for a long-term investment? Choose a neutral-coloured bag in a classic shape that will last for a good few seasons and will go with lots of different looks.

- Only smart bags will do when you're wearing a corporate suit to work. Pretty summer bags and baskets look frivolous in this situation.

- A pretty way of creating extra storage space is to hang a gorge bag on a cupboard handle and use it to store your tights and jewellery.

- Evening bags should always be smaller than day bags. But if like me you are one of those chicks who like to pack their party bags with lots of little bits and bobs then you're better off with a bag that is slightly bigger. There's nothing worse than seeing a delicate bag overstretched with worldly goods. And not only that, eventually you will ruin the shape of the bag.

- If you can't afford the real McCoy, but really want to tap into the must-have trend, then don't make yourself bankrupt by spending your last penny on an expensive bag. Market stalls and high-street shops will always do fake versions. And don't forget to try eBay for all sorts of designer goodies at slashed prices.

- Cheap or expensive, always check the seam of a bag to ensure it's in good nick.

- Don't store leather bags by hanging them by their handles – they quickly lose their shape. Instead, stuff them with an old towel to keep their shape and then store on a shelf.

- If you are looking for an everyday, runaround bag, then buy one that has easy access. Forget those bags that are like Fort Knox to get into, with buckles and straps, etc.

- Your everyday bag should have pockets on the outside and inside for your purse, iPod, lipgloss and mobile. If not, you'll be forever digging round in it and will ruin your freshly painted nails.

- When buying a tote bag, it's really important that you see how it looks when full. Try dropping your own bag into it, or your wallet and bottle of water and you should then get an idea of whether it will work for you.

- If you want a shoulder bag, then choose one with long enough handles. Short handles will drive you crazy – they won't sit on your shoulder properly, especially if you're wearing a big thick coat.

- If your bag is leather, then clean it with leather cleaner once every three months. Wash plastic with a damp sponge that has washing-up liquid on it. And don't forget to vacuum your bag once a week. If you look after your bag like this, it will last a good few more seasons.

- I always hang my little evening bags on the back of my wardrobe doors on small nails.

- If you are like me and you have to carry the kitchen sink around with you, buy a really big, stylish tote bag with good straps that you can throw everything into. It's better than being a bag lady!

- Always splurge on a bag that you plan to use every day (this could be a work bag or a shopping bag) and less on glitzy night-time bags that you take out only occasionally.

- When I'm not using my bags I always keep them covered in a special soft bag cover or in an old pillowcase.

- Plastic bags are so bad for the planet. Either re-use your old ones by carrying them in your handbag for when you next go to the supermarket or have a canvas one that you can roll up and keep at the ready in your handbag. You'll be able to use it time and time again for your groceries.

C E L E B R I T Y T I P !

Sungjoo Lim – owner of MCM Handbags

If you are the type that fears wearing colour, then the easiest way of injecting a burst of fashion's Seratonin into your outfit is by carrying a handbag in a stunning jewel colour. Believe you me, it will not only leave you on a fashion high, but it will make a dowdy outfit look dazzling!

Detox Your Out-of-date Wardrobe

I once turned on MTV *Cribs*, the show where you get a sneaky look round the house of someone who's mega-famous, and sat there for twenty minutes, green with envy and open-mouthed, while watching a guided tour of Mariah Carey's unbelievable wardrobe. She didn't just have a couple of wardrobes to put her bits and bobs into, but an entire floor just to house the most unbelievable clothes. It was like stumbling into Harvey Nichols. Her underwear was hung up individually on little silk hangers and zillions of shoes were caressed and parked up like Cadbury's chocolate fingers. What's more, there was even a maid for them twenty-four seven for TLC on tap. Insane, but totally fab!

Sadly, most of us don't live with our clothes colour coded and sorted out into seasons. Clothes explode out of drawers, every handle, hook, door and chair is covered in a dress, top or necklace, while shelves puff and groan under the weight of the clutter you've managed to hide away for the past decade. As for the carpet, where is it? It's no wonder most of us girls are always moaning that we never have anything to wear. Chicks, if this sounds like you, then you desperately need to give your wardrobe a workout NOW!

This detoxing experience will streamline your wardrobe into one that you can rely on at all times. If you can't see what you've got in there, then how are you going to find something to wear? It's very similar to clearing out an office filing cabinet – you have to sift through the lot to weed out the dead wood, leaving only the important bits that you actually need. But the best thing about it is that, by getting rid of the old, you've got a really good excuse to fill it up again with the new.

I recommend that you invite one of your best friends over so that she can give her honest opinion on your wardrobe. Make sure you choose someone who doesn't have the same taste as you, though – or she may only be telling you it looks bad so that she can pocket it for herself! Now take out one item at a time and ask yourself why you love it or hate it. Does it flatter your shape and does it make you feel good? You then need to make two piles: one to keep and the other to give to your local charity shop. So

that your friend doesn't feel like it's all one-sided, tell her you'll do the same for her too. Here are some ideas to get you started.

'KEEP-ME' PILE

- Key investments
- Classic items
- Basic foundation pieces such as white, grey, black, beige T-shirts, trousers, etc. in good nick (replace them regularly)
- Garments that you love and treasure
- Expensive designer clobber that you may be able to sell for a small fortune or that you can pack away and give to your children one day

'CHUCK' PILE

- Clothes that make you look like a tent
- Garments that pinch you in all the wrong places
- Anything beyond repair
- Clothes that make your ass look huge
- Anything that hasn't graced your body for the last two years
- Clothes that drain the colour from your complexion
- Scuffed shoes or bags

- I have to warn you that culling your closet can be a very painful experience indeed. It not only hits home that middle-age spread may have already started and that you can't even get your big toe into what was once your favourite pair of jeans, but it also means waving goodbye to old acquaintances that just hog precious space in your wardrobe and have been out of date since that rave when you were a teen; it can be heart-breaking. So, go out for some retail therapy, or get a big box of chocolates and share them with a friend who will help to make you see that you did the best thing.

- If loads of your gal pals are bored with their clobber and would love a new wardrobe without having to spend a dime, you could organise a 'swapping party'. Each person brings ten items along, swaps them and whatever is left over can be taken to the charity shop. (Note, you have to swap with people who are the same size.)

- Having your 'skinny days' clothes festering away in the dark depths of your wardrobe or staring at you every time you open the doors will only torment you — they will always remind you of how skinny you used to be. So give them away to charity or to an annoyingly petite friend and save yourself all that unnecessary heartbreak. However, keeping one or two skinny items may also inspire you to lose weight — so don't give everything away.

- A good way to update your ageing coat is to change the buttons for some cool and funky ones, or maybe sew a really unusual trim onto the pockets. A little facelift can totally transform them — it will almost be like having a new one.

- Once a year, put all of your coats into the dry cleaner's to be reconditioned. This will help to prolong their lives and prevent the dirt from becoming part of the coat itself.

- Never keep the plastic clothes bags that you get from the dry cleaners. They stop fabrics from breathing and clothes will begin to smell. Instead, store in fabric clothes bags.

- Did you know that studies show that 30% of handbags are contaminated with faecal matter? Yes, really, and it's probably because we dump our poor little bags on the floor when we visit a public loo. There are two solutions: clean your bag with a facial wipe, or hang it on the back of the door or around your neck, anything to avoid putting it on the floor!

- Try and match all your hangers. Bizarrely but psychologically, hangers that look the same will make you want to keep your wardrobe tidy.

- Sexy underwear is a great way to boost your mood and confidence, even if no one else gets to see it. So throw away any grubby or greying knickers and bras, or any with the elastic hanging out. And before you say anything, good underwear doesn't have to cost a fortune. There's no excuse for those hideous pants to lurk around in your knicker drawer.

- If your shoes are beginning to look like those that you see randomly in street gutters, then it's time to lob them, I'm afraid.

- Over the years our bodies change shape and we go up and down in size. If you bought a classic suit or jacket as investment pieces, make sure they still fit you – you may have to get them altered or else it's a trip down to your second-hand boutique to see if you can sell them.

C E L E B R I T Y   T I P !

Claudia Winkleman –
television presenter
and columnist
It's never OK to wear a beret.

How to Keep Those Jangle-bangers Under Control and How to Make Tiny Tits More Tantalising

Boobs are funny old things really, aren't they? Some big-boobed women find them useful weapons of destruction to lull stupid men into a false sense of security to get what they want (very good in a male-dominated office!). Other women find them very inconvenient, even annoying at times as they can attract a lot of unwanted attention from the meaty contents in men's underwear. They can also limit a girl's wardrobe, especially when it comes to summer dresses – big watermelons supported by tiny straps look desperately unhappy, as if they're clinging onto the fabric for dear life.

Then there's the tiny-titted girl, who looks like she's smuggling a couple of frozen petits pois around underneath her top, or a couple of cheap foam pillows into her bra. Whatever size you are, if you look like you've got two sets of boobies or a couple of fried eggs trapped in your bra, you're obviously wearing the wrong bra and it's time to learn a few tricks of the trade.

- If your boobies dance around like you're at a party each time you hit the treadmill at the gym, then you're not wearing the correct bra. Research shows that every time we exercise our boobs move an average of 9cm (3½in) each time we move. This will, of course, eventually put the ligaments under pressure, encouraging your breasts to head south. To avoid giving yourself a black eye as they uncontrollably smack you in the face, look for a Shock Absorber sports bra – they are amazing at keeping your boobies stuck to your chest while you work out.
- Armed with what they believe to be their correct bra size, women will then go into a shop, grab a bra in their size (and not try it on) just

because it's their size. Then, when they get home, they're surprised it doesn't fit. Every shop varies, so you might be a 32B in one shop, but a 32C in another. Always try before you buy and get yourself professionally measured (65% of women are wearing the wrong bra).

- The correct way to get yourself into a bra is to put it on your body (don't do up the back strap yet), then pull the straps up in place on your shoulders. Now lean forward 45° and wiggle into the cups. When they're firmly in place, stand up straight and do up the back clasp.
- Don't put your underwired bras into the washing machine – this will halve their life. Instead, wash them by hand with a gentle detergent and warm water.
- Make boobs look smaller by wearing a minimiser.
- If your bra strap at the back isn't running parallel to the floor and is creeping dangerously towards the top of your back, it's the wrong size and won't offer your boobs any support at all.
- Just because you can't see your bra because it's under your top or dress this doesn't mean your overall look won't be affected. A badly fitting bra distorts the shape of all necklines on dresses and tops.
- Tiny tits? You can afford not to wear a bra with a high-neck, backless dress.
- If you are the owner of a set of non-existent man magnets, then a gel-filled bra is brilliant. They are so much better than the padded ones (so fake-looking). Plus, it's much cheaper than plastic surgery!
- Never wear a bra with padding and push-up qualities if you are flat-chested especially if you're going to wear a T-shirt – they will look super-fake and it will be very obvious to the eye that you're trying to fill a void. Opt for a bra that does one or the other job.

- On a photo shoot, I once had to use real chicken fillets on the model as she had no boobies at all! Otherwise it would really have ruined the look of the Amanda Wakeley dress that I was photographing. I have to admit that the chicken breasts actually looked pretty authentic – they were amazing, I suppose, because they resembled real flesh.

- If your boobs are spilling out over the top of your bra, it's too small. Go up a size or two. Boob spillage will ruin your outer clothes. And if they're really saggy and wrinkly, wear a top with a higher cut, but display a bit of the top of your back instead. Very hot!

- A bra might look amazing on in its own right, but it's really important that you see what it looks like when you're wearing clothes on top. It may be totally different and could spoil the line of your clothes.

- Try to match the colour of your underwear as closely as possible to the outfit you want to wear. Dark underwear under a light outfit is a cardinal sin. It's the same when wearing dark clothes: avoid wearing light undies, especially if there's a camera around to capture the moment. They will illuminate through.

- Don't bother going anywhere near a corset if you have raisin-sized boobs! A corset is meant to emphasise your already ample chest so that it swells up and over.

- To make small boobs look bigger when wearing a bikini, try a light-coloured patterned halter top with dark bottoms.

- Wear patterns and ruffles across your boobies if you want them to look bigger – it's a great disguise.

- Different dresses need different bras – it's down to the colour and cut of the dress. For example, if you're wearing a halter-neck dress, a regular bra won't work. The unsightly straps will have the fashion police after you! Every girl should really have one halter-neck bra, a backless bra, a strapless bra and a few regular ones in shades of white, flesh and black.

- A halter-neck or an off-the-shoulder style top will divert the eye from tiny tits and put all the focus on the shoulders instead.
- If the underwire in a bra is starting to show, then I'm afraid it's time to say goodbye. Not goodbye for good, though. Take the padded bits out (if they have them, that is) and re-use by sticking them onto the ends of cheap hangers so your more precious and delicate clothes can hang in a little more comfort.

C E L E B R I T Y   T I P !

Theo Fennell - Jeweller to the Stars

Always wear colours that suit you, even down to the colour of gold. Essentially, darker skin suits yellow gold and paler skin white metals. The stone colouring is fairly obvious: red-heads and emeralds are a good combination, if you like that sort of thing, and blondes suit the blue colours better. Strangely, diamonds suit everybody but can, ironically, look very cheap on the wrong girl. Some of the really bright new colours suit some unlikely people and it is worth trying them on as, if one can find some unusual combination that suits, it can become a signature look...and, if you're lucky, a cheap one.

- Big-bapped? If you want your boobs to look less like two footballs stuck to your chest, then avoid wearing high-necked tops, T-shirts or dresses and opt for a V-neck or wrap style.
- If you're blessed with curves, show them off to the world! Think how good Kelly Brook looks. She's got big boobs, a great little waist and a shapely bum. You always see her having fun with her curves and assets, wearing pencil skirts and fab fifties dresses. Don't try to hide your curves in one big frock in the hope that this will drown them out – you'll only look like a big block of flats with no shape!
- A perfectly fitting bra should clasp the outer rim of your boobs, and to give them a lifting boost, choose a demi-cup bra.

Accessories

Clothes without accessories are a bit like going to Cornwall and having fish without the chips or going to the cinema and having an apple instead of penny sweets, a hot dog, a tub of caramel-covered ice cream and an industrial-sized popcorn. Accessories are meant to highlight your good features and won't highlight your wobbly bits. Clothes need accessories to come alive, and they make us feel good, too.

Accessories are more powerful than you might think. If you've got big boobs and you choose the wrong pendant necklace, then you could end up with one hundred pairs of unwanted male eyes staring at your cleavage as they interpret your necklace to be an arrow. Teaming your 'to-die-for' ensemble with a pair of tatty trainers is a similar no-no.

Learning how to manipulate your accessories successfully will teach you a multitude of great things. A bunch of eye-catching bangles will divert the

eye from your turkey-thigh upper arms, for example. But bear in mind that accessories can also highlight areas you hate. A choker-style necklace will turn your double chin into a quadruple one and a gorgeous pair of embellished summer sandals only draws attention to your Beast of Bodmin hairy toes. Whether you want your accessories to whisper or shout, here's how to transform your outfit from ordinary to extraordinary, from office to party, with a few simple tweaks.

- Your jewellery should always be in tune with what you're wearing. A diamond necklace won't look right with a hippy outfit and neither would a LBD work with daytime wooden bangles.

- I love, love, *love* market stalls and vintage stalls in all countries around the world for unusual nick-nacks, especially accessories, as they tend to be mega-cheap and won't weigh your luggage down too much. Actually that's total nonsense. Every time I go to somewhere lovely like Thailand, where everything seems ridiculously cheap, I always end up having to buy another suitcase to house my market-stall shopping and pay through my nose for all the extra weight! Oh well, at least there's amazing memories attached to them.

- Trying to divert attention away from fankles (fat ankles), or maybe a wobbly gut or a lard ass? Use gorgeous accessories to draw the eye away from those areas and keep them out of the limelight.

- If you lose one out of a pair of gorgeous and very unusual earrings, don't worry. You can always tell people it's a one-off and meant to be worn singly. But, if you lose a stud, it will only look like you've lost the other one.

- Wearing lots of gold jewellery at once is cheap and tacky. You can only get away with it if you genuinely come from the ghetto.

- If you've fallen in love with a colour, yet it doesn't suit your complexion, rather than ditching the idea of wearing it all together, just add hints of it around your outfit through accessories.

- Sunglasses are the LBD of the accessory world. They are as important as your lipgloss, so never leave the house without them! They make you look rock'n'roll and they're a good fallback as they hide a multitude of sins, including a hangover or a very late night! But when choosing them, take into consideration how big or small your face is. I always think Nicole Richie looks a little odd in some of her glasses because they're way too big for her and it can sometimes look like she is wearing two side plates on her face. Big, oversized glasses do add that Hollywood celeb feel to a look, just bear in mind that accessories have to be in proportion with you.

- If you have a double chin, then avoid wearing a choker unless you want three extra chins.

- The general rule is don't wear loud earrings and a loud necklace together. Choose one or the other – it's just too complicated otherwise.

- A heavily textured handbag, such as fake snakeskin, can add so much visual richness to a plain beige outfit. Fake is always better than real when it comes to snakeskin.

- Ever noticed how a belt can quite often rise up your back? Well, that's because it's a straight style. Opt instead for a curved belt that follows the contours of your hips and stays there.

- The quickest way to update a look without having to spend a fortune is

to invest in high-street accessories. Choose carefully, though – sometimes cheap can look cheap.

- An alternative way to accessorise your neck if you don't want to wear a necklace is to tie a gorgeous scarf around it. If you're trying to draw the eye away from another part of the body that you don't like with the use of a patterned scarf, then that's great, but, if you have a spotty face or wrinkly neck, bear in mind that a scarf will naturally draw attention to those areas.

- The neck and cleavage will unkindly give away a woman's age. So, if your neck is starting to look a little wrinkly, rather than drawing attention to it with a choker or a very short necklace, wear a necklace in a slightly longer style that attracts the right kind of attention to the right place.

- If you have an oblong face then you can wear big eye-catching earrings. Avoid tiny little studs, though, as they will make your face look even longer.

- A cute little scarf can be just what you need sometimes to jazz up an outfit, but they also come in very handy for when you need to hide greasy hair.

- Store your accessories in transparent plastic boxes from Muji so that you can see exactly what is in each box at all times.

- The smaller the brim on a hat, the more daytime it is – and vice versa.

- A belt totally transforms a boring outfit, but because you will be creating the focal point around your tummy, just make sure it's in trim shape. A darker colour belt is always more flattering than a lighter one.

- A little bit of razzle dazzle goes a long way with us chicks who love a bit of glamour in our lives, but if you can't afford the real thing, stock up on fake diamonds. Swarovski is incredible, especially with a LBD.

- If you work in a smart office, leave the funky accessories at home and opt for smarter (and more conservative) studs.

- Short legs? To make them look longer, wear the same colour belt as your trousers/skirt. If you have a short back and would like it to look longer, then wear a belt in the same colour as the top half of your outfit.

- If you're going to invest in a pair of gloves that you can take from day to night, then buy a pair of leather ones. They'll go with lots of things and look smart; also they won't show any dirt and will last for years.

- It's so worth building up a collection of gloves so that you have every colour under the sun to go with any outfit. Don't have just a black pair to wear with everything.

- I always collect cheap beaded necklaces on holiday, and for some reason they tend to fall apart (probably because they only cost me 20p). And I know what it's like: you keep the loose beads for years with the intention of getting them restrung, but it never happens. Just dump them!

- If your bag has gold in it, then so should your jewellery. A bag with silver in it should be highlighted with your accessories.

- Wear angular glasses if you have got a round face. Round glasses suit a long and square-looking face.

- It's amazing how you can transform your LBD from day to night simply by changing your accessories (from flat shoes and plastic jewellery to high heels and diamonds).

- Matching your bag with your shoes is sooooooo naff!

- Only wear a gorgeous, attention-grabbing ring if your hands are worth showing off too (see page 34). Bitten nails and/or smoke-stained fingertips won't do your ring justice.

- If your outfit allows you to wear opaque tights, then you can definitely get away with wearing a skirt that is slightly shorter – the tights are so flattering.

- Goliath-sized bones? You're better off wearing slightly chunkier jewellery than somebody with twiglets for bones. If that's you, wear delicate jewellery.
- Choose a purse in proportion to your body. A small purse can make a larger body look even bigger.

C E L E B R I T Y   T I P !

Dahlia Shaffer - Director of clothing brand Lipsy

You don't need to spend a lot of money to look a million dollars! When I want to go designer bargain hunting, TK Maxx is where I bag the really big game. I've found über-gorgeous designer pieces in there that I've seen later in the gossip mags... for half the price of what the beautiful people pay. This place is literally every fashionista's best-kept secret.

Fast Fashion & Long-term Investments
(Your Safety-net Wardrobe)

Looking good isn't about flashing the cash, it's about training the eye, learning where to source and what to buy once you're there. Wearing half the collection from one store all at once is seriously sad and just makes you look like a fashion victim. For a unique, eclectic mix, put high street, designer and vintage together – it's the best way to stamp your personality on a look without breaking the bank. You don't have to be minted to be stylish – in fact, some of the super-rich can end up looking super-cheap. 'It takes a lot of money to look this cheap,' I remember Dolly Parton once saying.

- Mixing is not about having lots of clothes, it's about being resourceful: you can create the maximum wardrobe with minimum investment. Different jewellery can change a dress dramatically each time you put it on. Just use your imagination.

- Some fashion, I think, is very similar to fast food. You buy it, wear it once or twice and lob it! So don't go spending a fortune on designer clobber you're hardly ever going to wear; make a trip down the high street and get your quick fix down there.

- There's nothing better than having a good old flick through the pages of a fashion magazine, but it's another thing if you start to copy them from head to toe. Remember, models and super-trendy celebs dress in certain ways either because it's an arty photo shoot and they're trying to make the picture visually unusual to give readers a treat or the celeb will be donning a particular outfit just to get the attention that guarantees them magazine space. So, don't be too literal. By all means, pick out elements of a look that you like and mix them in with clothes that you feel and look good in, but don't be a fashion victim!

- Saying that, our fashion magazines can be our fashion bibles, too. If you're in a rut and you don't know how to start building a new wardrobe, check out the magazines.

- It's worth spending some dosh on a classic trouser or skirt suit that you know you will wear all the time (think of Yves St Laurent and Le Smoking, the first ever trouser suit). You will really get your money's worth as they're timeless, chic, sharp and look wickedly sexy.

- A beautiful suit will actually become one of the most versatile things in your wardrobe because it's multi-functional. You can wear it to work as

a full suit, or mix and match as separates. For instance, you could team the jacket with a cool cami and a pair of jeans, or the trousers with a gorgeous shirt or jumper.

- Tailored clothes are always going to make your body look more feminine and shapely. And if you want to give the impression that you're taller than you are, wear your hair up high.

- If you want to get value for money from your clothes and for them to be as versatile as possible, choose colours and fabrics that go with the rest of your wardrobe.

- Similarly, if you don't want your clothes to date quickly, then go for classic shapes, cuts and colours.

- If you can't afford a new dress, dig out an old favourite. Now go and get your barnet washed and blow-dried. I swear you will feel as if you're wearing a new frock.

- Remember, high-maintenance clothes are like high-maintenance friends: they need a lot of attention and looking after.

- If you feel uncomfortable in what you are wearing, it will come across in your personality and will knock your confidence. Minis are for those with toned and tanned pins, not anyone with shot-putting trunks. And if you're over 50, it will look cheap and nasty.

- The older you get, the longer your skirt should be. You should also follow trends less religiously. Instead, it's more about style. Work out what looks good on you and flatters every part of your body.

- Never show boobs, stomach and legs at once unless you want to look like a slut. One at a time, please!

- Have several pairs of jeans in different styles for heels and flats to avoid scuffing the hems. They go with pretty much anything and are great with flat pumps and a cute sweater when you're buying your groceries, or seriously hot with killer heels. It takes a lot for them to wrinkle too.

- You are better off buying clothes in one block colour than patterns and prints, etc. Not only will people remember the patterns more, you'll also be able to mix your plain-coloured clothes with a lot more things.

- Colour is a very powerful tool: it can make us look twice as fat, twice as thin, happy or sad, short or tall, so make sure you choose wisely. Just because a colour looks good on your best friend, this doesn't mean it's going to look as good on you. If you're unsure where to start, begin with a neutral palette and add a touch of colour at a time. Hold colours up to your face to see how they react with your skin. Some will make you look healthy, others a little rough!

- If you want to buy a winter coat, it's worth spending a little more money so that you get a good few years out of it. Colourwise, you are better opting for a black one that will go with most of your wardrobe.

- Going to really good vintage shops can be a great way to add some zest to your capsule wardrobe, plus you'll be investing in something that is both unusual and most likely to be a good label. This is a great place to find a stunning and unusual overcoat. Just make sure the lining is intact and there are no moth holes!

- Designer fusion ranges are a really great way to look cool without having to pay through the roof.

- When buying an investment overcoat, don't pick one in a hard-to-match colour. Go for something that matches the rest of your wardrobe and without high-fashion details that will date by next season.

- If you're not too sure how you look in something, have a friend take a picture of you from every angle in that item. Load it up onto your computer and check it out. Photographs really help us see what we look like from all angles.

- You can get away with mixing two trends if you know what you're doing. Any more and you'll look like you're wearing your whole wardrobe at once.

- Whether you're heading off to the beach or going to a barbecue, or simply enjoying the sun, summer dresses are meant for fun. Don't spend a fortune on your frocks as you will be forever worrying about getting something on them and will therefore never feel totally relaxed in them.

- When the hot summer months kick in, you don't have to expose your worst wobbly bits just to stay cool. Hide what you don't like, but always focus on your more positive points, highlighting those areas that you are happy with.

- Because your shoes get a lot of wear and tear, you are better off spending more on these items and less on your clothes. Plus, if you are wearing designer shoes, everybody will assume that your clothes are designer too (the same goes for bags).

- There's a time and a place to wear stripes. If you want to look a little more business-like, opt for vertical. For a more casual approach and for a nautical look, go for horizontal. The wider or thicker the stripe, the more informal the look will be.

- Setting yourself a budget – and sticking to it – is a great way to stop yourself becoming too greedy and also means you can pay your bills. But what should you be spending on, and what should you be saving on? Read on.

SPLASH THE CASH

Shoes, especially hot evening strappies

Overcoats

Jackets

Daytime leather tote

Trouser and skirt suits

A trench coat (they always come back into fashion)

Smart jumpers

Fitted blazers

Knee boots

A striking watch

SAVE ON...

Funky accessories

T-shirts in all colours

Gorgeous summer dresses

Cardigans

Glitzy evening bags (hardly any wear and tear)

Bras and knickers – the high street is crawling with them

Accessories – earrings, bracelets, necklaces, scarves, belts, rings, etc.

Sunday squidgy jumpers

- If you choose wisely, the expensive items above should last you a good few years. Change the cheap items every six months before they start to become shabby.
- A gay male friend is the best person to take shopping. Why? He will not

only have a brilliant eye for what looks good on you, but he isn't direct competition so he will want to see you in something that makes you look your best.

- On the whole, plain-coloured clothes tend to look classier than brash colourful numbers. So as not to look as dull as dishwater, inject some zesty colour into your outfit to zing things up, though. This could be through your accessories, for instance.

- Don't go shopping when you're in a bad mood or have PMT. You will make all sorts of mistakes because you will be impulse buying, thus your wardrobe will begin to burst at the seams with items that you don't want to wear.

- I know it's been said a million times before, but every girl needs a little black dress in her wardrobe to fall back on. If you change your accessories every time you wear it, then your dress will take on a different persona. Make sure you buy one with a classic and simple cut.

- Black is a great backdrop to other colours. For example, wearing acid yellow and black looks sharp and a floral pattern is so good on a black background, as is metallic and white.

- No one ever manages to keep up this next tip for long, but it does work! Colour-code your wardrobe. It will make your life a lot easier when you next have to decide what to wear. Depending on your mood, you will naturally gravitate towards the right colour to match it. This will save you time in the morning when you're trying to get inspiration.

- If you were on a bender last night, all the wheels fell off and you're now wallowing in the hangover from hell, don't wear black – it will make you feel worse. Pop on a soothing colour like green or blue. Don't wear headache-inducing shades such as red or orange.

- Every girl needs at least three pairs of smart trousers that go from day to night with smart trainers, ballet pumps, corporate court shoes or hot stilettos.
- If you and the weather need a bit of cheering up, wear yellow to bring some sunshine into your life.

Fashion Faux Pas That Should Really Be Extinct By Now

It's obvious some people don't own a mirror, otherwise they wouldn't have left the house looking like they got dressed in the dark. For instance, you get so many women parading down the street in leggings so skintight that the whole world knows exactly what they had for breakfast. Honestly, stylish women should know that second-skin leggings are only for use in the gym, nowhere else!

- Although fashion trends come and go with every season, there are some things that are always wrong. If you're going to commit a crime against fashion, then I sincerely hope you have a good friend who likes you and points it out so that you don't make the same mistake again!
- Trying to do the whole 'cute girly' thing is just so wrong when you're a fully grown woman. OK, a sweet little hairclip can work, but putting your hair into pigtails is taking it too far.
- There's only one person who can get away with wearing white socks with dark sandals and that's the amazing Michael Jackson. Keep away from this look!
- Attaching your mobile to a belt on your trousers is so nerdy.

- Bum cleavage/arse crack – ugh! Only boobies need apply (and only if you're not wearing a mini skirt at the same time).

- What's with the whole logo thing? Wearing rip-off designer fakes looks *really* fake if it's from head to toe. Logos on your shoes, bag, jumper, coat, T-shirt, etc. is just taking it too far. One ironic piece maybe, but that's it.

- Leather worn head-to-toe is fine if you are a biker (and actually have a bike), but, other than that, it's a huge no-no.

- Baggy trousers (where the crotch is worn down around the ankles) – if you're not a gang member, don't dress like one!

- Jean shorts – wear them with caution. Micro style looks good, but only if you have hot legs like Pamela Anderson. Knee-length ones look shocking. If in doubt, don't go anywhere near them.

- Chunky sweaters can make a chunky person look twice the size. If you're big, you're better off opting for a finer knit.

- Wearing no underwear. Britney and Paris do it, so it's definitely not cool! Go for flesh-coloured undies, especially little G-strings.

- Some women will pick a pair of trousers with a super-high waistband in the hope that it will disguise their bulbous belly. Well, it doesn't – it only highlights it. Instead, opt for a waistband that ends just below the belly button, wear tummy-controlling knickers and wear a top that loosely covers it all.

- Christmas jumpers should be thrown out with the wrapping paper.

- Denim worn head to toe was cool back in the seventies, but it certainly isn't now!

- Don't hide haggis arms under a long top. Instead, wear a three-quarter-length, bell-sleeve top. This will act similarly to a flared trouser leg, where it balances out the whole limb.

- Cheap and tacky materials such as polyester, lurex and spandex tend to stick to you with friction.
- Wearing red jeans and a red T-shirt together will make you look like a giant sweet red pepper.
- Fanny packs (they highlight camel toes) and bum packs. Yep, they may come in handy for carrying your cash and passport but they do nothing for a fashion-savvy lady. In fact, however cool your outfit is, if you wear one of these, it will totally kill your look.
- Low-rise jeans worn with a beer-gut belly shirt/love handles and a stomach hanging over the top of your skirt or trousers: cover it up or do some sit-ups! Skinny jeans are called skinny for a reason, too.
- Toilet paper on your shoe and skirts tucked into knickers are never a good look!

CELEBRITY TIP!

Lionel Richie - Singer

Don't buy trend, buy style – if you buy the style that works for you, you will always look good.

- VPLs – it's amazing how many women will spend hours deciding what to wear out, only to neglect their underwear. You can't just wear the same underwear for all your clothes. Each outfit requires different undies. Dark underwear under light clothing is also out – you're not Pamela Anderson!
- Wearing too many patterns at once is a no-no.
- Showing off your ten-year-old greying and fraying white(ish) bra straps. Only display straps that are hot and worth highlighting.
- And finally, trying to squeeze into anything is an absolute no-no. If it doesn't fit, don't wear it!

SOS EMERGENCIES & HOW TO FIX THEM IMMEDIATELY

We've all done it, haven't we? Sitting in someone's chewing gum in your favourite trousers. And unless some kind soul lets you know, you've probably been walking around like that all day. Then there's the moment your heel decides to kick the bucket, always at the most inconvenient of times. You're either out on a hot date and trying to impress new potential boyfriend material or on your way to the most important job interview of your whole life. There's no immediate solution, so what do you do? Do you hobble around, or style it out with confidence? Don't get your knickers in a twist – try these tips instead!

- If you ladder your tights (and you don't have a spare pair in your bag), stick a thin layer of clear nail varnish onto the offending area to stop them from laddering any further.

- Deodorant marks are as just as bad as big old sweat patches. So how do you get rid of the blighters? It's easy, just dampen a white towel or flannel with warm water and dab until it's all gone. I use a deodorant that is actually designed not to leave marks in the first place.

- Another good way to banish that BO-basher is to get a breakfast bowl or a Tupperware box, pop some hot water (about 1.5 pints/900ml) into it, along with three teaspoons salt. Give it a mix, dunk a tea-towel or sponge into it and dab onto the soiled patch until it's all gone.

- You can, of course, buy sweat pads to attach to the armpit section of your clothes and they absorb all of the sweat.

- If your hem comes down, put it back in place with double-sided sticky tape. Only until you can get it properly mended, mind!

- When you put a top on over your freshly made-up face, put a silk hanky or a tea-towel gently over your face and slip the top over your head. This will prevent your make-up from getting on your clothes (useful when you're out shopping, too). If you do get make-up on it, don't panic and drown your top in water or the mark will just spread. Only ever use a tiny bit of warm water on a white cloth (it must be white) to remove a mark. If you still can't rid of it, then use a little washing-up liquid as a last resort.

- If one of the handles on your handbag kicks the bucket when you're out and about, tuck both handles in and carry it like a big clutch bag.

- When the hem on your trousers comes down, take it down totally on both of the legs, iron over the crease and wear higher shoes.

- If you've been good and gone for a swim at the local swimming pool, then rather than waiting till you get home to put your swimsuit in the washing

machine, give it a little rinse at the gym. This will prevent the chlorine from discolouring it. The same applies when you've been to the beach for the day.

- Once you've got bleach on a top or trousers, then I'm afraid you can't reverse the colour. Rather than throwing all of your toys out of the pram, think how you can use this mistake to your advantage. Put some rubber gloves on and splash a bit more bleach artistically around the place and your top will no longer look like a mistake, but a unique one-off piece.

- Chewing gum stuck to your clothes? Don't worry. When you get home, pop your trousers or skirt in an old supermarket plastic bag and then into the freezer. Leave for a few hours to freeze, then use a knife (not a super sharp carver, just an everyday eating one) to pick it all off. If you are in situation where you can't just whip your kegs off (let's say you're out in a bar), then dunk your hand into your cocktail, grab an ice cube, suck the liquid off and then go into the bathroom and rub it onto the offending area. Once it's cold and hard, pick it off.

- If the heel on your shoe breaks and someone stops and quizzes you about your one-heeled look, give them a really condescending look and tell them they obviously don't get fashion. Say it with confidence and they'll believe you. Anyway, you may just set a new trend. Watch out, Kate Moss!

- Red wine splashes? If you get red wine on your top, cancel it out with a splash of white wine immediately. Another good way of getting rid of fresh red wine stains, but less practical in public is to soak the garment in soda water and then pat dry with a clean tea-towel.

- If you're one of those girls who is prone to losing her coat, umbrella or bag when you go out on the razzle, then pop your business card into the pocket or somewhere it can be easily spotted. Anyone who finds it will be able to phone you.

- Avoid Lycra if you have to travel quite a lot and you sweat big time. Wear cotton clothes that absorb all the sweat.
- The transitional time between winter and summer can be a nightmare. Do you wear a jumper today or a T-shirt? So you end up deciding on the jumper as it looks a little nippy outside, only to be hit by a heat-wave a couple of hours later! The best way to combat this problem is to leave the house wearing a few thin layers. If it's cold, you can wear them all and, if it's hot, you can remove some of them.

Choosing Swimwear

Play up your good points and disguise your least favourite body parts with this figure-fixing guide.

SHORT BODY

If your body looks like it's been chopped in half and you want to give the illusion that it's longer than it really is, then wear thin vertical stripes.

LONG BODY

If your body is too long and you want to shorten it, wear horizontal stripes. You can also go for a bikini where the top half is an off-the-shoulder-style crop top. A two-piece will always be more flattering than a swimming costume, because the flesh on show will break up the expanse of material, therefore the length of your body.

FLABBY TUMMY

Invest in a double-layered structured bikini that will hold everything in

the right place. Wearing a dark colour with a small print is great for disguising lumps and bumps. Choose a swimming costume with ruching on one side – this will totally disguise the rolls.

FRIED EGGS

Look for a bikini with a bit of padding, not too much padding though or it will only look like you're carrying a pair of foam pads around with you. Crochet and ruffled tops are great for disguising tiny boobs. Halter-necks are better than a regular bra-strap shape. The angle squeezes what boobies you have together.

BIG BUM

Stick on a layer of fake tan before you hit the beach – it will always look more flattering, but never wear white to highlight it. This shade will make you look twice the size you really are. Always wear double-layered material too. A sarong will make you feel more comfortable especially if you are tottering up to the beachside café for lunch or going for a stroll.

Some women think that a huge piece of fabric hung over their butt will reduce the size of it, but it only makes it look bigger. Go for a shape that draws the eye up your figure and a pattern in a small, dark print. Wear a strapless swimming costume, too. The focus will be on your shoulders, not your bum.

SHORT, STUBBY LEGS

Go for a bikini with a high cut as this will make your legs appear longer. Chilled-out-looking wedges also add length.

BROAD SHOULDERS

Halter-neck styles will make your shoulders seem less broad.

NO WAIST

Create one with a belted swimming costume or buy a super-cool swimming costume with trendy cut-outs around the waist area.

Sales Shopping: How to Work Your Way Through the Crowds

When it comes to sales shopping, it's dog eat dog out there. This is no time to watch your Ps and Qs and be all ladylike; it's elbows out as women across the land are driven by desperate cravings for bargains. So here's my guide to the survival of the fittest.

- Keep your eye on the newspapers and look out for stores advertising their sale days.
- First, make a list of the shops you want to hit so you have a game plan. Don't be too glued to your purchasing path, though – you may stumble across some amazing little shops.
- Set yourself a budget and try not to go over it or your bank may just suffer a hangover the next day. It's so easy to get sucked up into the whole sales thing. Have some willpower!
- A good supply of energy is vital when it comes to battling the sales, so go to bed early the night before so you can jump out at 4am, bright-eyed and bushy-tailed.
- Avoid the hours between 11.30am and 2pm. Sales tend to be at their most crowded then because people are on their lunch break.
- Do be ruthless. If there's only one item left and four women want it, only the strongest and fittest will survive, so be assertive. When you see something you like, grab it before it disappears!

- Don't wear earrings unless you don't mind risking ripping your ear lobes off when you're taking clothes on and off. Actually, this goes for all jewellery. Sales shopping is not a fashion parade, so you may as well make it as easy as possible.

- Wearing the right footwear is most important. If you hit the shops in your strappies, you'll only last a couple of hours, so wear flat shoes. They will give your tootsies the stamina you need to hot-foot it round all the best shops in record time.

- Sometimes an item will be in the sale because it's damaged. Check carefully to see if it's repairable.

- Take along the same handbag essentials as you would for any other shopping trip (see page 170).

- Easy-access clothes are essential. And no, not in case you meet the man of your dreams! Wear clothes that you can slip on and off easy-peasy style. Having to undo twenty buttons, zip this and that up and down, tying laces, etc. will only slow you down.

- Bring some readies just in case the shop's machine is having a nervous breakdown. Just make sure you put it somewhere safe, though.

- If you're looking for bottom-of-the-barrel bargains, wait till the end of the sales. Some shops will literally give the stuff away.

- Don't let the size of the outfit put you off. It's fit that's important. There's no point in squeezing yourself into a size 12 when you blatantly look better in a 14.

- Always ask yourself this question before you buy something: if it was full price would you still want it? If the answer's 'No' or a 'Maybe', don't buy it.

- Just because it's a designer garment and it's got 75% off, this doesn't make it a bargain, especially if you're never going to wear it.

- A lot of shops open up their changing rooms at sale times to fit in the crowds. If you don't want to show off all your wobbly bits in a communal changing room, then try wearing a thin swimming costume (see also page 171).

- If you're wondering about an item, then the chances are that it doesn't look good on you, so don't get it!

- Sales assistants are there to make money out of you. If she/he is trying to force you into buying something or to convince you that something looks gorgeous when you know full well that it doesn't, then don't put up with harassment. Tell them to get lost – in a nice way, obviously!

- If you are looking for an organised shop to mill around in, then go in the morning. The afternoon can be absolute chaos and often looks as if it's been freshly burgled.

- The best thing about shopping in the sales, other than acquiring some fab new pieces for your wardrobe, is the calories you burn off while doing it! Yes, all that hot-footing around and stressing out about the queues, plus running back and forth to the car burns calories!

TLC For Shoes

Shoes! They're very expensive candy for the grown-ups. Since cave-woman time, we have formed a highly developed 'hunter gatherer' instinct that drives us on to search for the ripest and sweetest berry. The hunt to own a gorgeous pair of shoes satisfies this deep desire.

Why do women love shoes so much? Unlike clothes, which sit there

lifeless until you put them on, shoes look amazing in their own right, a bit like handbags with a life of their own. But the reason why I think we're so obsessed with them is because it doesn't matter how frumpy or fat you're feeling, a gorgeous pair of shoes will always fit your feet and takes the focus away from any flaws you might be thinking about. The experience is also like having two walking jewellery boxes stuck to your trotters, making them twinkle, as we totter and wiggle our peachy little bum cheeks. They make us feel tall, powerful and sexy too.

I once did a bit of research to see if a women's heartbeat is really affected by the sight of a gorgeous pair of shoes. So off I went to Bond Street, reporting for *Richard & Judy*, with a heart monitor stuck to my arm. Our first stop was a bookshop, but not much happened there and my heartbeat didn't change. Next was Charbonnel et Walker, the glamorous chocolate store, where it went up a smidgen. But then I went into Gina Shoes and, sure enough, the monitor went completely crazy; it was unbelievable! So, it just goes to show that shoes truly have a powerful hold on us. It's something that men will never understand.

So, whether you plan to keep your feet as temptingly naked as possible in a pair of 3500 BC bikini-like flip-flops or some 'too hot to handle' high heels, Sharon Stone style, just remember that, if you look after your shoes, they'll look after you!

- Keep all of the soft shoe bags that you get with your shoes (or buy some) – they will prevent your shoes from getting scratched and damaged when you store them.
- Having a dog poo stuck to the bottom of your shoe just isn't a good

look, nor is a price tag! To get rid of it in one nice old swoop, switch your hairdryer to the hottest setting and blast it really close to the label for roughly twenty seconds. It'll then peel off with ease.

- I'll tell you what works a treat for dull-looking patent shoes, and that's Vaseline. Pop a little bit onto a flannel or face cloth and gently rub over your shoes. Buff afterwards.

- Every year, you should re-heel and re-sole your shoes (you may have to re-heel certain shoes more often). This will give them a new lease of life and they'll last twice as long.

- Don't wait until soles have worn down to the actual shoe itself to get them re-soled because, once the scuffing starts, there's no turning back, whereas a sole can be scuffed, then changed.

- Shoes are like humans – they need feeding! Clean them with a good polish if you want them to look good.

- Store your boots and shoes in the boxes they came in (if you have space and want to be eco-friendly), wedged with shoe trees. Just write what's inside them on the box, then store under your bed.

- Pierce the sides of the shoe box with a fork so the air can circulate in a shoe box, keeping your shoes fresh.

- You can put a Polaroid of your shoes on the outside of each box so you know what pair is inside each of them. Or store them in clear boxes as an easier alternative.

- You might be a sporty person, but that's no reason for wearing high-heeled wedge trainers like the ones Victoria Beckham wore to watch LA Galaxy. They are beyond hideous!

- If you're going to wear a gorgeous pair of heavily detailed sandals during

the summer that will command a lot of attention, make sure your feet are in tip-top condition. Similarly, when you're wearing peep-toes, the focus will be on your tootsies. A pedicure is a must! Renew your nail polish regularly afterwards.

- High heels can make your calf muscles shorten, which in turn will make them look chunkier, so stretch your calves every time you wear them.

- To keep your long boots in shape and in tip-top condition, stuff them with tissue paper.

- Make your wellies super-comfortable by deluxing them up with some carpet. Yep, you heard me right: don't go throwing it out! Use an offcut of rubber-backed carpet and make a couple of insoles.

- The thinner the heel, the less support your foot has and the more pain you may encounter. It may be worth buying shoes with thicker heels if you don't want to be the first to leave the party.

- High heels do make us feel and look sexier, but this won't work if you can't walk in them.

- Uncomfortable new shoes can ruin a party by cutting your night short, so, before you give them a first outing, wear them around the house to break them in. Wear some socks when you're breaking in new shoes, too.

- Pop in some of those cushioned gel pads if the balls of your feet get sore when wearing high heels. They really do take some of the pain away.

- If you've got spotty legs, buy some long boots and hide the problem.

- Never, ever put your smelly sports trainers in with your most treasured high heels. Ban them from this sacred area and keep them somewhere like the garage.

- If you are buying a new pair of shoes, then you are better off doing so at the end of the day when your feet are all tired, hot and puffed up. You will get a true sense of how they fit and feel. If you do so at the beginning of the day when they're cold, then you might have problems if they swell up later and they begin to hurt. It'll be too late then to take them back to the shop for a refund.

- If it has been raining and your shoes are wet, or you've just come in from a run, then don't just chuck them into your wardrobe straightaway. Leave them by the door, where they can air and dry.

- If you've got fankles (fat ankles), choose open shoes and slingbacks as they will add leg length.

- Kitten heels are the most versatile style – they are great at taking your tootsies from day to evening.

- I get really bad shin splints and sore calves from wearing high heels if I don't warm up. If you also have this problem, then all you need to do is to stretch your toes and move your ankles slowly in circular movements. Following this, do gentle calf raises. After I've done this for a quick five minutes, I'm ready to put my strappies on and have a good old knees-up!

- Suede shoes look smart when they're well looked after, but they can look so scruffy if you don't look after them. Buff every time you want to wear them. For a more intense clean, hold them over the steam of a freshly brewed kettle for one minute. Now buff away (this also works with suede handbags). Use masking tape to remove any stray hairs or dust from them.

- Sexy, pointed closed-toe high heels, ooh, there's nothing quite like them! Just beware when buying really pointy shoes: make sure your toes aren't so crammed in that they can't actually move so the blood circulation gets cut off, resulting in numb and very unhappy trotters indeed!

- If, like me, you are a little shorty, go for shoes with an open toe. They magically make you look a little bit taller.

- If you are really petite, you may find yourself wearing mega-high shoes all the time. This can often lead to sore knees, bad posture and achy feet, however. If you want the height, but would like to walk in something really comfortable, then choose a wedge instead. They are still high, but offer lots of support.

- Never wear your shoes day in, day out. Always alternate them.

C E L E B R I T Y   T I P !

Angela Kardash –
International Press
Director for Gina

Polkadot peeptoes are very sexy and add that touch of playfulness for a glamorous summer's evening.

Wardrobe in Crisis

You've only yourself to blame if your wardrobe starts to resemble a flea market and your poor carpet hasn't seen daylight for the last five years. Rather than blaming your wardrobe for your string of fashion disasters, maybe it's time for a ruthless tidy-up session so you can set free the fashion icon that you always knew you were.

- To stop a little job becoming a mammoth one, tidy your wardrobe once a day. When you come home from work, rather than lobbing all of your stuff onto the bed, actually hang up your clothes and put the accessories back in their relevant homes. They will never pile up and you will always find what you're looking for in your wardrobe.

- Wardrobe organisation can save you precious minutes when they're most needed. Hang all your skirts and trousers, shirts, etc. in their own little areas.

- Belts can be mistaken for spaghetti sometimes, the way we just chuck them into our wardrobes without a care in the world. But don't mistreat them – they can be life-changing accessories. Not only will belts make an outfit look finished off, but they will also make our bums look a lot smaller, if worn correctly, so find a good home for them! If you are pushed for space, bang some nails into the back of your wardrobe door and hang them up and out of the way from their buckles.

- Use dead space cleverly to store things. Bang a nail onto the back of the wardrobe door, hang a bag and then fill it with little nick-nacs that would usually be stuffed at the back of the wardrobe or on the floor under the bed somewhere.

- No one sane likes ironing, do they? Don't cram millions of garments into your wardrobe so that there's nowhere for them to move. The more you ram them in, the more creases your clothes will have.

- Vacuum out the bottom of your wardrobe every few months to keep the dust from settling.

- Cigarette holes and moth holes are great if you want to look like a tramp, but if you don't then ditch your smoker friends and put lavender bags in your wardrobe to keep the moths at bay.

- Once a week open all your wardrobe doors and your bedroom window and have a good old blow-through of air to freshen up your clothes.

- Put your smart coats and suits into long clothes bags and hang them up. This will prevent the light from discolouring them and dust from settling on them.

- Don't go putting a smoky item of clothing into your wardrobe immediately after you've taken it off. Instead, put in on a hanger and hang it up on the door-frame to air for the night.

- If you have delicate clothes that you want to hang up in the wardrobe, always hang them inside out so they don't snag on a neighbouring sequinned top.

- Always hang your trousers from the hem. They will not only hang straighter, but it's actually quicker than hanging them from the waistband.

- A multiple skirt or trouser hanger is a great way to hang lots of things on one hanger.

- The heavier the item of clothing, the stronger the hanger should be.

- I have heaps of costume jewellery that I have collected over the years and, if it wasn't for my transparent mini drawers from Muji, I don't know where I would be. They are brilliant because you fill them up with your goodies and then stack them on top of each other. When you need to find something, you don't have to trawl through every single box or bag – you can just peer in through the sides of the drawers to find exactly what you want.

- Padded hangers are a must when it comes to hanging your delicate tops. You can always recycle old shoulder pads by sticking them to the ends of the hangers.

- Cedarwood hangers are great because they help to ward off any moths.

- Hang your clothes by the fabric support straps that come inside the actual garment as this will help to take the stress off the item and it will keep its shape. They are there for a reason!

- I know what it's like when you buy a new garment: you wear it do death – literally. So, rather than sending it to an early grave, don't wear your togs day after day. Not only will your friends get fed up with seeing you in the same thing, but repeated wear actually make your clothes stretch out of shape, so keep your wardrobe circulating.

- When storing clothes under your bed or above the wardrobe, always put them in airtight bags to keep them fresh and to stop the moths from getting too cosy.

- When you take off your clothes at night, empty the pockets of tissues, sweet papers and anything else that you may have stashed away in there. There are three reasons for this: it stops your clothes from moulding into permanent lumpy shapes, allows them to breathe and you won't have to pick out the gooey mess from them because you forgot to empty them before putting them into the washing machine!

C E L E B R I T Y   T I P !

Prince Azim of Brunei

A black outfit always looks expensive no matter what. So, if you want to lie about the price of something you are wearing, you'd better wear black!

- This may sound obvious, but always clean your clothes before you store them in airtight bags. Have them dry-cleaned regularly, too.
- Don't overfill your wardrobe or the clothes won't be able to breathe properly and will start to smell stale.
- Never try to re-use the horrid wire hangers that you get from the dry-cleaners. They offer no support for your clothes, create an indentation and, if they rust, they will stain your clothes.

How to Clean Your Bobby-dazzlers

When does gin on the rocks take on a new meaning? It's when you are soaking your rocks in it, of course! Our little bobby-dazzlers deserve nothing more than to be treated like princesses with gin to bathe in and velvet-cushioned boxes to sleep in. Here's how to keep your diamonds dazzling, gold gleaming and your silver shimmering.

GENERAL JEWELLERY MAINTENANCE

- Regularly check the setting on your rock to make sure it's still in good nick and that none of the prongs that hold the stone in place has come loose. Also, check that the clasps are all working as they should.
- If you live near the sea, then you have to be really careful with sterling silver as it doesn't suit salty air and will end up becoming tarnished. A great way to remove the tarnish is to wipe it with a 100 per cent cotton cloth. Any other cloth can scratch the surface of the metal (polyester, for example, often has wood fibres in it).
- Always keep the boxes that the jewellery came in to store it.

- Don't store your rocks all in one box or bag or they will knock, chip and scratch each other. Keep them separately.
- I have customised a big flat box for my jewellery. In the bottom are four kiwi protector trays (you could also use egg cartons) and it's lined with tissue paper. And that's where it all lives very happily indeed.
- Don't do your household cleaning while wearing silver or gold jewellery. Cleaning materials are quite corrosive and the stones will be discoloured.
- If you have a tongue piercing, always rinse your mouth out with water after you have eaten to prevent bacteria from building up.
- Belly piercings can become infected if you wear really tight clothing that rubs against them. Let your piercing breathe!
- Always rinse your belly ring/stud with warm water after exercising – sweat can sometimes irritate the area around the piercing.

Diamonds

- If you're going out to battle the bling, then you can't have your porky piggies donning a dull-looking ring! So pop your rock into a glass with some washing-up liquid and warm water, then leave to soak for 20 minutes. Use a clean toothbrush to gently scrub away the grime, then rinse with warm water and buff with a chamois.
- Diamonds might be the hardest gemstone in the world but if stored together they will scratch each other.
- Never store your diamonds with any other stones either – they will scratch all the other stones.
- Always clean around the prongs – this is where the residue builds up.

- The slightest bit of body oil can build up with you touching a diamond just once and this can take the shine off the stone. Avoid this as much as possible.

Gold

- If your gold jewellery is starting to look a bit black and grubby, then fill a glass halfway with some cola. Pop your jewels into it and leave for five minutes then rinse with water. Give it a good old polish with a soft, clean tea towel. Bring to a shine with a chamois.
- Always let your hand cream dry before you put your gold rings on – the chemicals can discolour them.
- Wash your bling in some soapy water and leave to dry on a clean tea towel. Buff it up with the same tea towel.
- My mum swears by washing her gold rocks in gin. Naughty Mama!
- The cleaning fluid I use for my glasses also comes in very handy for sparkling up my gold.

Silver

- When my silver jewellery needs a bit of a scrub, I use warm water, an old toothbrush and some washing-up liquid, then gently brush my treasures as I would my teeth. The toothbrush is great for getting into all the little nooks and crannies.
- Never clean your silver with toothpaste – it will very lightly scratch the surface.
- To store silver jewellery and to stop tarnishing, wrap it in a little bit of black tissue paper and then put it in a box.
- Never apply perfume after you've put on your silver or it will slowly tarnish it.

- The best way to prevent a build-up of skin oil on your silver is to give it a quick wipe after you've worn it and just before you put it back in its box.

- Tongue piercings only look good when the jewellery is clean and sparkly. If you don't keep the piercing clean, then you may end up with a serious infection, so brush it every day with your toothbrush when you're cleaning your teeth and, once every couple of months, clean the area with saline solution to keep it germ-free.

Emeralds

- Emeralds are very porous and fragile, so don't wash them in water – they will suck it up and your stone will crack.

- Do not use everyday soap to clean emeralds as it will leave a nasty residue.

Amber

Pop your amber bits and bobs into a glass of warm milk and leave to soak for 20 minutes. Remove and dry with a soft, clean tea towel and then buff with a super-soft chamois.

Opals

These stones are so delicate, so use a glasses-cleaning cloth to clean them or a chamois. Do not use everyday soap to clean opals.

Coral

Coral doesn't respond well to going from hot to cold and it may crack. Because it is so delicate, it is really important that you store it somewhere super-safe where it won't get knocked.

Pearls

- This may sound a little odd, but, rather than washing your pearls in washing-up liquid, the most effective way of cleaning them is to wear

them. Wearing them helps them to self-clean as they will naturally absorb your skin's moisture, which in turn keeps them healthy.

- Spritz yourself with perfume before you put your precious pearls on so not to discolour them with the chemicals, which may damage your stone.

- Pearls must always be stored separately as their delicate nature means they are prone to scratching.

- My granny Dorothy gave me my first set of pearls when I was 18 and she said the best way to bring them to their glory was to wash them in a little bit of salty water in a cup. When they have dried off, you should buff them with a silk hankerchief.

- To add a little bit of shine to your pearls, wipe a tiny bit of olive oil onto them.

- Freshwater pearls hate really dry or humid conditions, so, if you're thinking about going to Thailand in the rainy season or Dubai in the dry season, leave your pearls at home!

- Always store your pearls in a flat box or lid to prevent the strand from stretching out of shape.

- When you wash your pearls in warm water it's really important that you don't get any water in the drilled holes as this will eventually cause them to discolour.

- If you want to re-string your pearls, you will need beading wire (bend into the shape of a needle) silk or synthetic thread, a clasp and, of course, your pearls:

    1. Cut a length of thread about four times the length of your present necklace.

2. Cut a length of beading wire about seven inches long. Fold it in half and cut the ends at an angle to make a point.

3. Thread the silk or synthetic thread through the wire needle. Your 'needle' is now threaded and ready to go.

4. String all of the pearls.

5. Tie one half of the clasp onto the thread and pass the wire needle back through the last pearl, in the opposite direction from the clasp.

6. Once the needle has gone through the last pearl, tie a knot with the free end of the thread around the thread already in the pearls.

7. Pass the wire needle back through the pearls, one by one, tying a knot behind each pearl as you go.

8. When that's done, tie on the other half of the clasp.

C E L E B R I T Y   T I P !

Sarah Cawood - Television Presenter

To stop your jewellery chains from tangling up (and we've all known the frustration of trying to untangle one of Tiffany's finest, haven't we?!)... slide the chain into a drinking straw, cut to half the length of the chain, then fasten the clasp on the chain and leave it like this when you're not wearing it.

5

Diet, Food & Exercise

WOULD YOU RATHER have headaches from hell, mood swings galore, rotten breath, trapped poo, poor concentration and depression or feel alive, happy, sexy and ready to conquer the world? The difference between feeling the former and the latter is more often than not down to what you ram past your lips and down your gullet. Think of it as being like looking after your car – if you feed your car with dirty dishwater, it will break down. It's the same with your body: with the right fuel going in on a daily basis, you lower the chances of coming down with a brain-splitting headache and having bad breath and you increase your chances of feeling full of energy and of having a fruity sex life.

De-bloat Your Gas-filled Stomach

So you've been on your hot date, teased him Sharon Stone style up in the bedroom, taken full control of the situation and now you've slipped into your hot negligée and it's all looking pretty damn good. He thinks he's the luckiest man alive and he can't wait to tell the boys tomorrow about his hot sizzling night, and you – yes, *you* – all you want to do is *fart*!

Come on, girls, be honest: we've all been in that situation, locked inside the bedroom of your Brad Pitt (or Arm Pitt)-like date and all you want to do is squeeze cheese! So what do you do? You lie there, squeezing your bum cheeks for Britain, trying to re-absorb it, hoping it's just going to disappear and that your vixen image and babe-like reputation will still be intact the following morning. But a fart doesn't just go away like that. Angry that you've tried to trap it, it will come out bigger, bolder and stinkier! Oh yes, it will wake you up with a vengeance just as you've relaxed into a lovely peaceful sleep. So how do you get out of this one? The bed has just experienced a volcano-like eruption, you daren't lift the duvet or move a millimetre for fear of your fart wafting up and smelling like you've taken either a dead cat to bed and, worse still, did he hear it? Yikes!

Well, that serves you right for guzzling far too much at dinner! You see, that's what happens when you don't know when to say 'No more, thanks,' and you'll only have yourself to blame when he doesn't reply to your text messages the following week.

So, to stop yourself having a heart attack because of your rotten farts, here are some crucial tips to prevent them ever happening again! But I have to note here that, if you're going to bed alone, there's nothing nicer than knowing you can happily fart your head off, drop them left, right and centre, even have the windows up and no one's going to give a damn! Heaven, eh?

- So many of us get so hungry that, when we eventually come anywhere near food, we literally guzzle it back like some old vacuum-cleaner-head without even chewing. As my best friend Ems would say, 'It went down like a bride's nightie.' This can result in tummy pains, indigestion, heartburn, trapped and not-so-trapped wind, burping and a stomach so rounded and air-filled you could take flight up and over the hills like a hot-air balloon! So make sure you chew, chew, chew your food thoroughly as this will enable you to digest it more efficiently.

- Trapped wind can be so painful and it can also ruin the appearance of your LBD or any other skintight outfit you may be wearing as your tummy increases in size. So, if you are in this unfortunate situation, excuse yourself from the dining table, go into the bathroom and lock the door (believe me, you really don't want anyone else seeing this!). Get down on the floor. It's like doing a yoga position: put your hands and feet on the floor and turn yourself into a doggy. Now raise your bum as high as possible so that you are creating a triangle shape (your bum being the very highest point). Hold this position for two to three minutes. This forces the wind right up to your bum, so when you lower it back to the doggy position it will force its way out! Which means that, when you get back to your table, you will be looking more ironing board than Space Hopper!

- We all love a little bit of bubbly or a refreshing sparkly lemonade, but for some this can ruin a good night or the look of a tight dress as they can fill your stomach up with lots of the unwanted wind that causes gut-ache. Instead, opt for non-fizzy drinkies. Also, try not to drink too much at the same time as eating – again, this will lead to a fart-filled tum.

- A lovely mug of peppermint tea (make your own by pouring boiling water

The Lazy Goddess

over fresh mint leaves and add a slice of lemon and a spoonful of honey) can really ease a gas-filled tummy and definitely sorts out indigestion.

- If you are going out to dinner and you know you might suffer from trapped wind, chop up some fresh coriander and put it in a little bag to take to the restaurant and sprinkle on your dinner. When people ask, tell them you just love the stuff and have to have it on everything. It's better than sitting there radish red because you're desperately trying to hold one in. Or you could always ask the waiter if the chef could kindly put some on for you.

- After you've guzzled a massive dinner, the worst thing you could do is go and lie down on your sofa. Instead, get up and go for a twenty-minute stroll outside and this will prevent you from getting indigestion.

- If you are going to have a little snack, then you're probably better off munching on some dried apricots, prunes, pineapple or bananas as they all have de-bloating enzymes in them.

- Don't go mindlessly filling up your trolley at the supermarket with white bread and white pasta – they will make you look as if you are carrying triplets! Instead, opt for wholegrain bread and wholemeal pasta.

- Maybe you're one of these people that only has to look at a car and it makes you want to bring up your breakfast. If so, guzzle this smoothie beforehand. What you need:

- 1 or 2 ripe bananas
- 1 tsp fresh grated root ginger (this will stop you from feeling sick)
- 300ml (½ pint) natural bio yoghurt (freeze beforehand because the colder it is, the more soothing it will be)

  Whiz all the ingredients in your blender and drink. It's lovely and thick like an ice drink.

Diet, Food & Exercise

Keep Those Sticky Little Mitts Out Of the Fridge: Substitute Choccies For Cherries

How to say 'no' or 'I don't need any more', eh? This is something I've been trying to master for years and I'm crap at it! Do you find yourself constantly staring at the fridge or the bread bin, on the hour every hour, umming and ahhing about what you can snack on next because your stomach's rumbling so much that it's actually beginning to sound like a knackered old washing machine?

I know us girls absolutely love eating – in fact, if we're not ramming something down our forever open gullets, we're talking about it! Asked whether we'd rather go on a hot date with Brad Pitt or get stuck into a toffee cake with ice cream, it would be the latter, hands down. But why are we *always* so hungry, even when we've just eaten a meal for ten? Let's face it, if we put as much effort into our work as we did thinking about what we're going to have for breakfast, elevenses, lunch, mid- and late-afternoon snacks, dinner and naughty treats, then us girls would all be multi-millionaires, wouldn't we? But I think one of the main reasons why diets go tits up is because of the lack of healthy food to hand for when those dreaded hunger pangs rock up. Read on...

- So, tip one – always keep your house and workplace full of healthy snacks such as ready prepared celery or carrot sticks, home made low-fat hummus, dried fruit, lots of lovely fruit bowls filled to the brim with plums and bananas, etc., unsalted nuts and rice cakes.
- Don't starve yourself or you'll only end up having a blow-out and eating everything you shouldn't. Instead, snack on healthy foods every four hours to keep cravings at bay and your metabolism high.

- Sometimes your body will mistake thirst for hunger, so, before you allow your monster-munch-like hand to delve into the cheese drawer at the back of the fridge, drink a glass of water to see if your hunger subsides. Always carry a little water bottle with you in your handbag.

- If you want to be able to resist the cake trolley when it whizzes past your desk at work, then eat breakfast before you leave the house. This also prevents your metabolism from slowing down. If you can't bear the thought of eating breakfast so early, then take a portion of cereal to the office and eat it at your desk.

- Fatty snacks should be your worst enemy if you want to make your ex regret dumping you. You need to plan your meals for the week so that, when you walk into the supermarket, you know exactly what you want to buy, rather than impulse buying only to get home and find that a box of chocolate brownies and a tube of Pringles have accidentally fallen into your bags. Remember, little pickers wear bigger knickers!

- If you keep denying yourself yummy things, you will drive yourself crazy – all you will be thinking about is what you're trying *not* to think about! So, rather than becoming a miserable sod to be around, have a blow-out day and stuff your guts until they pop. One naughty day will really help to strengthen your willpower – you know that, if you are good all week, you can have a full-on, naughty treat day.

- Love it or hate it, *never* go shopping at the supermarket when you're hungry. You will just end up filling your trolley up with lots of junk food that you would never usually go for (and definitely don't need). When you're hungry all sense goes out the window, especially when you come face-to-face with a macaroni cheese plus four extra full-fat cheeses on top!

- Look, we've all got super-skinny legs-to-die-for, peachy, pert-bummed friends who can snack on anything they like. While they're sitting there devouring a whole pack of chocolate, cream-filled, caramel-drizzled éclairs that won't make the slightest difference to their never-ending, streamlined, goddess pins, there's you, sucking reluctantly on a tasteless stick of celery, still only just able to zip up your jeans after forcefully ramming your thighs, bum cheeks and several rolls of stomach in! It just isn't fair, is it? But the worst thing you could do is to compare yourself to these freaks of nature, especially if you are on a diet. It will only depress you big time, and then you'll have to join in the chocolate-éclair eating just to comfort yourself. The best thing you can do is accept your friends as they are, accept who you are – and just be clever and don't invite them on any beach holidays, where you have to parade around in a bikini.

- Combine exercise with dieting healthily and focus on your good points, rather than shedding tears over your bad bits. It will do wonders for your self-esteem.

- It can be such a fag sometimes having to peel and prepare fruit, especially if you're out and about, or at work. Before you leave the house, peel your fruit, cut it up into chunks and put it in a plastic box. When you feel like snacking, all you have to do is take it out. How easy is that?

- Try to eat any snacks and meals as slowly as possible. I know what it's like, you get your snack and you want to wolf it down in one go, which may leave you wanting more because your stomach hasn't told your brain that it's had enough. Count to ten before another snack just to give your brain time to work out whether it really wants more.

233

- The office canteen can be like a death trap with all those amazing temptations right under your nose. If that sounds like yours, avoid it like the plague! You might not be in the mood for anything naughty at all, but setting foot over the canteen threshold can cause you to misplace your rabbit-food lunch-box. Be honest, you know as well as I do that the smell of freshly cooked chips or home made hot treacle tart with custard and cream on top is virtually impossible to resist. So, prepare your own really yummy, but healthy food at home to take in with you. You'll know exactly what's in there (no hidden fat, etc.) and it will give you a good excuse to go outside, eat on a bench and get some fresh air.

- Try to sit down at the table to eat your dinner rather than retiring to the sofa to gobble your grub. The reason for this is that it's always nice to have a change of scenery and if you concentrate and appreciate your food then your brain will register that you have eaten, meaning you won't be reaching for the snacks later. But if you sit there, gripping the edge of your seat, while biting both your nails and your corn-on-the-cob because Phil Mitchell has just remembered that somebody owes him a hundred quid and he's got the hump and wants it back (which is cool, if you need entertaining, but not so good on the waistline as you're so busy soaking up the storyline), your brain will completely forget to tell your mouth you've been eating – which results in your being back in the fridge after *EastEnders* has finished.

- The thing about supermarkets these days is that everything's just getting bigger and better. When you stroll into one, what are you bombarded with? Millions of offers and discounts – 'Buy One, Get One Free', etc. It would be wasteful not to pick up that freebie because we all love to save money, but, when you only go in there to pick up a newspaper, you have to ask yourself, do I really need thirty chocolate bars in mega king-sized packets, with another one for free? Don't do it! I can see it now: you will leave the shop, open the bag up, consume the lot, get home, shout at your boyfriend and blame him for allowing you to wolf the lot! So don't be tempted by these offers unless you really need them.

- Pretzels are a good low-fat snack when you fancy something crunchy.
- If you can't live without your coffee and you're about to bust the padlock on your sweet cupboard and gobble up everything, have a coffee with a little protein snack. This should help to keep cravings at bay. I would recommend the little protein bars you can get in Holland and Barrett (low in carbohydrate and high in energy), a handful of almonds or a slice of chicken.
- Ditch the unhealthy biscuits and go for oatcakes, mini rice cakes or crispbreads. They are so much better for you.
- Eating the same thing every day, week in, week out will leave you feeling unsatisfied and searching for naughty snacks. So, to prevent this happening, try to introduce two different ingredients every week so your tastebuds don't get bored. Variety is the spice of life after all.
- If you're on a diet and you find yourself gravitating towards the kitchen constantly with absolutely no willpower, then stick pictures of yourself not looking your best in the worst offending areas such as the fridge, bread bin or sweetie cupboard – anywhere you think your little trotters might delve into. Seeing a picture of yourself on your most recent holiday in Spain, all lagered up and sporting an apron of a stomach might just put you off emptying the fridge and will remind you that you don't want to look like that any more.

- Eat your dinner as early as you can every night. Eating late will force your body to store food and this results in weight gain.

- If you really aren't in the mood for cooking when you get in, buy pre-washed and chopped vegetables that are ready to cook.

- Low-fat biscuits only work when you don't vacuum up the whole lot and just have one or two! So, if you do want to eat a couple but don't trust yourself to live in the same house as the rest of them and worry that you may sleepwalk during the night and eat them all, buy small packets. Eat a couple of biscuits and feed the rest to the birds or spray with disinfectant or washing-up liquid and lob into the bin. If you don't spray them, you might find yourself scooping them out of the bin.

- A good little substitute for chocolate or sugar cravings are frozen dates. Pop them into the freezer and they will become really sweet and chewy.

- Carbohydrates lead to a short-term fix of happiness. When you get stressed or sad, you reach for something starchy and this releases the hormone serotonin into the brain, which chills us out. But there's no point shovelling in a loaf of white bread, white pasta or white rice followed by a family pack of gooey cakes as this will just make you feel lethargic, moody and fat; you'll be really high, then tired and wanting more. So choose unrefined carbohydrates such as rye bread, brown rice, sweet potatoes, wholemeal pasta and lentils. These will cause a slow increase in blood-sugar levels, giving you more energy at a constant rate and for longer.

- If you are someone who doesn't keep their fridge stocked up, but needs to eat as soon as you get in from work, rather than reaching for the box of cereal or ordering a takeaway, make a batch of food and freeze it in portions. For instance, I always make enough soup or spaghetti bolognese for ten people when it's just me eating it. I let it cool down and pop it into freezer bags and then into the freezer. Remember to write the date of freezing on the outer packaging (I tend to chuck it if it's not been eaten after two months). Remember, you can't freeze egg-based sauces or any food with a high water content such as cucumbers, lettuce and strawberries. Meat, fish, bread and herbs can all be frozen well.

- Christmas parties can be a double-edged sword: on the one hand, it's great to be out and about, having a blast, but it can also be an absolute nightmare, especially when the host (probably skinny) has selfishly laid out the daddy of all hog-out banquets. The problem is, we are genetically programmed in that, if we see food, we have to eat it. It's so annoying, but it's true and that's why we're left trying to burn off the banquet bulge come January. So before you enter 'banquet hell' eat a banana or low-fat yoghurt to line your stomach and to take away the feeling of a dangerously empty tummy.

- At a party, don't just load your paper plate up with vol-au-vents, sausages and crisps, etc. Put some greenery on your plate too. It's low in fat and has a high water content that makes you feel full.

- If you are one of these people who miss out on eating the bulk of your dinner and instead snacks on all the nuts and other bits and bobs, don't be fooled into thinking that you're being good by not sitting down, having a proper dinner and saving calories. In fact, you are probably eating twice the amount because that's how fattening snacks can be. So, instead of eating your way around the room, serve yourself a proper dinner and eat it with a knife and fork. You will feel so much more satisfied.

- Some people will wolf their dinner down so quickly it's as if they're scared it's going to run out! They then go back for seconds and thirds. If that's you, you don't need to do a million trips: try taking your time over eating rather than consuming it all so quickly.

- If you are a chocoholic, opt for a good-quality, dark variety with a high cocoa content rather than reaching for cheap chocolate bars. Dark chocolate can also help to reduce high blood pressure and is packed with antioxidants. So back up the chocolate truck and enjoy!

- Have your thighs morphed into a pair of thunder trunks so they constantly rub together when you walk? Does your hand have a crisp packet permanently stuck to the end of it? If so, it might be time to consider giving up crisps. If the thought is just too much to bear, how about weaning yourself off them gradually? Our brain is trained to finish what is in front of us, whether it's a plate of food or a bag of crisps so use this to your advantage. When you next buy a packet of crisps, empty half of it into a re-sealable bag or straight into the bin (drizzle with detergent or washing-up liquid) and carry on eating as usual until you reach the bottom of the packet. Your brain will trigger that you are at the end and will feel satisfied. If your bag of crisps was huge and you ate the top third of it, you would probably find yourself re-visiting it every ten minutes until it was all gone. This applies also to meal portions. Give yourself a smallish one to start off with, finish it and see if you feel satisfied rather than serving yourself a massive portion and eating it just because it's there.

- Proteins such as chicken and fish give you loads of energy and, because they keep our blood-sugar levels stable, you won't go through that roller coaster of ups and down with your energy mood levels.

- Most humans crave something really yummy after dinner and I don't mean a measly old apple, I mean a good old pud with all the trimmings. Of course, this is bad news for our 'svelte' shape in the making. Rather than denying yourself totally, do have something scrummy but without the fat content. This is where you need to have willpower or a friend by your side to stop you from doing the inevitable. Arm yourself with a teaspoon and head on over to the fridge – I know, it's dangerous territory. Take your little (notice how I wrote 'little') spoon and dunk it into your fat-free crème fraîche or fat-free yoghurt and honey (or even a low-fat choccie pudding). Shove it into your ready-and-waiting trap, savour the taste, swallow slowly and close the fridge door. Now, one little cheeky mouthful is fine and won't make a difference at all, but it's quite another thing when your little spoon goes in and out, in and out, until there's nothing left!

- Studies show that those who have one bowl of soup a day for one of their meals are more likely to lose weight than those who don't. If you have loads of leftover vegetables and some chicken, let's say, rather than give it to the dog, chuck it into the blender. Whizz it up into a yummy soup and have for your lunch the next day. Eating soups tends to make you feel full sooner so you are less likely to keep on scoffing.

- Be warned, though: soups can be misleading. Yes, they are a healthy option, but some are crammed full of hidden sugars and lashings of cream. Not particularly good for our waistlines! Make your own (as above), if you have the time. Creamy-based soups are packed with calories, so make sure that you go for a low-calorie vegetable broth.

- If you are trying to shed a second pair of bum cheeks, then it's time to buy a tape measure so you can measure your waist and other points on your body. Chuck your weighing scales out because they don't measure your shape or fat loss, but your water loss. And, as we all know, if it's the time of the month our body retains a lot of water, therefore a pair of scales won't give an accurate reading. Plus, muscle weighs heavier than fat (and fat takes up more room in the body), so if you are being good and going to the gym, then a set of scales which says you are getting heavier will make you feel really disheartened.

- Food is more powerful than you might think and eating the wrong snacks can make you feel seriously grumpy. It's like a car: if you fill it up with good petrol, it will get you from A to B very easily. If, however you fill it with mud, you ain't going anywhere! It's the same with our bodies. If you keep feeding your body bad sugars, white bread, cakes and other junk, then it will leave you looking like crap and feeling as if you're a time bomb waiting to explode. So, if you want to have more energy and look good, eat well.

- Breaking old habits and making new ones can sometimes be the recipe for successful dieting, so avoid all the old haunts where they sell your favourite cream buns and bacon butties and start going to new ones with healthy options.

- If you were born with a mega sweet tooth, then a stick of celery just isn't going to do the job! Instead look for fruits with a really high sugar content that will give you the same fix, such as figs, grapes and peaches.

- For most people, munchie attacks happen around 3.30pm just when our bodies and brain lack energy and get that mid-afternoon slump. Others may find it happens around 11am. The important thing here is to work out when your dips occur and to fill them with activities that take your mind off food, such as a phone call to a friend for some serious gossiping, or a bit of gardening. If you work in an office, walk to another department and say hi to someone.

- Why is it that, when we go into the kitchen to get the ironing board, we come out with a hunk of cheese and a little round of biscuits to wash them down with? OK, it's not a massive calorie-killer but, if you end up stuffing your face with a little something every time you go into the kitchen to do a non-foody chore, then over the course of the day the calories will start to mount up big time – and so will your gut, bingo wings and fatty back. And, although you've eaten three relatively healthy meals, you won't understand why you can't fight the flab. I know I've said this before but, remember, little pickers wear bigger knickers!

- Although eating a banana is better than eating chocolate cake when peckish, just be aware that, as far as fruit is concerned, bananas are more calorific than some other fruits such as pears or apples.

C E L E B R I T Y   T I P !

Brian Turner CBE - Chef

Always have your own Bloody Mary mix ready in the fridge for adding to vodka for when unexpected guests arrive – if nobody arrives, then drink it yourself and stay happy!

- If you want to get rid of sugar cravings, take a whiff of vanilla essence. Put some into a burner or on a tissue.

- Before you go out for dinner, have a little mixed salad at home. This will prevent you from ordering the wrong thing because you're starving and your greedy head is on.

Foods To Keep You Looking Like a Little Ripe Peach (and The Ones That Make You Look Like An Out-of-date Prune)

- When you get up in the morning, eating fresh fruit on an empty stomach is one of the best ways to cleanse your stomach.

- After you've had a wee, have a peek down the loo. If it's dark yellow/orange and makes your nostril hairs curl up, then you are dehydrated. Your pee should be the colour of a light-yellow diamond, so drink lots of water.

- Chicken is low-fat, scrummy and filling. Most of the fat is under the skin, so remove it before you cook it. Try and eat the white breast meat if you are watching your calories – this is the part with the least fat. With lamb or beef too, remove most of the fat before cooking and you will lower the fat content considerably.

- I know that, if you want to eat organic food, you almost have to take a second mortgage out but it isn't packed with all those toxic pesticides. Did you know that organic fruit and vegetables contain 40% more antioxidants than other varieties? So, instead of eating yourself into poverty, try swapping to just a few organic foods. Certain fruits have more pesticides than others, such as really soft fruits (they are like little sponges and will suck up all the pesticides sprayed onto them), spinach, lettuce, tomatoes, bread and milk. Also note that organic food isn't quite as pricey if you eat it when it's in season. With non-organic fruit and vegetables, just make sure you give it a really good clean under running water to get rid of all the pesticides.

- It's tempting to purchase fruit and vegetables from stalls at the side of the road because they are so convenient and cheap. But there is a negative side that comes with this and that is that they will be crawling in pesticide residue and car fumes, so always rinse them thoroughly.

- If you spend most of the year looking like Rudolf the Red-Nosed Reindeer having one cold after the other, if you suffer badly from PMS or if you're constantly tired and hungry and therefore put on weight, try taking zinc supplements. Zinc is renowned for zapping colds and helps to relieve PMS. Now, you can either take a zinc supplement or you can eat it. Also, trying beef, oysters, Cheddar cheese, baked beans, muesli and Brazil nuts in your diet.

- No one likes waking up looking like they haven't been to bed, do they? So, to avoid that startled, slightly glazed-over look because you haven't been able to sleep, munch on some lettuce and red onions before you go to bed. Or have a mug of hot milk. All of these will have a calming effect on your body and will help lull you into sleep. Having said that, it might not be advisable to eat onions if you have a boyfriend or if you are on a hot-date sleepover. You might get kicked out of bed!

- Winter always makes us reach for the naughty fatty foods because they make us feel better for a moment, but this also means we have to buy clothes in the next size up or go on a regular twenty-mile run! Try eating baked apples with soya yoghurt on top instead. Yum!

- If people stand a million miles away from you, and your love life (and breath) needs a boost, get your choppers round some beetroot! It cleanses bad breath and it's supposed to be an aphrodisiac because it contains the mineral boron, which stimulates your libido.

- If you're going to eat canned food because you're a lazy so-and-so, then make sure you go for no-sugar ones.

- When your skin looks like a slab of slate and lacks any healthy colour, it's time to get your choppers around some broccoli, blueberries and unsalted nuts – they are packed with good essential fatty acids and will re-plump and re-hydrate your lifeless skin.

- Avoid sugar where possible as it slows down your metabolism – you know, the thing that helps you lose weight when it speeds up. Have a cup of green tea instead, to speed things up.

- Animals are like us: they too store their toxins in their fat and that's why you should always buy lean meat and cut off all the extra fat before you cook it so you don't overload your body with even more toxins.

- I know it's very glam, having a chocolate croissant or a Danish pastry for breakfast and they taste really, really good, but what's not so good is that eating high-sugary foods on an empty stomach will give you such a sugar high for twenty minutes, followed by a mega-crash. This forces you to head back down to your local corner shop to load up on another batch because your energy levels are dwindling. You are better off going for a wholemeal bagel. Warm it up in the microwave for ten seconds for an extra-yummy taste.

- Ready meals are packed full of hidden fats, sugars and preservatives. Not particularly good news for your mood or skin. But if you can't resist a cheeky little ready-made meal, then you are so much better off buying vegetable- or lentil-based ones or make yourself a mega-quick dinner using fresh foods such as chicken with wholemeal pasta and vegetables.

- Don't be fooled by cereal bars. Some of them are packed full of fat and sugar, so always check the label.

- Eat a portion of pineapple after your meal. Pineapple is packed with digestive enzymes that will help you digest your grub and also reduce bloating.

- If you are going to the cinema, take your own popcorn (hide it in your handbag so that you don't get caught). Make it at home and don't go showering it in sugar! Instead, sprinkle cinnamon on top for a great low-calorie snack.

- If you are going to have a naughty treat and frozen chips are on the menu, be sure to check the label for any added fattening seasoning.

- If you are a sweet-tooth fairy, try munching on ultra-sweet dried apricots. They are low-fat, too. Guilt-free pleasure, that's what we like!

- Low-fat foods tend to have lots of sugar in them to give them flavour so try to avoid buying them.

- I'll tell you a brilliant snack to get your choppers around and that's gherkins! If you're craving something crunchy and sour, these little slug-like pickles are just the ticket.

- Nuts are good for us in small quantities, but fattening otherwise. Always choose raw over roasted.

- If you are a jacket-potato lover but would rather have a lower calorie option, try eating a sweet potato. They not only have half the amount of calories but are also packed with lots of lovely nutrients, too.

- Rather than blitzing your porridge with sugar, which will make you hyper for twenty minutes, swap some of that sugar for cinnamon or nutmeg.

C E L E B R I T Y   T I P !

Mike Brewer - Motoring Expert

My ultimate way of being lazy is to get my lovely wife to do everything for me – that's why she's 8 stone and I'm 16 stone!

What to Keep in Your Fridge & Storecupboards

Here's what you need to fill your fridge and storecupboards with to slow down the ageing process, preserve youthful looks and keep you looking healthy on the outside and feeling healthy on the inside.

FRUIT

Apples – low-fat and full of satisfying crunch factor.

Apricots are a great sweet snack for dieters. They are a mild natural laxative and also relieve period pains.

Bananas – although one of the most fattening fruits around, they are very good as a snack when you are starving as they keep your blood-sugar levels steady.

Blackberries are good for fighting off poor health.

Blueberries slow down the ageing process.

Cherries – eat loads of them if you have drunk too much alcohol. They are amazing detoxifiers.

Dates give you loads of energy.

Figs are a good natural laxative and great for those on a diet as they are really sweet.

Goji berries are full of antioxidants.

Grapefruit – the wonder fruit. Eating these can actually help you lose weight because they reduce insulin levels (insulin makes you hungry). Eat one half an hour before every meal.

Grapes – their lovely sweet taste is good for sorting out sugar cravings. They are full of antioxidants and are great for cleansing the digestive system.

Kiwi fruit will sort out water retention during your period and bloating.

Lemons and limes are a great liver cleanser and high in vitamin C, which is great for warding off colds and other infections. Lemon is good for digestion.

Mango puts you in a good mood and cleanses the kidneys. It also helps ward off any infections.

Melon is low in fat with high water content. It's good for a bloated stomach and fab for combating those sugar cravings.

Papaya – always have some in your fridge. It's one of the best detoxifiers. Papaya helps digestion (and therefore weight loss); it also encourages a healthy immune system.

Pears keep your digestive system working and your colon in good order.

Pineapple is full of enzymes that help you digest food. It also helps clean out the intestines.

Prunes – an excellent sweet snack for dieters as they are low in fat and will fill you up. Brilliant for easing trapped poo!

Raspberries are brilliant for a dwindling sex life – a good little revver-upper.

Strawberries are full of antioxidants that are great for slowing down the ageing process.

Watermelon keeps your kidneys clean. It re-hydrates the body, is packed with vitamin C and almost fat-free.

VEGETABLES

Asparagus is a good 'un for digestion and great for de-bloating.

Avocado is so good for your skin as it's packed with vitamin E and the 'good' fats that help to keep our blood-sugar levels constant, which in turn stop us from getting the munchies.

Beetroot tastes like mud, but it's amazing for that little energy boost and is also a great cleanser. It helps to relieve constipation, aids digestion and also speeds up your metabolism.

Broccoli is full of vitamins that promote healthy hair, bones and teeth. It is high in fibre and very cleansing for the liver.

Carrots help keep infection away and also cleanse the liver.

Celery is one of the best foods you can eat when you're on a diet. Because it tastes a little bit salty, use it as a substitute for salt in a dish (salt makes you retain water, which makes you look bloated). Did you know that you burn up more calories trying to digest celery than in the vegetable itself? It also lowers cholesterol levels.

Courgettes are filling and a good diuretic.

Cucumbers have such a high water content that they are a mild laxative and brilliant for cleansing the digestive system and the bladder, which prevents you from getting water retention and cystitis.

Garlic – stinky, tasty – but a natural antibiotic!

Green beans are full of vitamin C. Essential to ward off infections and great for strengthening your immune system.

Kale is a rich source of nutrients. It has more calcium than any other vegetable and is packed with vitamin C. Good for strong bones and teeth. Use it in omelettes and soups.

Leeks and celeriac – shovel these in like they're going out of fashion when you have your period! They are great for helping to reduce water retention.

Lettuce promotes a good night's sleep and is great for fighting off water retention as it's a diuretic.

Mushrooms are filling and keep hunger locked up for a bit.

Parsnips are good for healthy-looking skin.

Potatoes are packed with fibre and will give you loads of energy. They only become unhealthy when you fill them up with full-fat cheese, butter, Coronation Chicken, etc.

Radishes speed up the metabolism, which in turn helps us to burn calories more quickly. They are also packed with anti-ageing antioxidants.

Red cabbage is great for relieving constipation.

Red peppers help us to burn fat as they kick-start the digestive system.

Spinach protects you against heart disease. It's a great stress-buster, pumps us up with energy and is also a good laxative.

Watercress – use raw in salads or in soups. It's full of antioxidants and great for cleaning out your digestive system.

TINNED FOOD

Lentils, kidney beans, chickpeas (full of antioxidants and fibre), sweetcorn, baked beans, tinned tomatoes, sardines, tuna in water and salmon are all OK to buy, guilt-free. Avoid any with sugar or salt, though. You are better off buying tinned tuna in water than oil, as water is much healthier. Carrots and peas in tins tend to have sugar in them, so fresh is best. Tinned fruit is packed with naughty, tooth-decaying syrup – always go for fresh unless you like the black-toothed look!

FISH, MEAT & POULTRY

Cod – don't go for fish covered in batter – it's very unhealthy. Instead, steam or bake cod. It's a very low-fat fish and full of magnesium, which boosts the metabolism.

Duck – very hard not to have when you're ordering a Chinese! It's quite high in fat, so just bear that in mind before you eat the entire thing. Like chicken (below), remove the fatty skin before eating – this is where all the fat is stored.

Free-range chicken is low in fat and filling. Always remove the skin before eating it – this is where the fat is stored.

Mackereal is full of vitamin D, which is good for healthy bones and teeth. It's also rich in the antioxidant selenium and vitamin E – great for a healthy heart.

Oysters – the lovers' grub! It's full of zinc, which helps to ward off illnesses and cleans out the liver.

Prawns are full of zinc, which helps to ward off illnesses.

Salmon is really creamy-tasting and full of omega-3 fatty acids, which are essential for good health; it improves your digestive system, which in turn helps to burn fat.

Tuna is the dieter's best friend. Super-filling and a great detoxifier, it helps to rid the body of those nasty free radicals and builds up our immune system to ward off illnesses.

Turkey – again, remove the fatty skin before eating. It is full of zinc, which is good news for our immune system. The darker meat has a lot of iron in it and this is great for us girlies, especially during our period when we lose a lot of iron.

Go easy on buying bacon, anchovies, scampi, beef, duck and mussels. Red meat is a lot harder to digest than white and lean meat. White fish is easy to digest and full of good oils, which are vital for good skin, bones, hair and teeth. Shellfish have a lot more fat than normal fish.

HERBS & SPICES

Basil destresses and makes you feel more chilled out.

Bay is a natural medicinal herb that is great for sorting out chest infections and depression.

Chillies are fat-free and add some kick-ass to your meals. They rev up your metabolism, helping you to lose weight. Chillies are also good for keeping colds at bay, especially during the winter.

Coriander is great for putting a stop to your farting (see also pages 227-230).

Ginger eases travel sickness. It's also good for keeping colds away as it's a natural antiseptic.

Mint prevents indigestion.

Parsley helps relieve PMS.

Rosemary stimulates your memory.

GOOD GRAINS & SEEDS

Flaxseed is a good one to have in your diet as it's packed full of omega-3 fatty acids. It's also good for relieving constipation. I put flaxseed oil in my salads.

Lentils – amazing stuff! They are known as the road-sweepers of the gut as they totally cleanse it. Lentils are also mega-filling, versatile, full of fibre, iron and minerals.

Nuts – unsalted cashews and almonds are full of vitamin B and packed with minerals and antioxidants.

Oats – they fill you up, relieve constipation and are great if you suffer really badly from PMS as they help to even out your blood-sugar levels – and this prevents you emptying out the fridge!

Pumpkin seeds help to relieve constipation and are a powerful cleanser.

Quinoa regulates your blood-sugar levels, sorts out a bad mood and is full of calcium.

Rye is full of fibre and a slow-release energy food. Great, if you can't keep your face out of the fridge as it really fills you up!

Avoid buying white rice and white pasta – they will not only bloat you, but also offer no nutritional value whatsoever and play havoc with your blood-sugar levels, which causes cravings. Instead, go for brown rice, which is great for cleaning out your digestive system. Also, try wholewheat pasta, which contains more nutrients than white and is also high in fibre.

OTHER BITS & BOBS

Bio yoghurt contains friendly bacteria, which keep our intestines working well. It also has antibiotic qualities. If you suffer from candida, bio yoghurt will help.

Bread – white bread has no nutrients in it at all. Instead, opt for wholemeal.

Eggs – don't eat too many or they will make you constipated. They are high in antioxidants and zinc, which cleanse the liver and keep colds away.

Honey is a great substitute for sugar and a lot sweeter, too.

Olives are great for anti-ageing because of all the vitamin E.

Tofu is full of calcium, which is good for our bones, hair and teeth, and a good source of protein for a vegetarian. It also has a lot of fibre in it and keeps our energy levels high.

DRINKS

Camomile tea – drink a cup of it before you go to bed. It's great for a good night's sleep.

CELEBRITY TIP!

Jean-Christophe Novelli - Celebrity Chef

To make life easy...

- *Peel root ginger with the inner curve of a teaspoon.*
- *Leave the skin on tomatoes when making tomato sauce – you can easily pick them out at the end.*
- *Crack whole cloves of garlic, adding them near the end of cooking, you get more flavour and the most from the garlic. This principle is applied to soft herbs as well.*
- *Place a few uncooked grains of rice in your salt shaker, to absorb any moisture and keep the salt flowing.*
- *¼ par boil potatoes before roasting, allow them to steam dry first before roasting as normal to give fluffy roasts.*

Green tea helps you to lose weight as it breaks down fat and stimulates the metabolism. It's also full of antioxidants, which are great for slowing down the ageing process. Drink about four cups a day.

Peppermint tea is brilliant for digesting food after a meal.

Red wine is the most heart-healthy alcohol. It's full of antioxidants, reduces cholesterol and blood clotting – so pop that cork and raise a glass (just the one, mind) to red vino!

Buy lots of fruit to make your own fruit juices, or buy ready-made ones that are unsweetened. Don't go filling your fridge up with lots of artificial fizzy drinks and booze. They're no good for you and offer you no goodness. Substitute full-sugar soda with diet soda – every little calorie counts!

The Gym Sucks! Going from Pork to Pert

Of course, every girly wants to be the owner of a dream-like body, with never-ending peachy pins, a stomach as hard as a concrete breeze block and a couple of Pamela Anderson men magnets stuck to her chest. But let's be honest, this isn't going to happen if you spend half of your life parked up on the sofa, ramming cup cakes and burgers down your throat while working your way through every single film from your local video shop. You need to exercise!

Doing exercise doesn't necessarily mean padlocking yourself to the running machine at the gym until you go red in the face and pass out, or cycling absolutely nowhere on one of those stationary bikes. If you don't like the gym, don't go! It's as simple as that.

You can spend your savings on plastic surgery to re-sculpt your walrus-like body at the risk of looking like a patchwork doll with all the seams on show, or stop using your stomach like a kitchen cupboard, filling it up till the door is unable to close with all the snacks you've crammed in. Do something active like cleaning the house or going on a fabulous shopping spree. Get up off the sofa, leave the cakes alone and let's get those gooey, full-fat figgy-pudding butt cheeks and turn them into delicious hot poached pears.

- If you can't be arsed to go to the gym or you can't afford it, turn your house into your gym. Run up and down the stairs holding your weights (or two bags of sugar) until your legs and bum cheeks are quivering.
- Do your errands in your trainers; run from one thing to the other. Not only will you get everything done in a super-quick time, but you will also burn lots of calories, tone up and it hasn't cost you a penny.
- Throw away the car keys and do your shopping on foot, then carry the bags home. And no, you're not allowed to take the bus or a taxi back either.
- Ditch the Naan next time your fingers dial up that Indian takeaway and opt for something healthier such as wholemeal pitta bread.
- The more fun the exercise is, the more likely you're going to do it. So burn off 400 calories and do an hour of gardening. If someone you know needs to re-decorate or they are moving house, get right in there and offer your services. Decorating or lifting heavy boxes up and down the stairs is a fantastic calorie-burner.
- If you are feeling a bit down in the dumps, then even a little fifteen-minute run will do your head the world of wonders. Notice how after only five minutes you will feel ten times more amazing.
- There's no point in joining a gym on the other side of town because you'll never go. Try to find one that's near your work or home.

- Put your gym kit on and see if this encourages you to get off the sofa and to stop wearing those comfy pyjamas.
- Cleaning the house on full speed will tone you up quicker than you can imagine.
- If you exercise at night you will end up feeling full of beans and unable to sleep. But if you go in the morning then you will kick-start your metabolism and burn calories for the rest of the day; you'll also feel full of energy.
- Next time you need to get a fresh box of tea bags from the top of the shelf, don't take the easy option and get a chair to clamber onto. Instead, lean up onto your tippie toes and reach and stretch for Britain! This is a great way to stretch out your back and spine.
- Whenever you are standing (while you're waiting to pick up your coffee or on the phone, for example), squeeze your pimply bum cheeks as hard as possible, hold for ten seconds and then release. Repeat ten times. Be careful not to squeeze too hard – you don't want to force out a little fart, do you?
- If you are tied to your desk with no hope of getting anywhere near the gym (phew!) and your stomach is beginning to flop over the top of your pants, don't let that stop you from doing a few sneaky abs exercises at your desk. While you are sitting there, breathe in and, when you exhale, tense your stomach muscles, hold for ten seconds and then release. Do this about fifteen times.
- Next, your legs: sit with your back up straight, extend your leg out, and raise it about 7.5cm (3in) off the floor. Hold for as long as you can, then release. Repeat on the other side. Do this daily for toned thighs.

- Make your bed every morning and burn twenty calories.

- Don't waste money on a workout video – they only ever sit there in the sealed packet, collecting dust. Instead, put MTV on full blast, dance for twenty minutes and burn lots of calories and tone up.

- If your house is looking like a bombsite, rather than taking handfuls of junk up the stairs in one go, move one thing up at a time to get those thigh muscles working and toned up.

- While you are waiting for your potatoes to boil, take this opportunity to do some exercises such as some calf raises while holding onto the edge of the worktop. Or do some bicep curls holding onto two pineapples (or use full bottles of mineral water or baked bean cans).

- Invest in a cordless phone so that every time you make a call you can walk about the place rather than sitting on your derrière and by doing this you will lose about 2.25kg (5lb) a year!

- When you come in from a hard day's work, the last thing you feel like doing sometimes is preparing vegetables. All that washing and peeling! So, be prepared. Peel and cut up different types of vegetables, divide into portions and put into freezer bags, then chuck into the freezer. When you get home, all you have to do is get a bag out of the freezer and cook it. You can do the same with fruit. Fat-free yoghurt on top of frozen berries is a delicious snack.

- Ditch the remote control for your TV. Instead, get up and change the channel manually. You will burn more calories getting up and down than moving just one finger.

- If there's a set of stairs, take them. Don't be a lazy so-and-so and take the lift!

- If you must take the escalator then walk up it, don't just stand on it and wait for it to transport you to the top.

- Nothing beats a good old gossip session with your best mate in Starbucks, but after one too many hot chocs and a cheeky little muffin, there's only one place for those nasty calories – and that's on your behind! So, instead of cleaning out the cake cooler unit, arrange to meet your friend in Starbucks, ask for low-fat hot chocolates to take away, then walk and talk outside (around a park, for example) while you drink them. You can enjoy your drink without any guilt and you won't be tempted to eat or drink anything else.

- Do you know what, you can be having a really good, healthy day where you haven't eaten any junk and you're feeling proud: it's 8pm and you're out of the danger zone of wanting to stuff your face, plus, it's nearly bedtime, so you don't need anything to eat. Cool? Yes, but then you turn on the TV and the adverts come on. It's OK to watch the boring car or banking ad, but as soon as an advert comes on for gooey, sticky chocolate cakes, you're in trouble. That larger-than-life vision of heaven and hell just stares you straight in the face, telling you that you need that chocolate. So you put your coat on over your nightie, get into your slippers and run out of your house with your mission face on (do let alarmed neighbours know you're not running away from a burning house!). The long and short of this tip is: when the adverts come on, get up and go and do something, even if it's to go and have a pee or hang your washing out! Foodie ads will encourage you to eat.

- There are two reasons why you should eat with chopsticks. First, it takes you four times longer to eat your dinner, so it's much more satisfying because you take many more mouthfuls so you feel like you're eating more. Normally it would take all of three seconds with a knife and fork. Second, because chopsticks are really difficult to use, they force you to focus on your meal, therefore you concentrate on what you're eating, not what's on TV – again, it's a satisfying feeling for the brain, as it remembers that you've eaten and you will be less likely to reach for the snacks later.

- There's nothing like a curry on a Friday night after a hard week at work, but vacuuming up a creamy korma means you will eat four times more calories than you actually need. So, instead of picking out the creamy, saucy dishes, opt for oven-cooked tandoori dishes with salad – they don't have any sauces and are far healthier.

- When you go for a Chinese, be careful. A hungry stomach can lead you astray. So eat some fruit before you go, so that you aren't starving and order all the wrong (and naughty) things. Swap fried rice for steamed rice, order dishes with plenty of vegetables and go for shrimp and chicken rather than pork.

- You don't need to tie yourself to the treadmill to get fit or swim like a fish until you become more wrinkly than a prune. You can do sneaky exercise, but have super fun doing it. When you go to a party, don't be the loser wedged in the corner on the sofa. Get up and dance your little socks off! Burn lots of calories while having an absolute blast with your friends.

- Rather than drowning your salad in olive oil, try drizzling balsamic vinegar on it. It's sharp and doesn't come with all the fat.

- Always brush your teeth after you have eaten. A fresh minty mouth and the psychological feeling that dinner is over may just put you off heading back to the fridge. Oh, and while you are brushing your teeth, why not do thirty squats just to burn a few extra calories and tone up? Remember, every calorie helps.

- Everybody needs encouragement when it comes to doing exercise. No one normal likes doing it, really. So why make it any harder for yourself? If you wear cool, trendy workout gear that makes you feel good, you'll be down the gym in no time. If, on the other hand, your kit looks like an ancient car-seat cover, but somehow you do manage to dig it out and get yourself down the gym, what happens if you catch a glimpse of yourself in the workout mirror? Well, let's put it this way, I just hope you live near a hospital where you can get emergency access to oxygen – one look at your dog-like appearance will leave you gasping for air while having a heart attack!

- A little blast on the running machine or once round the park will lift the blues and make you feel a lot happier.

- Leave your running trainers by the fridge. Exercise is an appetite suppressant so if you've already eaten your breakfast or lunch, but for some reason you find yourself gravitating towards the fridge, throw on your trainers and go for a twenty- or thirty-minute run. When you get back, you won't want to go near the fridge for a while. Why? Because exercise helps to release a certain hormone that tells the brain your stomach is full. Plus, by running you will have raised your metabolism, meaning that, when you do eat, the fat won't go straight onto your hips as you will burn it off a lot quicker.

- Instead of making sandwiches with unhealthy white bread, try super-tasty variations such as rye bread.

- Rather than reaching for a cake or a full-fat pud after dinner, eat some baked fruit. It's both sweet and healthy.

- OK, so if you're thinking about going on a diet, rather than just *going* on a diet and trying to lose weight here and there, give yourself a deadline. It could be a special party, for instance. That way you will give yourself an incentive to conquer your goal.

- Roasting and frying will put a good old roll of fat around your waist. So opt for steaming or grilling, where possible.

- OK, so these pictures may not be for the family album, but they will be your best photos ever as they will help you gauge how much weight you have lost or how your love handles have seen the light of day. Persuade your best friend to take a picture of every angle of your body possible. Every week, have her take a whole new batch from the same angles and compare what you looked like at the beginning of your diet and the end.

- When you next go to the cinema, don't bring your greedy glasses and load up on the hot dogs, ice cream and a big box of penny sweets. Instead go for a tub of plain popcorn (bring your own little pot of paprika, if you want to spice things up a bit). However, if your porky little mitts can't control themselves and they need penny sweets, rather than filling your sweetie bag up with calorie-laden chocolate-covered brazil nuts, go for jelly babies: they are so low in fat.

- Hula-hoops aren't just for kids, you know! All that twisting and twirling does wonders for those unwanted wobbly bits that seem to cling onto a six-pack of stomach muscles, which are dying to be unleashed!

- Being taken out for dinner is always a luxury and having three courses is a must. The only thing about it is this can be catastrophic for a dieter.

Instead, have a starter for both your first and second course. Or how about a salad for the first course and then a normal main? That way you will be able to walk out of the door rather than waddle out.

- A dinner isn't worth going out for if you can't finish it off with a scrummy pud, is it? So rather than ordering a pudding each, share one with your date so that you still get the taste but haven't blown the diet.

- Try to vary your exercise. Not only so your brain doesn't die of boredom, but also because your body will get used to the exercise you repeatedly do and will stop performing; therefore, you won't see a change in tone and shape. Ask a friend if they'd like to play tennis once a week or go for a run. Then the next week, you could go swimming or power walking.

- Skipping, too, is a brilliant calorie-burner. Just make sure you don't do it in your living room while watching the TV. I'm not sure if smashing all your vases and lampshades is a particularly good thing to do.

- Most of the time I look like I've got ants in my pants as I never actually sit still. I'm always twiddling and fidgeting – even at night when I'm in bed I'm like a Jack-in-the-box! But, although at times I probably look like one of those one-man bands (you know, the ones who play a harmonica, drums, symbols and accordion and sing all at the same time?), I'm actually doing my waistline a lot of good. The more you fidget, the more calories you lose! It's believed that you can lose up to 350 extra calories a day. This is not a substitute for the gym, it's just a little bonus.

- Whatever the dish, ask your waiter if you can have the chef put the sauce on the side rather than on the food itself. That way you can control how much goes onto your fish, salad or meat.

- Before you go out to paint the town red, throw yourself on the floor and do 100 sit-ups. This is a super quick-fix for tightening your stomach muscles and is especially good if you are wearing something that's clingy and you've been shovelling in naughty foods all day long!

- When you buy a pot of chocolate ice cream, it's very difficult to eat just a little bit and put the rest into the freezer. You spend the rest of the evening drooling about the darn stuff! So, if you are one of those people who only feel satisfied when they see the bottom of the pot, buy a tub of chocolate or any other pure fruit sorbet. They are practically fat-free and you can polish off the lot guilt-free.

- Double up on exercise and chores. Multi-tasking is something only the female species can do! While waiting for the kettle to boil, get two big bags of flour or baked-bean tins out of your cupboard and do some bicep curls to tone up your arms. When you want a break from the ironing, do leg raises for your bum muscles – simply lift your leg up behind you, doing it slowly and repeat ten times, then do the same on the other leg. Using a ledge (this could be the bottom step of the staircase or a chair), you can help tone up the flabby bits on the backs of your arms with tricep dips. Remember, the more muscle you build, the more calories you will burn.

- We all love the taste of butter but one little knob can take a couple of hours of walking to burn off! Rather than loading your mashed potato up with shed-loads of fattening butter, try a healthier option – a drizzle or two of olive oil.

- As mentioned before, if you make your bed in the morning you will lose about 20 calories. Change the sheets, etc. and you will burn about 100.

- If the munchie attacks have invaded your body, then you're better off having something that is higher in sugar than higher in fat. Fat has twice the amount of calories as sugar. Meringue nests are the perfect solution as they are high in sugar but are virtually fat-free. They taste lovely with fruit and fat-free crème fraîche.

- It's strange, isn't it, but when it comes to doing stomach crunches we always think of a reason why we haven't got time to do them! Maybe the dog is looking really hungry and needs feeding or you've got to sort out that pile of elastic bands because they're causing a right mess! If you can't be arsed to do them, don't! Just don't get upset when you look in the mirror and see one big flab pack, rather than a trim six-pack. But you can do a little to help, and in a really super-lazy way. When you are next sitting there watching an episode of *Sex and the City*, hold your tummy muscles in really tight for a minute, then relax. Repeat five times. The great thing about this sloth exercise is that you can do it anywhere, any time.

- If you're trying to shift a couple of stubborn old unwanted pounds from your bum, etc., then here's one thing that you should always remember: eat foods that have a really high water content. You can stuff your face with them and they will fill you up, but they don't come with a whole host of calories. Choose things like watermelon, celery and other yummy fruits and vegetables (see page 246-248). Just make sure you incorporate low-fat protein-rich foods and starch into your meals, too.

- If you want to get rid of those out-of-control chicken wings that seem to be a permanent fixture on the back of your arms, then dust high and low!

- If you can't see your muff because an apron-like tummy is covering it, then vacuum! Dance while you do it and watch that tummy hone and tone. By getting your heart-rate high you will burn calories for up to fourteen hours afterwards. Vacuuming builds muscle, which uses up more calories than fat.

- Next time you're taking your make-up off or doing a facial or waiting for something to cook in the microwave, use this time to tone. Stand on one leg and lift your other leg slowly up to the side and back down. Repeat about ten times and then do the other leg.

- Every little helps when it comes to trying to reduce the amount of fat that you gobble down. Instead of buying cream to drown your fruit in, get fat-free crème fraîche or low-fat yoghurt.

- There's no point in being good and steaming your veg, only to load it up with super-fattening sauces or butter. But then I also understand that steamed veg with nothing on it tastes bland. So opt for healthy options such as sprinkling fresh garden herbs on top (mint on peas or spring onions on broccoli). Also, chopped chilli tastes yummy on everything and puts some va-va voom into any dish.

- It's so annoying how, when you get into a full bath, your entire body just magnifies under the water. So, either fill up the bath with loads of bubbles so you can't see anything, or do something about it. Massage your tummy for five minutes to help the lymphatic drainage system to circulate and to give your stomach the appearance of a more toned one.

- You know when someone's sitting down and they want to fart, then they kind of lean over to one side and lift one bum cheek, don't they? Well, this next exercise is similar but the difference is, you won't be farting (unless you want to), but doing sneaky bum clenches instead. All you have to do is squeeze your bum for a minute, then relax and repeat another five times. If you do this every day, you will soon have a bum that looks and feels as firm as an eggshell.

- If you are one of those greedy guts who like to fill their plates to the brim and polish the whole lot off (including the pattern), then try eating from a child's plate. Fill it up to the brim and wolf the whole lot down, guilt-free. Psychologically, your brain will feel satisfied as you have finished what was on your plate.

- Don't let freezing-cold weather put you off exercising outside. In fact, working in cold conditions will make you lose a lot more calories because your body is fighting to keep warm. For the same reason, don't have the heating up too high in the winter.

- It's bad enough that you've ordered yourself a big greasy burger with chips on the side and some fried onion rings to wash it all down with, but even worse if you keep licking your fingers between mouthfuls. By doing this, you are probably consuming an extra eighty calories! So use a napkin or a tea towel!

CELEBRITY TIP!

Brendan Cole - Dancer

Exercising is sometimes difficult to fit in. You can achieve quick results and save time from the comfort of your own living-room. Whilst watching a film, choose an exercise (for example sit-ups or press-ups). During every ad break repeat this exercise until the end of the film. Because your focus is on the length of the ad break rather than how many repetitions you are doing, the routine is less boring and psychologically more easy to achieve. This is not recommended for movies on the BBC as there are no ad breaks!

6

Cigarettes & Alcohol

CIGGIES

THE CORNER SHOP has closed and cravings and desperation have set in. You've run out of yellowy nails to bite and your waistline's rapidly expanding because you can't keep your porky little mitts away from the cream cakes in the fridge. Like a sheepdog, you round up all the butt ends around the house. It doesn't stop there, though.

This is the dark life that comes with smoking, lowering your standards just to satisfy your addiction and becoming a prisoner to the habit. Giving up isn't easy, but surely it's better than risking your health? As with quitting any addiction, to be successful you must really want to do it. If not, it won't work. So, here are a few helpful tips to make the ride easier and to stop you from rummaging around the dustbins for

The Lazy Goddess

those fag ends you chucked out three days ago. After all, do you really want pursed-up, unkissable lips that look really old and BO breath?

- Addiction is hard. If there's a packet of biscuits in the house, my life's hell, it's as simple as that. I start drooling like a dog, my eyes become dilated and I can't think of anything else! But if they're not sitting there under my nose in the first place, then I won't think of them (well, I didn't until one of those very convenient, but equally annoying 24/7 garages opened up right next to my house, so temptation is right on my doorstep, all day and night long!). So, keep temptation out of sight. Hide all matches, lighters, ash trays and of course the ciggies. Even better, throw them out. Out of sight, out of mind.
- Ex-smokers say that it's the ritual of putting a cigarette in your mouth and having the actual contact that's the hardest thing to give up. Well, this is where pencils and pens come in handy. Get down to the Cash & Carry and buy a bulk load of them. When you get the urge to smoke, instead of picking up a fag and shoving it into your mouth, shove a pen in instead and chew the hell out of it!
- When you're down at the Cash & Carry picking up your pens, don't forget to fill your trolley with some super-chewy, fat-free sweets, mints and chewing gum. These are great substitutes for fags, especially if your mouth is in need of some action. If you want to go for a much healthier version, then keep hummus, carrot and celery batons in the fridge and munch away on them. They are very satisfying as they have lots of crunch.
- As soon as you stop smoking you will not only notice how much bigger your bank balance will be, but also your circulation and the condition of

268

your skin will improve. You'll have much more energy and all that coughing and spluttering up mucus will totally go away as long as you drink lots of water to loosen it.

- If you're finding it hard to go cold turkey, start to take smaller drags of your fags. The less you suck them to death, the more likely you will have longer to live.

- If you always have a ciggie with your coffee, then you may have to cut coffee right out of your daily routine. It's psychological – every time you have a coffee, you will crave nicotine. If you drink a lot of coffee and smoke every time, then don't cut it all out immediately: you will only end up having mega nicotine withdrawals and feel depressed. As with any form of giving up, do it gradually, one thing at a time.

- Some people find smoking acts as an anti depressant. If this is the case for you, then go to a health-food shop and buy St John's Wort. It will really help if you are struggling with withdrawal symptoms. If you are taking other medication, then consult your doctor beforehand.

- Smoking is expensive. You may just as well burn your money. So, instead of buying a pack of fags, put the money into a little box. At the end of each month go out and treat yourself to a fab new handbag and go for a relaxing facial. Far better to look fresh-faced and carrying a hot new handbag than a dried-up old hag with a pursed mouth!

- Another horrible side effect when giving up smoking is insomnia. Lying there wide awake can be so stressful. Try taking a herb called Valerian (from health shops). Take one just before you go to bed.

- Boredom can leave you thinking you're in need of a cigarette. So, rather than sit there twiddling your thumbs and staring at the cigarettes, do something to take your mind off them. The more physical, the better. It could be a brisk walk (this is one of the best, as exercise will help to reduce the stress and tension that comes with giving up smoking), a quick vacuuming session around the house, culling your clothes from your wardrobe (see pages 181-185), or doing a bit of gardening.

- I've seen so many people have a fag, then dash to the bog for a big old dump. When they reappear, they not only have a smile on their face, but their tummy looks flatter, too. Great! But what isn't so good is that, when you give up smoking, it can make you severely constipated for over two weeks because nicotine is a bowel stimulant. Yep, that means a bloated, hot-air-balloon-like stomach, filled with two weeks' worth of crap (literally!). It'll leave you feeling so agitated and snappy.

- But fear not, there is a solution. Get your piggy trotters down to your local health-food shop and buy the whole shelf of Puritee by Ideal Health. This delicious little tea bag will detox your whole system – a God-sent gift to those who can't squeeze cheese! Also, up your intake of water (this will always help to relieve constipation) and go for a run or a brisk walk as these will stimulate your bowels and kickstart them into action.

- If you are at a friend's house party and you have the urge to smoke, put an ice cube into your mouth and suck away. It's far healthier than having a fag or vacuuming up 3,000 calories of nuts.

- So many smokers believe that a cigarette helps them de-stress in needy times. Research has proved otherwise, so don't give in! Put a few drops of lavender essential oil onto a hanky and, when you feel stressed and are reaching for a cigarette, have a few sniffs and this will make you feel less anxious.

- Try to avoid going into areas where people are going to be smoking. All it takes is one whiff or to see somebody light up a fresh ciggie and you'll melt under the pressure as your willpower flies out the window. There is of course the whole passive-smoking thing to think about, too. You may have given up, but by being in a smoke-filled room means you are theoretically smoking three or four cigarettes too.

- If your friends smoke, ask them not to tempt you and to help you through that cold-turkey stage until you are able to sit with them comfortably without wanting a drag.

- Rather than reaching for a ciggie after dinner, go and brush your teeth immediately and get ready for bed. Actually, brush your teeth after every meal just in case. It helps with all kinds of cravings.

- Research has revealed that if you are trying to give up smoking then eating a bowl of porridge oats with soya milk and raisins for breakfast really helps to curb the cravings. As an alternative, you can also mash up a banana and spread it onto an oatcake.

- Start hanging around your non-smoker friends. When the cravings start to kick in, give them a bell and get them to remind you why smoking is so bad for you.

- Fiddling and doing creative things is a great way to keep your hands occupied rather than thinking about smoking and all that hand-to-mouth action. That's why it's best to choose fiddly foods that are time consuming and healthy to eat, such as oranges or nuts in their shells, when you've got the munchies.

- Nicorette patches are a great solution to help you deal with the cravings and withdrawal symptoms that you suffer when giving up smoking. They are small patches that you stick on to your skin; they filter nicotine into your blood to help relieve the cravings.

A Little Greenie

This fixer-upper drink will really sort out and help that phlegm problem when you're coughing your guts up!

You will need:

- ½ large cucumber, cut into pieces (cucumber is very cleansing)
- a big bunch of fresh watercress (amazing for breaking up and getting rid of phlegm)
- 1 big floret of broccoli, cut into pieces (broccoli is a great cleanser and detoxifier)
- 6 fresh tarragon leaves (they taste good and help to get rid of the nasty toxins that are floating around)

Put the broccoli and cucumber through the juicer and then transfer the juice into a blender. Next, throw in the tarragon and watercress and blend the whole lot together, then drink.

- Binge smoking (having twenty cigarettes on a Friday night because you're totally trashed) is just as bad as spreading them out throughout the week. So, to avoid this happening every Friday night, note down when and how you start to smoke. Is it maybe after five drinks that you beg for a ciggie? If that's the case, then make sure you don't drink more than four. Alternatively, try something different on your Friday night to vary the routine.
- Believe you me, when you decide to knock smoking on the head, your mouth will want entertaining and will become a permanent fixture in the

fridge if you're not careful. To suppress an unnecessary appetite, try drinking a lovely mug of hot camomile tea.

- And finally, here's a little bit of info that might put you off lighting up your next cigarette: every time you take a drag of your fag, you are actually sucking in 4,000 different chemicals, some of which are poisonous (lead and arsenic are just two of them). On top of this you will be inhaling carbon monoxide, which prevents your body from absorbing oxygen.

THE BINGEING BIRDS BRIGADE

What is it about Friday nights, men and alcohol that transforms some of them from perfectly respectable businessmen extraordinaire into what are best described as escaped scientific experiments from the zoo? Why do they need to shove their hairy bollocks into an empty beer glass, and what's so appealing about dropping their trousers and trying to unsuccessfully light a fart? And which part of their now-dehydrated and microscopic brains thinks stealing a traffic cone and wearing it on their heads will make them the most original and funniest man alive? Not to mention redecorating the pavement outside some poor old person's house on the way home with an unexpected arrival of last night's kebab, vindaloo and twenty pints of lager.

And then the next day arrives, and boy does it hurt! Not only do the birds outside sound like they're doing karaoke with the volume turned up full blast, but there's also the headache from hell to deal with, not just because of the obscene amount of alcohol that was consumed but also the damn loo seat kept hitting them as they hurled up last night's produce!

But there's a big difference between men and women getting drunk. For men, strangling their balls in a beer glass, projectile puking over the pavement and pulling any poor girl is notching up 'lads' points' and gives them cool credit. But a drunk girl can lose her dignity, her purse, her knickers and could be forever tarnished with a derogatory nickname such as slapper, slut, village bicycle or, worse still, open all hours. So, to prevent you from becoming a drunk and disorderly, beer-guzzling bloke and waking up in a stranger's bed with the hangover from hell, I strongly advise you to read this section over and over again. Binge drinking and being arrested for drunken behaviour seriously isn't cool and never will be.

How To Be a Good Drunk

- Take note, girls – alcohol might make you feel sexy but drink one too many and I can assure you that you will begin to look decidedly unsexy. That lopsided, distorted, drunken face doesn't really do much for anyone – so read on and absorb...
- Drink like a fish. And I don't mean that you need to stand there, propping up the bar all night. This can lead to lost knickers and, well, getting lost in general, having absolutely no idea what your name is or where you live. So, drink like the fish do and drink lots of water. Alternate every glass of alcohol you have with a glass of water and this will hydrate you again. Being dehydrated gives you a headache, so glug, glug, glug the stuff back!
- Before you go out on your big night, make sure you close the curtains, put a 'Keep Out' or 'Be Quiet' sign on your door, a huge glass of water by your bed and, most importantly, a big pair of Joan Collins-like sun glasses beside your bed (an even better idea is to go to sleep in them!). I'm telling you this now because when your far-too-chirpy mum (or flatmate) comes in at 7am, whistling away, and proceeds to open the

curtains, you won't be feeling strong enough to mumble 'bugger off'! By cleverly pre-planning beforehand you will save yourself some hell.

- Everybody loves a Christmas party: it's the one time of year when you can dress up and really let your hair down with your colleagues. But it's an entirely different thing when you get totally trashed, the wheels fall off entirely and you decide it would be a brilliant idea to tell your boss what you really think of him/her. And it doesn't stop there. The office geek over in the accounts department, who usually makes you want to hurl, suddenly looks really cute, almost Brad Pitt-looking. 'Where has this little hunk of spunk been hiding?' is the question you'll ask yourself as the alcohol slowly seeps into your blood, distorting your vision and your furry dip-covered tongue becomes desperate for a drunken snog.

- To stop yourself becoming the casualty that everyone will be gossiping about the next day, don't binge drink and, for goodness sake, drink a glass of milk before you go out, or take 200g milk thistle (from health-food shops) the night before. You could also try an energy-boosting drink or having something to eat just before you go out (see page 237) to line your stomach, otherwise it might not be just your reputation that you'll be trying to save but also your job when you find a P45 on your desk the next day. Oh, and I'd better mention here, whatever you do, keep away from the photocopying machine!

- If the drinks are going down like a bride's nightie (ie without touching the sides) and you find yourself becoming more relaxed, if someone put a bowl of salted nuts or a fresh batch of cheesy chips right under your nose, you'd eat the whole lot, wouldn't you? Before you know it, you'll have blown your diet, big time. Never order bar snacks and, if they do come in your direction, push them away. They are full of hidden calories and salt, and the more salt you eat, the more you want to drink. It's a vicious circle. Every nut you cram in will take you one step closer to that next cocktail (and that extra tummy tyre) and every cocktail you bolt down will take you even closer to looking like a train wreck – and the hangover from hell the next day!

- This goes without saying, but I'll say it anyway – never ever ever drink and drive. It's the most selfish thing a person could ever do.

- Instead of diving straight for the gin bottle, pour yourself a tonic water, tart it up with all the trimmings of ice and lemon, then dip your finger into the gin bottle and rub it around the rim of the glass. Your sense of smell will convince your brain that you have got a proper full-blown gin and tonic. P.S. This also works well with rum and coke.

- Cocktails in coloured glasses can sometimes be potent as you can't always see what's in there. Opt for cocktails in clear glasses to be on the safe side.

- If you are going on a bender, then leave all expensive jewellery safely at home.

- Before the wicked side of your brain tries to convince you that life won't be worth living without that extra cocktail, think about the consequences. Imagine your poor little pooch cross-legged by the front door, holding his lead and trying desperately not to wee, as he looks at you in the hope that you'll move your lazy fat bum out of bed.

- I know how it is... Sometimes you're pouring a little drinkie-poo and your hand accidentally jolts. Before you know it, you've poured too much vodka into your glass. But rather than tipping some of it back in the bottle, you just top it up with a little bit of mixer. This accidental jolt is a sure way to becoming super-sloshed. The moral of the story here is to put more mixer than alcohol in the glass if you don't want to get too trashed too quickly. A little Buck's Fizz is a good drink as it's half-champers and half-orange juice – meaning you're getting your hit of booze, only diluted with some healthy orange juice.

- If you 'quite rightly' order yourself a large glass of vino at the bar, just be aware that some places have bigger glasses than others. If this is the case, then don't have as many drinkies as you normally would.

- If you are one of those people who only has to look at a cocktail and the room starts spinning, always opt for drinks that aren't made up of carbonated mixers as they will speed up the rate that the alcohol is absorbed into your blood (you will get trashed quicker). So remember, anything with fizz will make you whizz!

- Believe me, falling head over heels and flat on your face while showing off your Bridget Jones super-sized, 'hold everything in'- style pants in front of a crowd of cool clubbers really isn't that clever. Look, I'm a chick, I know what it's like when you want to look good in your new dress and so you throw out the Starbucks card, padlock the fridge and basically starve yourself to squeeze into that little frock, but all your efforts to look Angelina Jolie super-hot will fly right out the window if you get too intoxicated and show yourself up. So, if you're going to be knocking back the drinkies then you *must* line your stomach with something substantial (a little bit of shepherd's pie or pasta with tomato sauce). And, no, it won't make you look pregnant in your dress! What it will do is to slow down the rate at which the alcohol enters your blood, meaning you won't get too drunk too quickly and your hangover won't feel so bad the next day.

- How gutting is it to reach the end of your glass of white wine and you don't even remember drinking the darn thing? Well, to save you from ever experiencing that empty feeling, make your wine go further by putting a few ice cubes in it.

- If you have a habit of getting totally trashed and can never remember where you live (or even what your name is for that matter), then organise your transport home. Book a cab with a reliable company or persuade a teetotal friend to take you home. Always make sure that you have plenty of cash on you so that you don't have to stop at a cashpoint.

- We all know booze is super-fattening, and that every glass we devour will take us further away from our Kate Moss superwaif dream and closer to being a fat-filled walrus. Now if skipping the trip to the burger bar is out of the question after you fall out of the club, but you still want to watch your weight, there are a few drinks that you should avoid like the plague because of their calorific content and others that you can drink guilt-free (well almost!).

  Avoid: anything creamy, such as Baileys, White Russian, Pina Colada, rum & cola, Screwdriver, Tequila Sunrise and Bacardi Breezer.

  Opt for: dry white wine, Bloody Mary, vodka and diet cola or diet lemonade, gin and diet tonic, champagne and vodka with orange juice. Always opt for a clear spirit and low-calorie mixers. It all adds up, remember!

- Alcohol is sooooo fattening! But don't go skipping a meal to save calories for drinkies. Alcohol upsets your blood-sugar levels and gives you an appetite anyway, so you may as well eat something healthy so you don't over-munch on all the wrong things.

Cigarettes & Alcohol

- Did you know that by drinking too much booze you are encouraging your body to expel calcium, the stuff that's vital for good bones, hair and teeth?

- Every girl needs a little bit of glitz and glam in her life: if you're home alone and you fancy a bit of bubbly, why not? But to add a bit of swish into your cocktail, try dropping in a fruit cube. Simply wrap lots of strawberries up separately in clingfilm and whack them into the freezer until they are rock-solid. Mid-week, if you fancy a cheeky little tipple then you can crack open the bubbly and pop one of the strawberry ice cubes in your glass. They not only look pretty and taste good, but they also keep your drink lovely and cold. You can, of course, do the same with lemons and limes. If you only fancy a wee bit of champers, then rather than cracking open a big bottle, open up a mini-sized one: it's less expensive and means that you will drink less.

- There's a general rule and that's the darker the alcohol, the worse it will make you feel, especially in terms of a hangover the next day. It's probably too late to try to remember anything once you're in no fit state, but try to engrave this into your brain and maybe consider drinking clear spirits instead of a brandy next time.

- Never take on a man in a drinking competition, especially a man you don't know that well – unless your sides are made from iron, he will always win. Because men are bigger than us, they don't get so drunk as quickly. We chicks absorb more alcohol into our blood even if the guy is the same size as us.

- Young wines (under two years old) are again the worst offenders when it comes to a terrible hangover as they have a higher level of hangover-producing chemicals.

- No one likes not being able to squeeze cheese in the morning and drinking alcohol can make you constipated as it irritates the lining of your digestive tract.
- If you don't want a hangover from hoggily polishing off that vodka bottle, then don't drink! It's the best solution.
- Did you know that drinking booze before you eat will probably make you eat an extra 250 calories?
- Here are some signs to watch out for, in case you are worried that you might have a drinking problem:

  Being drunk often

  Gulping down your first glass of wine as if somebody is going to snatch it away from you

  Ordering doubles

  Having frequent alcohol-fuelled arguments with friends and loved ones

  Having accidents and getting into fights

  Having the shakes and the sweats

- And here are some ways to cut down on your drinking:

  Buy and use smaller wine glasses to drink from at home

  Arrive at the bar about an hour later than everyone else – this will cut your drinks down by about two

  Replace your usual drink with a less alcoholic one

  Buy low-alcohol beer and wine

  Decide to have two booze-free nights and, instead of going to the pub, go and do something that's both entertaining and fun – try a yoga class, a trip to the cinema or a long walk around the park

C E L E B R I T Y   T I P !

Dean Piper - Entertainment Editor at
Closer *Magazine*

A great trick at a party for not ending up the drunk loser in the corner is to have sparkling water with a load of chunks of fresh lime with a straw. Everyone thinks you are necking a large vodka and tonic but you will easily escape the hangover.

How to Feel Like a Human Being Again (& Less Like a Disembodied Zombie)

If you've woken up with a pink oval ring embossed on the side of your face, you may just have spent the night hugging the loo while hurling up what seems like the entire insides of your stomach. If this is you, make sure you eat something from the list below to re-energise and revitalise your frail body, stocking it back up with all the vital minerals and vitamins that will sort out your blood-sugar levels.

- To prevent your porky-pie fingers hitting those digits on the dog and bone and accidentally ordering a Chinese set menu for ten (this sort of food will knock your state of recovery five steps back again), do a little supermarket sweep the day before your big night and fill your fridge with healthy stodge such as eggs, lean bacon, tomatoes and brown bread and make yourself a delicious fry-up. Fry-ups will replace lost nutrients and boost your blood sugar. Plus they help to settle your stomach and, more to the point, they taste damn good!

- Because you're probably incapable of doing anything other than grunting and dribbling after a binge-drinking session, this is when you're more likely to burn the toast. But a bit of charcoaled bread works wonders because the carbon will help to soak up some of the toxins that have entered your system.

- Sometimes reaching for a strong black coffee in the hope that it will take away your hangover from hell only makes the problem worse as it will dehydrate you, giving you a stonker of a headache. Also, coffee is a stimulant, which will highlight just how bad you feel. It's also a diuretic so you'll forever be scraping yourself from your pit-like bed to go and empty your bursting bladder. Why add salt to the wound? You're supposed to be putting yourself back on the road to recovery. So brew up a lovely jubbly cup of fresh mint or camomile tea (add a little sugar) instead.

- If you've been chucking up chunks all night then get your gnashers around a big old banana – it will help replace all the potassium that you lost last night, making you feel you might just survive another day.

- Sometimes your leftover curry comes in really handy. Dig it out and retrieve the Naan bread (clean it off, if needs be). Now make two little balls by ripping off a couple of bits and roll them in the palm of your hands and shove them into your ears. The sound of somebody eating a bag of crisps will no longer be like a pneumatic drill!

- Now if you have a hairless egghead, don't bother reading this tip! If your head feels like you're cooking up some popcorn in it, as if it's about to explode, then gently massage it and very carefully pull your hairs at the roots. This will help to stimulate the blood flow in your head and take some of that headachy tension away. If you're wearing black, expect a snowfall of dandruff!

- If you feel at death's door but you have to make it to a really important family gathering, then just phone them up, pretend you're sober, on fab form and can't wait to join the celebrations, but are just waiting for the telephone engineer to come round and fix your landline. Now turn off your mobile phone (it ran out of battery, remember) and go back to sleep. It's your call: either lie really well and remain part of the family, or go, start to get the shakes and projectile vomit *Exorcist* style over a crowd of shocked faces and your grandma and grandpa's very special 60th wedding anniversary cake. The choice is yours! If, however, you do decide to go, make sure you take a cab or public transport if you are over the limit.

- A natural reaction is to reach for a painkiller when you're suffering from a hangover, but sometimes you maybe doing more harm than good. The liver absolutely hates paracetomol as it irritates it. Your stomach will not thank you for feeding it aspirin either as it destroys vitamin C, the thing you most need for a swift recovery. So, instead, try something natural that isn't going to upset the body's balance, like Nux Vom (from health shops). This is a homeopathic remedy which is brilliant for treating sickness and big, bad-ass headaches.

- If you want breakfast in bed, but no one's going to make it for you, drag your mattress down from your bedroom and park it up on top of the kitchen table before you go out. When the morning comes, you won't have to move a millimetre and you can just stretch out your leg, open the fridge with your piggy-trotter toes and devour the contents of your fridge! How easy is that?

- Rub two drops of fennel oil and two drops of juniper oil into your mitts, massaging the area between your forefinger and thumb. This is of course an acupressure point, which will calm and soothe your headache.

- Depending on how wasted you got last night, you may be better off avoiding public transport altogether and going on foot. The swaying, stopping and starting of the bus, tube or train may well leave you wanting to chunder all over your fellow travellers. So think of others before yourself. Or you could always ram a plastic bag into your handbag just in case you do feel like you are going to hurl. And don't forget the peppermints!

- If the taste of water makes you want to hurl, on top of the fact that you want to hurl anyway because you're so hungover, munch away on watermelon. It's great for re-hydrating a water-deprived, shrivelled-up old prune-like body because it's made up of 92% water. And, hooray, it's virtually fat-free!

- After you've made yourself a nice cuppa, don't go throwing out the tea bags. Instead, chuck them into the fridge and, when they have cooled down, go and get them, lie on your bed and pop them over your eyes. They will be so soothing.

- Alcohol zaps the oxygen levels in our body, leaving us feeling incredibly lethargic, so you may want to try this simple exercise to regenerate your sluggish body. It's so easy, all you have to do is get yourself comfy on the sofa. Take a deep breath in, filling up your lungs and tummy (your tummy should look bloated like you've just porked out on a curry), hold for three seconds and then slowly let it out. Repeat six times. You really will notice the difference.

- There are two reasons why you should take a shower after a big night out on the town. First, you probably look like a yam and smell like an onion, not to mention that lovely coating of dried sick in your hair and beer in between your toes. Second, by having a shower that consists of hot water for two minutes, followed by thirty seconds of freezing cold water, this will perk you up and re-energise your sluggish, sloth-like body. Repeat this action three or four times in one go while you are in the shower. However, if you are so drunk that you had trouble remembering where you live, I would strongly advise you not to shower and deal with your sicky hair the next day – after all, you don't want to slip, knock yourself out and drown.

- Rather than getting irate with your flatmate because he or she has yet again left the top off the cola bottle, they may have just done you a favour. Drinking flat cola will help you feel less sick.

- A brisk walk can help fight off the demons and make you feel more human – and if you break into a sweat, all the better. The more you sweat, the more your body will be able to get rid of the toxins through your pores.

BODY-BOOSTING DETOX DRINKIES THAT WILL HAVE YOU FEELING GORGEOUS AND SPARKLING IN NO TIME

Bloody Mary

You will need:

- 1 measure vodka
- 4 measures tomato juice
- a dash of Worcestershire sauce (add to your taste)
- a dash of Tabasco (add more if you like a bit of kick ass!)

- Just under a measure of lemon juice (get the bottled version, not fresh. First, because it's a lot easier and, second, because, if you squirt yourself in the eye, it will make everything worse)
- a couple of slices of lime
- a sprinkle of pepper, salt and celery salt
- ice
- 1 stick crunchy celery

Lob it all into a glass of some sort, using the celery stick to stir.

'Help!'

This is a real good 'un, especially if you feel like death. It cleanses your liver and pushes all of those nasty old toxins right out of your 'temple'. It will give you the encouragement you need to use your legs again.

You will need:

- 3 lemons (peel and cut into pieces. There's lots of vitamin C in these beauties and, because they are a good diuretic, they will help eliminate all the alcohol and the toxins)
- 2 or 3 apricots (so yummy and a good natural sugar. They are really good for getting rid of the bad toxins)
- 2 apples (don't peel – that's where all the goodness is. Get rid of the core, though. Apples have lots of fibre and are a really good detoxifier. They are also great for giving your skin a healthy rosy glow)
- 26 seedless red grapes (you can use white, but red have more antioxidants – always good for beautifying because this is this what makes us look younger and slows down premature ageing)

All you do is put them all through your juicer and drink – and watch the life flow back into your corpse!

Carrot Sorter-outer

- Get a bunch of carrots with their skins on, but remove the top. Give them a blast under the tap to wash off any mud. You mustn't peel them as all the good vitamin A, which will bring you back to life, is under the skin
- I pear, cored (pears are a great colon cleanser and will help to keep those dreaded cravings at bay)
- a big pinch of root ginger (ginger is fantastic for settling your tummy if you feel like chucking your guts up!)
- a couple of drops of fresh lemon (if you can't be bothered to cut one up, use the lazy lemon that you can buy in bottles. Lemons are the daddy of liver cleansing: they are amazing for cleaning out all of those toxins and contain lots of vitamin C, which will again re-energise a sluggish body)

Pop it all into a blender, along with a couple of chunks of ice. Blend up and guzzle!

A Tiddly-widdly Buck's Fizz (my mum's favourite)

Champagne not only brings a bit of glamour back into your sorry day, but it certainly does what it says on the label! Having the one drink is fine and it will definitely take the edge off your hangover, but don't have any more! Just use half-champagne and half-orange juice.

Bright-eyed & Bushy-tailed Again

OK, so you've been using your stomach as a dustbin over the weekend and filling it up with all sorts of crap. Well, now it's time for the mother of all detoxers, so get ready to clean your body from head to toe, leaving you feeling bright-eyed and beautiful again.

Hell-raiser to Heaven

You will need:

- 3 little carrots, topped and tailed (carrots aid digestion and help the kidneys and liver to work. They also help relieve tiredness and bloating)
- 3 beetroots, washed and chopped into small pieces (I hate the taste of beetroot, but it's one of the most powerful detoxifiers out there as it totally cleanses out your intestines and liver)
- 2 crunchy apples, unpeeled and cut into slices (this has loads of fibre and adds sweetness to the drink)

Again, an easy-peasy one to make. Just chuck it all in your juicer then drink straightaway.

Plummy Paradise

This next body-boosting drink is also called 'Watch out, tummy, you're about to go on the roller coaster ride from hell!'

You will need:

- 5–6 plums, halved and stones removed (again these have loads of fructose, but they are also a good source of iron and malic acid, which will help the absorption of iron)
- 2 lovely ripe pears, chopped into pieces (they have lots of fructose, which the body will convert into energy)
- 1 avocado, peeled and stone removed

Put the plums and pears through the juicer. Take this juice and put it into the blender with the avocado until yummy, scrummy smooth, and then drink it.

How to Deal With the Next Day

How you got home last night remains a mystery. Now we all know that having to face the music the next day is always a shocker and totally humiliating, especially when your so-called 'friends' phone you in hysterics, gasping for air, to refresh you on what you got up to last night and then of course you've got the photographic evidence caught on somebody's phone to deal with, which by now has been posted on Facebook! So here's a little pick-me-up (off the floor!) to help boost your fish-like memory, shift that thunderstorm of a mood and promote positive thinking. Having said that, if you were really bad, and I mean totally off the scale, maybe you're better off blissfully ignorant!

My Saviour

You will need:

- 4 apples (the sugar will help to kickstart your concentration levels)
- 30 blueberries (research shows that blueberries help to slow down age-related troubles with memory loss)
- 30 white seedless grapes (white grapes are a must-have in the fridge, as they are good to munch on, but in this case they really do sort out sugar cravings and also help your concentration levels)

Juice everything separately, stir when in the glass and drink.

Eggnog

This body-booster contains raw egg. Yuck! But if you want to bust that bad-ass hangover, then this is the one for you and it's a classic.

You will need:

- 1 egg
- 1 measure rum
- 1 measure brandy
- 1 dessertspoon cocktail syrup

- 4 measures milk
- a pinch of ground nutmeg

If you haven't got one of those James Bond cocktail shakers, then use an old jam jar with a lid. Lob in the egg, rum, brandy and syrup and shake it as hard as you can. This is pretty exhausting stuff, just to warn you. If you are going to use a proper cocktail shaker then pour the mixture into a glass, add the milk, stir, then lightly sprinkle the nutmeg on top and drink. If you are using the old jam jar, then just put everything in it, including the milk, and drink directly from it (a great way to save on the washing up!).

Cabbage Cure

This one will help to sort out stomach upsets, bloated stomachs – and farting! You will need:

- ¼ cabbage, cut up into bits
- 2 fennel bulbs, cut up into chunks (fennel gets your metabolism going again and is a great cleanser for the digestive system)
- 4 small carrots, topped, tailed and cut into pieces

Put the whole lot in the juicer and drink!

Wave Goodbye to Toxic Waste

This sweet and yummy cocktail won't want to make you gag (unlike that Eggnog number!). This is a bit like sweet and sour Chinese with tangy grapefruit and strawberries.

You will need:

- 12 strawberries, hulled (strawberries are rich in vitamin C and soluble fibre, which will send all the waste in your body on its merry little way!)
- 1 grapefruit, skin removed and cut into pieces (very good for removing toxins)

- 300ml (½ pint) ice (measure it out into a plastic freezer bag and freeze)

Chuck everything into a blender, blast and guzzle!

CELEBRITY TIP!

Judy Finnigan - Television Presenter

Whatever needs doing, just ask Richard – it's no trouble at all!

So, all you bone-idle, lazy goddesses out there – you've read it, you've tried it, you've tested it. With your newfound skills there's absolutely no reason for you to ever again leave your house looking like a dustbin bag that's been ravaged by the foxes! You're gorgeous, you're a wizard in the kitchen, and you look like you have just stepped out of the pages of *Vogue*! Good luck – and remember, if there's a shortcut to a glam goal, take it!

LAZY GODDESS
SHOPPING LIST – THE BEST
PLACES TO GO SHOPPING FOR
THE ULTIMATE ADDICT

Fashion

CLOTHES

High street

- TK Maxx – it's designer bargain heaven – if you haven't experienced it, then boy have you been missing out big time
- Oasis – I practically live in Oasis – need I say more?
- Lipsy – hot, must-have clothes all year round. A favourite with the celebs
- M&S – great bits and bobs from glitz and glam to comfy and casual
- Gap – the place to stock up on your staples
- French Connection – always have fab winter coats
- H&M – for brilliant basics and funky bits
- Vanilla – it's where all the celebs go to get their winter gilets. It's just off the Kings Road in London. It does the best handbags too at really good prices
- Zara – it's like going into Prada, sometimes the cuts and designs are so good, only the price tag is a darn lot cheaper
- Topshop – it's basically an Aladdin's cave for fashion addicts
- Miss Selfridge – bang-on-trend wardrobe fillers from street to bo-ho chic, etc.
- All Saints – loving the vibe in this place if you are into your quirky Vivienne Westwood style of stuff

- Reiss – GREAT shoes, bags, belts and hot sassy skirts for the office
- Joy – this shop really is a joy! Has loads of sexy and quirky pieces at a really affordable price. I get everything from shoes and maxi dresses to birthday cards and dirty joke books here
- Warehouse – always has a little Friday-night problem-fixer in store
- Mango – I always get my Christmas sparkly dresses in here
- King's Road Sporting Club – officially the best gym gear in the universe! Their stuff magically makes you look twice as thin when you put their clobber on – proper cool LA stuff

Designer

- Jenny Packham – heavenly dresses for the most glam of occasions from cocktail to weddings
- Cricket in Liverpool is a great one-stop-shop boutique where all the wags go to stock up on designer treats
- DKNY – whatever you buy here, you are guaranteed to love forever
- Chanel – every lady needs a piece from here
- Novamio – dresses to die for. SJP would kill for anything from this designer
- Diane Von Furstenberg – the ultimate wrap-around-dress designer that covers a whole host of sins
- Ben de Lisi – dresses that ooze elegance and sophistication
- Joseph – they do fantastic, flattering jeans
- Mathew Williamson
- Prada – for the James Bond-esque babe

Lazy Goddess Shopping List

- Dolce and Gabbana – if you fancy a bit of slick razzle dazzle then pop in here
- Nicole Farhi – chic and sophisticated clothing
- Chloe – hot body sculpting jeans
- Burberry – from ladylike dresses to cute little jackets. Scoop up some cool bangles while you're in there

BIKINIS

- Melissa Odabash in Harvey Nichols and Heidi Klein. Somehow they make peanut-sized boobs look huge! They're incredible! And what's more, they keep all of those wobbly bits locked away!
- Topshop – great 'kinis for your hols in really fun and funky colours and patterns
- Accessorize – girly gorge bikinis in all styles

UNDERWEAR

- By Caprice lingerie – if you see it, get it! It's the solution to spicing things up in the bedroom, plus the fit makes your body look fab! www.bycapricelingerie.com
- M&S – there's sporty, there's sexy, supportive and there's formal. They've got the lot
- Agent Provocateur – whoo-eee! Some seriously kinky and stunning stuff in this store. Don't forget to treat yourself to some hot perfume and fluffy mules while you're in there
- If you want to treat yourself to some naughty undies but don't want to leave the house, then order them on line from Figleaves. They have everything

- Pussy Glamour in Topshop and Selfridges. Sexy sets for those who dare – really cool, for the ultimate rock chick

ACCESSORIES

- Theo Fennell – treaty diamonds for a magpie minx
- The Earring Boutique – gorgeous gorgeous gorgeous!
- Aspinall of London – for personalised diaries and passports, and matching bags
- MCM – handbags for day or night, for a stylish lady
- Accessorize – I could spend a day in there, it's so rammed full of goodies
- Russell and Bromley handbags are perfect for fitting the kitchen sink in
- Philip Treacy – the most creative and sculptural hat designer
- Erickson Beamon – breathtakingly beautiful jewellery
- Radley – umbrellas that last for ages and fab luggage labels which match passport covers
- Butler & Wilson – unique vintage-inspired bags, jewellery and clothes
- Links of London – simple and modern jewellery
- VVRouleux – they do the most amazing ribbons and trims if you fancy customising something
- Butterfly at Selfridges – beautiful, delicate jewellery, perfect for summer dresses and Christmas jollies!

SHOES

- Gina – goddess shoes! This bootilicious boutique will make your heart-rate go through the roof. Bring your sun glasses because there's more twinkle here than in a star-filled sky

- Fit flops – they are officially the most important pair of shoes that any girl should purchase this year. Brilliant at giving you a bum-lift and a firm favourite with all the A-List stars
- MBTs – hone and tone chubby cheeks and thighs. A great solution for perfect pins
- Moda in Pelle – heavenly shoes that won't break the bank
- Kate Kuba – hot heels and Ugg boots for the babe in the making
- Strutt Couture – if you want to strut your stuff in some hot-mama booties, then this is where you need to get them
- R.Soles – the place to get the real McCoy cowboy boots
- Ugg Australia – the most comfortable and heavenly shoesies ever designed, the A-list must-have for all year round

DIY

Its B&Q through and through – it's the best sweetie shop of the DIY industry! Paints, furniture, homewares, cement, wallpaper, lights, pictures, blinds, curtains, plants, tools – you name it, it's all there. Beware, though! Expect to come out with a lot more than you went in there for. It's all just too tempting!

INTERIOR DESIGN

- B&Q – cushions, curtains, blinds, throws, wallpapers, etc. etc… to suit all styles from Elton John-like country style to Lilly Allen hippy-like lovers
- Habitat – for great rugs, tableware, vases and furniture
- Heals – fantastic kitchen bits, bed linen and nick-nacks

- Volga linen – anything can be personalised and embroidered with your name
- Oka – beautiful things from outdoor living to a cosy night in
- Lombok – for the uber-chic stylish house
- Louise Bradley – couture for a cool pad oozing with elegance
- Mo-Mo interiors – Moroccan masterpieces! www.momo-interiors.com
- Only Roses – just roses in their full glory
- Cath Kidston – pretty oven gloves, picnic baskets and tablecloths
- Jo Malone – all their candles and linen sprays
- Shuttersinc.co.uk – shutter paradise for your windows
- Spaceslide – sliding wardrobes that are super modern and edgy
- Woven Ground – rugs and more rugs and more rugs!
- istock – a huge photo library of any picture you could imagine. Order it and have it made into wallpaper. I use it on *60 Minute Makeover* all the time
- Ikea – it's got absolutely everything you can imagine and is excellent if you are on a shoestring budget
- M&S – scrummy candles, luxurious bath towels (hotel style), fab dressing gowns (perfect for getting ready before you go out) and a whole range of dining clobber and vases, etc.
- The White Company – they do beautiful candles, china and pot pourri
- Unlisted Room Spray – great for disguising nasty smells
- My deco – a fantastic website that helps you plan your dream room with the help of a handy 3D room planner
- Joanna Wood – trinkets, nick-nacks and all sorts of goodies for the home
- Thomas Sanderson – the place to go and find your perfect window treatment

- Range Master – colourful kitchen appliances such as cookers and fridges
- Harlequin – Chelsea design centre with out-of-this-world wallpapers
- Tesco, Sainsbury's and M&S – for fresh, pretty and cheap flowers

CLEANING PRODUCTS

- M&S – Naturally derived anti-bacterial kitchen cleansing wipes. I keep these by each of my sinks in the house, so that I can easily give them a quick clean down every day to keep things sweet and fresh
- Persil Non Bio – washes and looks after your precious clothes really well
- Lenor (clothes softener) – the smell is almost edible
- Comfort – for the delicate-skinned out there. Heavenly fragrance too!

Beauty

FACE

- Olay – A Touch of Sunshine – fantastic moisturiser that gives you a gradual tan
- Elemis – Papaya Enzyme Peel – purifies and regenerates tired skin
- Bliss Triple Oxygen Instant Energizing Mask from Bliss – great for pre-date beauty as it refreshes tired and dull-looking skin. The effect is out of this world, and you will feel like you have just paid a visit to the spa. It also acts as an anti-bacterial treatment helping to keep blackheads and breakouts at bay and it's brilliant at relieving tension in your facial muscles
- Bliss Youth As We Know It – heaven packaged in a pot. This moisturiser for the face is simply outstanding. Lovely to use after you have used your Triple Oxygen Instant Energizing Mask

- Elizabeth Arden Eight Hour Cream – the best for nourishing dry lips
- Dermalogica Active Moist – gorgeous light face cream. I put mine on before I put my make-up on as it has this amazing ability to make your make-up stay where it should for a lot longer
- Clinique Repairwear – intensive eye cream. Pat it on daily to reduce lines and puffiness
- Simple Cleansing Wipes – remove all make-up leaving your face feeling fresh and fab
- Normandie Bare-faced Cheek – great face wipes for removing make-up. Available in Boots
- Bliss fabulous foaming face wash – I use this day and night, and I definitely credit it as to why I have crystal-clear skin
- Zelens radical defence serum – a powerful antioxidant which protects you against grubby environments, such as smoking, car fumes, sunlight, stress and alcohol – great if you want to put premature ageing on hold
- Bliss Scrub your nose in it – if your nose is beginning to look like a pebble-dash wall because you have so many blackheads, then I strongly advise you scoop up one of these masks/scrub

BODY

- Bliss Body Butter – yummy cream for your body. Such a treat!
- Holland and Barrett Aloe Vera Gel – clears your guts out big time
- Vichy Auto Bronzant – I swear by it for a sun-kissed-looking brown face and body
- Avene – gentle body scrub for sensitive skin

Lazy Goddess Shopping List

- Papaya Body Polish — smells good enough to eat and leaves your skin glowing
- Jo Malone Lime, Basil and Mandarin Shower Gel — it smells amazing. Once you start buying this stuff, you will never stop
- Jo Malone Lime, Basil and Mandarin Body Lotion — the partner in crime with the shower gel
- M&S or Body Shop Exfoliating Gloves — they remove dead skin cells really well if you are going to be applying fake tan
- Michael Kors perfume — it's a man magnet!
- Rimmel Sun Shimmer — instant tan cream for your face and body. I use it on my legs if they are looking a bit pasty and I have to wear a dress. When you get back home after a night out, you can rinse it off
- Dry Skin Body Brush — you can get it from most pharmacies and from Boots. Helps to fight cellulite and removes dead skin
- Christian Lacroix for Avon perfume
- All Avene sun-protection creams are great for sunny climates
- Bliss Fat Girl Sleep — I LOVE this creamy stuff like I do a new Chloe handbag. It reduces the look of existing 'orange peel' cellulite. It helps to take away that bloated look that we all get when we get our period and it makes any future dimpling think twice about settling on your thighs and bum cheeks
- Soap and Glory Sugar Crush Body Scrub — flaky skin fighter. This scrumptious smashed brown sugar and sweet lime oil scrub is nothing less than pure delight to smear all over your body
- Soap and Glory Butter — no it's not to spread on your toast but, instead, all over your body. It's lush!

HANDS

- Adcal D3 – you can get at a pharmacy – chewable tablets for rock-solid healthy nails
- L'Occitane – moisturising gloves – for soft hands
- O.P.I nail lacquers – they really 'hit the nail on the head' every time. The colours are fab and, what's more, they just don't chip
- Lemon and Zest Hand Wipes – M&S – handy to have in your handbag for when you need to clean your mitts

HANDS AND FEET

- Gillette Venus Breeze – you can buy them in all good chemists and supermarkets. It's the Rolls-Royce of razors worldwide! All Gillette razors are, but the Venus Breeze is particularly brilliant because it is a shaver that comes with built-in gel bars, meaning you don't have to lug foam around with you. It's a great solution for downsizing your bag if you are going away on holiday
- One-coat fast-finish nail polish by No 17
- Neal's Yard pumice foot scrub – for sparking tootsies
- Pumice with a handle – Origins – scrapes away all the hard and dead skin
- Bliss softening socks – if your toes are tough as manky old potatoes and your heels are as hard as rhino skin, then these will bring them back to their former glory. You simply pop them on (for 20 mins), and the gel lining inside cuddles and soothes your tootsies and feeds them moisture and love, taking away dryness and any painful hard corns and calluses
- Bliss sock salve – it softens and tenderises rock-solid feet just like it does when you smash the 'you know what' out of a steak to make it tender

Lazy Goddess Shopping List

HAIR

- Batiste – dry shampoo for when you can't be bothered to wash your hair
- Richard Ward – Ultimate Repair Mask from Superdrug. It gives you instant Jennifer Aniston glowing locks as it nourishes and strengthens hair. I wash mine, apply it, then sleep in it overnight and wash it out the next day – wow is all I can say!
- Kerastase Resistance – found in most hair salons. Incredible shampoo for coloured and weakened hair. I swear by it
- L'Oreal Volume Extra – an excellent hair mousse that keeps your barnet looking salon sexy and polished

TEETH

- Oral B Triumph electric toothbrush cleans your pegs like a Dyson vacuum. It really is the daddy of the toothbrushes
- Oral B Dental Floss
- Smile Dental Floss
- Colgate Advanced Whitening toothpaste – cleans those pegs gleaming white

MAKE-UP BAG ESSENTIALS

- Max Factor mascaras – a make-up bag isn't complete without one of these
- Max Factor Miracle Touch, liquid illusion foundation – for doll-like skin
- Nivea Caregloss and Shine (natural colour) – fantastic for Pammy lips
- Liparazzi – officially the most fun lipgloss in the universe – comes with mirror and light so you can see what you are doing.
- Suqqu Mascara Volume Long – it's pure luxury for those lashes. Plus, all

of their make-up brushes are out of this world and make putting on make-up a doddle

- Mac make-up – I love everything in there from eye shadows to silk-like foundations
- Fake eyelashes from Boots and Sally Hair and Beauty
- Portable Pout by Avon – fantastic lipstick colours
- Non-Bio Travel Wash – it's a tiny little bottle of washing liquid that you can pop in your bag, meaning you can wash your clothes (or knickers) any time, any place
- Penhaligon's silver lipstick holders to protect your lippy while it's in your handbag
- Tampax Compak – always best to be prepared

Cures

- 4head – great for headaches
- Carpet burn – Calamine and Witch Hazel. You can get it in all pharmacies
- Dulco-lax – relieves poos that are hostages inside you
- Night and Day Nurse – kills colds like no other product
- Pepto Bismol – sorts out icky tummies, heartburn and indigestion
- Berocca – an intense tablet full of vitamins and minerals. Great for boosting your energy supplies and for when you've had a booze-fuelled night – it replaces all the goodness that you lost
- Migraleve – kills off those migraines like ant powder kills off ants
- Ear Wax Remover from Boots – cleans out all of the stubborn wax
- Optrex Brightening drops – sorts out and soothes red and dry eyes in an instant

Lazy Goddess Shopping List

Food

- M&S – the food section will make you feel like you have died and gone to heaven
- Little local butchers and market stalls at the weekend
- Chillies – brilliant for speeding up your metabolism
- Puritee – Holland & Barrett – flushes out toxins and poo
- Go-ahead bars – yoghurty yummy crunchy biscuits that are super-low-fat and sweet
- Low fat mango sorbet from M&S – it feels like you are eating something that's full of calories, but it isn't! What a joy!
- Green tea – from most supermarkets and Holland & Barrett – speeds up your metabolism
- Fry light from Waitrose – it's a bottle of extra virgin olive oil spray that pumps out 1 calorie's worth of oil per spray meaning you can control how much oil you put on your salad
- Holland & Barrett – yummy low-fat energy snacks
- Ryvita – if you fancy the crunch that crisps give you, but without the fat, then get involved with these little lovelies – the flavoured ones are to die for
- Moet & Chandon – an absolute must have for a chicks' night in!
- Peggy Porschen – the best cake- and biscuit-maker in the world! If you are getting married or having a special birthday, then this is the place to make that occasion a memorable one
- Rococco chocolates – every obscure flavour possible such as chilli, Arabic spices, sea salt, pink peppercorns, lavender, cinnamon, earl grey tea – the list goes on!

Cookery Books to Buy

Everyday Novelli by Jean-Christophe Novelli

India with Passion by Manju Malhi

Jamie at Home by Jamie Oliver

Step-by-Step Cook Book by Good Housekeeping

Easy Indian Cooking by Manju Malhi

Gidgey Gadgets for your Pad

- 15-inch LCD TV with freeview and dvd player
- I-phone – basically sorts your whole life out
- Pink Retro Radio from M&S – it's called Roberts Rd-50 'rivival' DAB digital radio
- Sony digital picture frame – exclusive for M&S. You can put all of your photos onto it. It's so novel
- Cordless phone – M&S – white in colour and proper P-Diddy looking for a super-slick house
- Le Creuset – roasting dishes and pots galore